WAR'S DIRTY SECRET

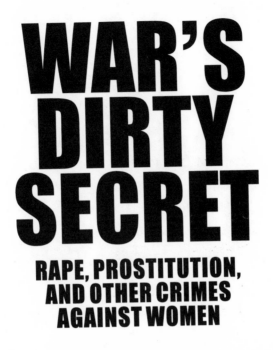

WAR'S DIRTY SECRET

RAPE, PROSTITUTION, AND OTHER CRIMES AGAINST WOMEN

Anne Llewellyn Barstow, editor

THE PILGRIM PRESS
Cleveland, Ohio

The Pilgrim Press, Cleveland, Ohio 44115

© 2000 by Anne Llewellyn Barstow

All rights reserved. Published 2000

Printed in the United States of America on acid-free paper

05 04 03 02 01 00   5 4 3 2 1

Library of Congress Cataloging-in-Publication Data

War's dirty secret : rape, prostitution, and other crimes against women /
Anne Llewellyn Barstow, editor.
   p. cm.
   Includes bibliographical references.
   ISBN 0-8298-1393-4
   1. Women—Crimes against. 2. War crimes. 3. Women and war. 4. Rape
I. Barstow, Anne Llewellyn

HV6250.4.W65 W374 2000
362.87'082–dc21

00-045644

*To the women
who are breaking silence
and speaking out*

Contents

Part Three
WOMEN AND THE U.S. MILITARY

Part Four
THE INTERNATIONAL RESPONSE

Abbreviations

ACWC	Advocacy Committee for Women's Concerns
AMNLAE	Association of Nicaraguan Women
AMPRONAC	Association of Women Confronting the National Problematic
CATW	Coalition against Trafficking in Women
CEDAW	Convention on the Elimination of All Forms of Discrimination against Women
CHR	Commission on Human Rights
CID	criminal investigative department
CUC	Committee for Peasant Unity
DOD	Department of Defense
ECPAT	End Child Prostitution, Pornography and Trafficking of Children for Sexual Purposes
FAIR	Fairness and Accuracy in Reporting
FDN	Nicaraguan Democratic Force
FGM	female genital mutilation
FIDA	Federation of International Women Lawyers
FRAPH	Front for Haitian Progress and Advancement
FSLN	Sandinista Front for National Liberation
GATT	General Agreement on Tariffs and Trade
ICC	International Criminal Court
INDE	National Institute of Electrification
JNA	Yugoslav National Army
K.W.S.J.	Korean Council for the Women Drafted for Sexual Slavery by Japan
KANU	Kenyan African National Union
KID	Konvansyon Inite Demokratik (United Democratic Convention), Haiti

NCCK   National Council of Churches of Kenya

NGO   nongovernmental organization

OAS   Organization of American States

PAC   Civil Defense Patrol

RPF   Rwandan Patriotic Front

SOFA   Status of Forces Agreement

SOFA   Solidarite Fanm Ayisyèn

SPS   Serbian Socialist Party

UCMJ   Uniform Code of Military Justice

UCR   Uniform Crime Reports

UN   United Nations

UNESCO   United Nations Educational, Scientific, and Cultural
                  Organization

UNHCR   United Nations high commissioner for Refugees

URNG   Guatemalan National Revolutionary Unity

VAWW-NET Japan   The Violence against Women in War Network Japan

WCC   World Council of Churches

WFP   Witness for Peace

WILPF   Women's International League for Peace and Freedom

WTO   World Trade Organization

Contributors

ANNE LLEWELLYN BARSTOW. Historian and author of *Witchcraze: A New History of the European Witch Hunts* (HarperSanFrancisco, 1994). Now retired from the State University of New York at Old Westbury, Barstow both studies violence against women in the European past and works for women's human rights today. She serves on the national boards of Witness for Peace and the Presbyterian Peace Fellowship.

JENNIFER S. BUTLER. Associate for global issues in the United Nations office of the Presbyterian Church (U.S.A.). Primary researcher and writer of the "Report on the Military and Sexual Exploitation and Abuse of Women," which was prepared for the Presbyterian Church in 1998.

IRIS CHANG. A Chinese American journalist who wrote the first full-length book in English in many years on the Rape of Nanking. She has spoken on this topic at the Simon Wiesenthal Center and on the *News Hour* with Jim Lehrer, among other venues.

CHUNG HYUN-KYUNG. Associate professor of world Christianity at Union Theological Seminary in New York City. Former professor of theology at Ewha Women's University in Seoul, Korea. Author of *The Struggle to Be the Sun Again* (Orbis, 1990).

MARION CIBORSKI. Fund-raising consultant in Pittsfield, Massachusetts. Coauthor of *A People Damned*, an exposé of World Bank complicity in the destruction of a Guatemalan village, and author of *Making Peace in Guatemala: An Unfinished Agenda* (Witness for Peace, 1997). She served for two years as a volunteer for Witness for Peace in Guatemala.

LAURA FLANDERS. Host of the radio program *Counterspin*, which is heard on one hundred stations in the United States and Canada. Former director of the women's desk at FAIR (Fairness and Accuracy in Reporting). Author of *Real Majority, Media Minority* and regular contributor to publications such as *The Nation* and *The Village Voice*. She visited Haiti and Rwanda with MADRE, the women's aid group.

MADELINE MORRIS. Professor of law at Duke University Law School in Durham, North Carolina. Special consultant to the secretary of the U.S.

Army, whom she advises about the army's senior review panel on sexual harassment.

PAULINE MUCHINA. Received her Ph.D. at Union Theological Seminary in New York City. Her research focuses on how faith can be used as an agent of political and social transformation: her dissertation is on poverty in Kenya and the role of the church to eradicate it. As a consultant with Women in Mission and Ministry of the Episcopal Church U.S.A., Pauline spoke and wrote about the global economic crisis and its impact on women and children. A citizen of Kenya, she hopes to return there to continue the struggle for liberation from all forms of violence.

AIKO OGOSHI. Professor of women's studies at Kinki University in Osaka, Japan. One of the founders of the Association for Research on the Impact of War and Military Bases on Women's Human Rights. Among her books are *A Feminist Criticism of Japanese Culture* (1996) and *Women and Religion* (1970).

TODD SALZMAN. Assistant professor in theology at Creighton University in Omaha, Nebraska. Author of *Deontology and Teleology: An Investigation of the Normative Debate in Roman Catholic Theology*. His interests include ethical theory as it pertains to social issues.

KIYOKO SHIMIZU. Professor of philosophy at Ottemon Gakuin University in Osaka, Japan, where she teaches the philosophy of Kant and Arendt from a feminist point of view. One of the founders of the Association for Research on the Impact of War and Military Bases on Women's Human Rights.

DONNA VUKELICH. Former coeditor of the *CEPAD Newsletter*, published in Nicaragua. Currently a graduate student at the University of Wisconsin.

Acknowledgments

For help with a book whose scope is global, one owes a wide debt of thanks. People who especially assisted me with issues surrounding the comfort women were Sue Babcock, Aiko Carter, Ruth Harris, Bev Harrison, Kim Kyung-In, Lee Eun Ja, Pat Patterson, Linda Scott, Sonja Strawn, David Suh, Wang Ching Feng, Michiko Hase, and Kazuko Watanabe.

For assistance with other parts of the book, thanks go to Carol Burke, Eleanor Conda, Paul and Becky Boyd-Driver, Cynthia Enloe, Sharon Hostetler, Wahida Naimar, Sr. Carol Rittner, Jennifer Rycinga, Vivian Stromberg, Marcia Wright, and Sarah Maguire of the Lawyers International Forum for Women's Human Rights. For an ongoing discussion of violence and its antidotes, special thanks to Helena Meyer-Knapp and the members of the Religion and Violence Seminar of the Society for Values in Higher Education.

Betty Peeler, Suzan Lipson, Debra Schwartz, and Betty Kersting were great companions at the Beijing Women's Conference at Hairou. They—and Sheila Brown, Peggy Andrews, and Dorothee Sölle—encouraged me to gather the pieces for this book; for their support I am grateful.

My firsthand introduction to violence against women in wartime was through Witness for Peace. On trips to Río Negro (Guatemala), La Victoria (Nicaragua), Port-au-Prince (Haiti), and Acteal (Chiapas, Mexico), I heard accounts from survivors that brought this violence home to me. My thanks to the workers in Witness for Peace for these opportunities.

Susannah Driver-Barstow helped edit the articles and offered much patient advice about the focus of the book. Tom Driver helped me cope with chapters arriving in half a dozen different computer programs and got me out of many a jam. They both deserve special thanks.

Most of all, I thank the dozen authors whose research and concern for this issue make this book possible.

Introduction

In war there is no victory for women, no matter which side wins.
Women are the worst victims of war and hence the highest stakeholders
for peace.   —NOELEEN HEYZER, UNIFEM

The purpose of this book is to change the way you think about war. I first
became aware of my own need for new ideas about war when I attended
the UN Fourth World Conference on Women at Beijing in 1995. Kazuko
Watanabe, a Japanese friend, invited me to accompany her to a press conference held by the Japanese ambassador to the UN. Because there was
much public criticism at the conference of Japan's refusal to do justice to the
"comfort women" of World War II, the ambassador had come to do "damage control."[1] We found the room jammed with people, mostly younger
Japanese women.

When the woman who presided announced that the first half hour was
reserved for questions from non-Japanese, the audience groaned but settled
into a traditional Japanese acquiescence. That half hour was monopolized
by Filipinas asking what protection the Japanese government offered young
women taken to Japan for the sex trade.

Finally my friend turned to me in tears: "No one has had a chance to
ask about sexual slavery and the comfort women. If you raise your hand,
they will acknowledge you." Not wanting to become involved in an internal
Japanese debate, I tried to beg off. But she insisted. Finally I raised my hand
and said, "The UN has declared that forcing women to render sexual services
is sexual slavery, a violation of their human rights, and that sexual slavery
imposed by the military is a war crime. Why does your government refuse
to accept that it practiced sexual slavery during World War II?"

Immediately the room burst into protest. Chants of "Sexual slavery, sexual
slavery! Say it, say it!" thundered out. Fists filled the air; people stomped their
feet. Standing in the middle of this turmoil, I wondered what I had unleashed!
When the ambassador waffled in his reply, saying that "Not the Japanese
government but the entire Japanese people are guilty of what happened," the

---

1. "Comfort women" is a bitterly ironic euphemism for the women (mostly teenaged girls,
actually) whom the Japanese army tricked into or kidnapped into military brothels ("comfort
stations") during World War II.

1

shouting grew. The minute the hour was up he made a fast exit. In order to leave, he and the woman who presided had to squeeze past me. As she hurried by, she took my hand and said, "Thank you for asking that question."

My research on this book has been my attempt to understand what I had unleashed that day in Beijing. How had traditionally polite Japanese women become so angry that they would shout in public at their ambassador? The first three chapters in this book refer to that story: how Japan forced 200,000 women, mostly Korean, into military brothels; how fifty years later the survivors broke silence, demanding recognition, recompense, and apology; and how many Japanese women stood with them, against their own government.

The research also led me to consider fundamental changes that have taken place in global society since World War II: how civilians have become the chief victims of wars, thus sharply raising the number of female victims; how women have found the courage to speak up about their victimization and to support each other in doing so; how some governments and the United Nations have begun to listen and to respond by changing international law and court procedures. I realized that the tumultuous moment at Beijing had opened a door for me into a pivotal moment in women's history: women as victims of violence, whether domestic, in global trafficking, or in conflict situations, were breaking silence, were demanding recognition and recompense. And their actions were beginning to have an impact everywhere.

I was drawn to do research on the comfort women because of the central role they had played in starting this movement. The elderly Korean women who with great courage spoke out in 1991 cleared the ground for a new way of looking at violence against women in wartime.[2] I soon realized, however, that the story has moved beyond the comfort women. Cataclysmic events in the former Yugoslavia and in Rwanda—events that victimized hundreds of thousands of women—had shaken world opinion. I had traveled to Central America and Haiti where I had seen and heard firsthand of widespread brutality against women by the armed forces and paramilitaries. I had to ask: Is this violence happening everywhere?

Those of us who are studying the evidence have begun to see that rape in conflict situations is often carefully planned, at high levels. It is systematic rape, even strategic rape—rape used as a weapon of war. The mass rapes in Bosnia and Rwanda made us urgently aware of the continuing nature of sexual assault against women. It has become a frequently used weapon. In this book a number of authors will document the military use of rape

---

2. They were soon followed by former comfort women from the Philippines, Malaysia, Indonesia, China, Taiwan, and the Netherlands.

and other sexual tortures against women. The crimes referred to here were committed by Japanese, Rwandans, Kenyans, Guatemalans, Haitians, Nicaraguans, citizens of the United States, and all sides in the Balkan war. These case studies are representative of similar violence in many countries.[3]

Changes in War, Changes in Society

One set of statistics tells it all: in World War I, the ratio of military personnel killed to civilians killed was 8:1; in World War II it was 1:1; in the many smaller wars since 1945, the ratio has been 1:8. This means that the victims of wars have changed: the great majority being civilians, they are now mainly women, children, and the elderly. This fact challenges our basic thinking about war. No longer is it a tragedy for which "old men do the planning and young men do the dying." No longer are warriors its only heroes. Now its chief actors are civilians who had little or no say about starting the war and who stand to win nothing and to lose everything because of the conflict.

These wars are fought very differently from the infamous trench campaigns of World War I or the massive aerial bombings of World War II. Many are guerrilla conflicts in which the main objective is to destroy villages and crops in order to starve out the enemy or force them to flee. Many utilize torture of men and women in order to demoralize the enemy. And most employ organized rape as a means of humiliating the enemy and destroying family and community life. Many of these wars have been genocidal, with the clear intention of wiping out an entire people or ethnic group. They have created refugees in larger numbers than the world has ever before seen—again, a type of atrocity that hits women with children very hard.

In this type of warfare, to gain control over enemy women's reproductive ability becomes a major goal. It is a war without heroes, a war in which we increasingly see that no one wins.

The Best-Kept Secret

This different kind of war creates not only new kinds of victims; it also demands new survival skills, cries out for new ways of peacemaking, and requires a new type of reporting.

---

3. We have evidence of systematic rape by military and paramilitary forces in these additional countries: Afghanistan, Algeria, Argentina, Bangladesh, Brazil, Burma, Cambodia, El Salvador, India, Indonesia, Liberia, Mozambique, Pakistan, Peru, Sierra Leone, Somalia, South Africa, the former Soviet Union, and Uganda. These cases have been documented by the United Nations and major human rights organizations. There is every reason to believe that there are more.

In some instances the press and other observers have risen to the challenge. In Bosnia, for example, reporters and NGOs were quick to alert the world to the existence of rape camps and of widespread massacre of civilian men and women.[4] But in far too many cases they have not seen what was before their eyes. Trained to report on war as what happens to men, observers and journalists have often not seen the torture and rape of women that occurs and is in fact part of the strategy.

An example of this strange myopia is found in the otherwise excellent account of the Salvadoran civil war compiled by Americas Watch.[5] The book documents the crimes of the Salvadoran army against its own people, criticizes the rebel forces for lawlessness, and exposes the weakness and corruption of the judicial system. It does not spare the United States for its role in training the army and supporting the abusive government. But on the subject of violence against women, it mentions only half a dozen incidents in which rapes were involved. Yet we know from other accounts that rape was a frequent tactic of the Salvadoran army throughout the thirteen years of the civil war (1979–92).[6] The book, however, does not comment on rape as a basic component of the terror of those years.

The only rape that it discusses is the rape and murder of four U.S. churchwomen (1980), but we know that many poor rural and urban Salvadoran women and girls were raped. Ignoring these assaults is a major omission in a study that attempts to be the definitive account of human rights abuses in El Salvador. While Americas Watch criticizes the U.S. government for not reporting on many of the atrocities that it knew about, the human rights agency must be criticized for not making a gender analysis of those same atrocities, for not asking, "And what happened to the women?"

Another inexplicable oversight can be found in Susanne Jonas's account of the first thirty years of civil war in Guatemala (1960–90).[7] Although Jonas gives an insightful analysis of the economic exploitation of women, she makes almost no mention of how they were exploited sexually. She refers to the plight of the thousands of refugees but does not ask what this meant for women fleeing with their children. In describing the horrors of the war, she mentions torture and massacre in the army's destruction of 440 villages, but she does not mention rape. Yet we know from many

---

4. Roy Gutman's work was outstanding in this regard. See *Witness to Genocide* (London: Element, 1993).

5. Americas Watch, *El Salvador's Decade of Terror: Human Rights since the Assassination of Archbishop Romero* (New Haven: Yale University Press, 1991).

6. For example, Mark Danner's evidence of mass rapes during the massacre at El Mozote in his book *The Massacre at El Mozote: A Parable of the Cold War* (New York: Vintage Books, 1994).

7. Susanne Jonas, *The Battle for Guatemala: Rebels, Death Squads, and U.S. Power* (Boulder: Westview Press, 1991).

sources that those attacks often included sexual torture and rape. Chapter 8 in this book, "Guatemala: We Thought It Was Only the Men They Would Kill," describes how the Guatemalan army and paramilitary carried out a massacre entirely of women and children. The overall story of military and paramilitary violence against Guatemalan women remains to be told.

Seymour M. Hersh won the Pulitzer Prize in 1970 for his reporting on the U.S. Army's atrocities at My Lai in Vietnam. That U.S. soldiers raped approximately twenty Vietnamese women that day in 1968 was documented by the Peers Commission investigations of 1970 and the court-martial of Lt. William L. Calley that same year.[8] These records also indicate that rape was practiced more widely than at My Lai alone.[9] Yet when Hersh wrote a thirtieth-anniversary piece on My Lai in 1998, he did not mention the rapes.[10] He recalled how the U.S. soldiers had systematically murdered all the women, men, and children that they could find and how some Americans had mistreated and killed prisoners and cut off the ears of corpses. But he did not remember the rapes.

An even more disturbing example of this kind of omission can be found in Philip Gourevitch's book on the Rwandan genocide of 1994.[11] The American public had first heard about the Rwandan genocide from reporters who missed the fact of sexual assault almost completely; women were simply invisible in their accounts. Not until March 1995 in the *Christian Science Monitor* were the mass rapes revealed.[12] One must ask how anyone could miss the fact of a quarter of a million rapes, but that is what happened. Gourevitch probed deeply into this genocidal morass; he succeeded in finding words to describe atrocity, no easy task. Yet despite the publication in September 1996 by Human Rights Watch of forty-eight pages of testimony about rape and forced impregnation,[13] and the eventual inclusion of rape in the mandate of the international tribunal trying Rwandan war criminals, Gourevitch does not reflect on sexual assault. Gourevitch refers to its happening, he mentions it in passing, but he does not include it in his overall

---

8. James S. Olson and Randy Roberts, *My Lai: A Brief History with Documents* (Boston: Bedford Books, 1998), 17, 22, 75–76, 89, 99–102, 107, 185.

9. Ibid., 17: "And in the villages some distance from Route 1, rape was not uncommon. When asked by investigators if rape was a widespread practice, [Michael] Bernhardt [of Calley's Company] replied, 'I thought it was, sir. It was predictable. In other words, if I saw a woman, I'd say, "Well, it won't be too long." That's how widespread it was.'"

10. Seymour M. Hersh, "My Lai and Its Omens," *New York Times*, Op-Ed page, 16 March 1998.

11. Philip Gourevitch, *We Wish to Inform You That Tomorrow We Will Be Killed with Our Families: Stories from Rwanda* (New York: Farrar, Straus, & Giroux, 1998).

12. Keith Snow, "Rape as a Weapon of War," *Peacework* 272 (March 1997).

13. Human Rights Watch/Africa, *Shattered Lives: Sexual Violence during the Rwandan Genocide and Its Aftermath* (New York: Human Rights Watch, 1996). See also Catherine Bonnet, "Le viol des femmes survivantes du génocide du Rwanda," in *Rwanda: Un génocide du XXe siècle*, ed. Raymond Verdier et al. (Paris: Editions L'Harmattan, 1995).

analysis. In chapter 5 below, the reader will find further information on the devastation of women's lives in Rwanda, where it is possible that almost every Tutsi woman and adolescent girl who survived the genocide had been raped.[14] An in-depth account of the mass rapes by the Hutu remains to be written.

The best-kept secret of all in the history of twentieth-century atrocities is the Rape of Nanking.[15] It was no secret in 1937 when it occurred: foreigners were able to slip out of Nanking within days and telegraph to the world the terrible news that Japanese soldiers had massacred about 350,000 civilians, many of them women who had first been raped, as well as killed up to 200,000 military prisoners who had put down their arms. The world was shocked, and "the Rape of Nanking" became a stock phrase for "military atrocity."

But as time passed, this event received less attention and gradually even dropped out of the major studies and texts on the Pacific War. That an atrocity of this size with enormous implications for the understanding of both sexism and racism in war could disappear from sight indicates a high degree of denial on the part of scholars and the public. It seems that we remember what we want to believe. Chapter 4 offers an excerpt from Iris Chang's groundbreaking 1997 work on Nanking, her attempt to bring these events back into the light of historical consciousness.

Fortunately, in recent years the documentation of violence against women in armed conflict has begun. Considering only major works, in English, that include a gender analysis, one must begin with Susan Brownmiller's groundbreaking work, which appeared in 1975.[16] Thereafter for a decade or so, scholarship on violence against women concentrated on the (related) issue of domestic violence. However, Kathleen Barry's 1979 work on female sexual slavery and Ximena Bunster's 1985 article on the political torture of women helped to keep issues of women and war alive.[17]

In 1994 the Australian writer George Hicks published the first book in English about the Korean comfort women.[18] The year before, Marjorie Agosin had edited a collection of pieces on women's resistance to political

---

14. Ibid., 24.

15. Iris Chang, *The Rape of Nanking: The Forgotten Holocaust of World War II* (New York: Basic Books, 1997).

16. Susan Brownmiller's *Against Our Will: Men, Women, and Rape* (New York: Simon and Schuster, 1975) contains a long opening chapter on rape in wartime.

17. Kathleen Barry, *Female Sexual Slavery* (New York: Avon Books, 1979); Ximena Bunster, "Surviving beyond Fear: Women and Torture in Latin America," in *Women and Change in Latin America*, ed. June Nash and Helen Sage (New York: Bergin & Garvey, 1985).

18. George Hicks, *The Comfort Women: Japan's Brutal Regime of Enforced Prostitution in the Second World War* (New York: W. W. Norton, 1995; first published in Australia in 1994).

violence in Latin America.[19] The conflict in Bosnia inspired an anthology by Alexandra Stiglmayer on mass rape and rape camps.[20] An excellent anthology on Asian women appeared in 1998 based on papers from the Tokyo Conference on Violence against Women in War and Armed Conflict Situations.[21]

At about this time the major human rights organizations began to show more awareness that women were being victimized in war; for example, in 1995 Human Rights Watch published an impressive compilation of its recent reports on abuses against women's human rights, most of them dealing with armed conflicts.[22] By this time also, the United Nations and the NGOs that work with it began to publish important pieces calling attention to the increasing wartime violence against women. The report of the Center for Women's Global Leadership on the Vienna Conference on Human Rights, along with its account of the testimony of thirty-three women victims, and the publications that came out of the Beijing Conference added to our knowledge.[23]

Cynthia Enloe contributed an important book challenging the effects of a militaristic society on women's lives.[24] Katharine Moon's study of state-sponsored prostitution around U.S. bases in South Korea should also be mentioned.[25]

But the task of documenting, analyzing, and working against violence against women in war is only beginning. Most reporting and commentary still fails to ask, "And what happened to the women?" The effect of these omissions is to render the suffering and deaths of women unimportant. Furthermore, when rape is not mentioned, the historical record is distorted; given the strategic importance assigned to rape in some recent wars, its omission becomes ludicrous. When it *is* mentioned but is neither reflected

---

19. Marjorie Agosin, ed., *Surviving beyond Fear: Women, Children, and Human Rights in Latin America* (Fredonia, N.Y.: White Pine Press, 1993).

20. Alexandra Stiglmayer, ed., *Mass Rape: The War against Women in Bosnia-Herzegovina* (Lincoln: University of Nebraska Press, 1994).

21. Indai Lourdes Sajor, ed., *Common Grounds: Violence against Women in War and Armed Conflict Situations* (Quezon City, Philippines: Asian Center for Women's Human Rights, 1998).

22. *The Human Rights Watch Global Report on Women's Human Rights* (New York: Human Rights Watch, 1995).

23. Charlotte Bunch and Niamh Reilly, *Demanding Accountability: The Global Campaign and Vienna Tribunal for Women's Human Rights* and *Testimonies of the Global Tribunal on Violations of Women's Human Rights* (New Brunswick, N.J.: Center for Women's Global Leadership, 1994).

24. Cynthia Enloe, *Does Khaki Become You? The Militarization of Women's Lives* (Boston: South End Press, 1983).

25. Katharine Moon, *Sex among Allies: Military Prostitution in U.S.-Korean Relations* (New York: Columbia University Press, 1997).

on nor incorporated into the total condemnation, it becomes a lesser crime, a footnote to what is traditionally seen as the more pressing problems of war.

The purpose of this book is thus not only to illustrate the increasing amount of wartime violence against women but also to call attention to the need for more gender awareness in analyzing and working to prevent these tragedies.

The Nature of Late Twentieth-Century Military Violence against Women

The major new awareness that we have gained is that, in this new kind of warfare, women have a strategic importance. Whether as "toilets" (Japanese soldiers' name for comfort women), as surrogates for men's honor, as unwilling child bearers, as (literal) targets, or as prized symbols and measures of how destructive an armed force can be, women now figure regularly in military strategy. The forms of "using" women are various, but the ultimate effect is the same: the combination of familiar forms of sexual objectification of women with the extraordinary power of the military in wartime has created enormous possibilities for new violence against women. As Rhonda Copelon observed, "War tends to intensify the brutality, repetitiveness, public spectacle, and likelihood of rape. War diminishes sensitivity to human suffering and intensifies men's sense of entitlement, superiority, avidity, and social license to rape."[26]

One form of that violence, already discussed, is military sexual slavery. Part 1 of this book alerts us to this crime of forced prostitution, when the crimes of entrapment and kidnapping are added to gang rape, in a prisonlike environment from which there is no escape. Drawing mainly on the testimony of Korean and Taiwanese comfort women, these chapters document a practice that should have been condemned by international law as soon as Japan was defeated in World War II. That this was not done made it more likely that these horrors would be repeated, and indeed they were, in the rape camps and detention camps where Serbs incarcerated, tortured, raped, and killed Bosnian Muslims. The reader can trace that story in chapter 5.

"Systematic" or "strategic" rape is the second new concept to emerge when one studies armed conflict with an awareness of gender. Planned rape, commanded by higher authorities, used in order to enable men to fight better (as in the Japanese and Serbian armies) and to humiliate and demoralize the enemy, has become a major strategy in a number of armies (see chaps. 5–6, 8, and 10). When commanders (Serbian) and political leaders (Rwandan)

---

26. Rhonda Copelon, "Resurfacing Gender: Reconceptualizing Crimes against Women in Time of War," in *Mass Rape*, ed. A. Stiglmayer, 213.

add forced impregnation as a goal, the societal chaos that follows is almost indescribable. This new "war by rape" works almost as effectively as the usual war of bombs and land mines, and fulfills as well the old promise to soldiers of receiving women as booty.

Another version of rape as a weapon of war, one not documented in this book, is the kidnapping of women to serve as "wives" for soldiers, as practiced today in Sudan and by rebels in northern Uganda. A further variation on using human beings as spoils of war is the practice during massacres of singling out young boys, old enough to work, to be used as household slaves; chapter 8 documents this custom.

It is not surprising that one kind of violence breeds another. That is never more true than in the connections between military and domestic violence. Some of these crossovers are examined in terms of Kenyan society (chap. 7) and Nicaraguan society (chap. 9).

Behind all of these customs lies the training of soldiers. What attitudes toward women are they taught? What basis is laid for killing civilians and raping women? When ordered to kill unarmed civilians, especially children, soldiers sometimes balk.[27] What makes a man, initially unwilling, finally agree to rape a woman prisoner?[28] In order to understand questions like these, chapter 11 investigates the military milieu in the U.S. armed forces, probing into what difference it makes that it remains a mostly male society.

In chapter 12, the line between "free" and forced prostitution is found to be very thin; in fact, the exploitation of "voluntary" Korean prostitutes around U.S. bases there today turns out to have similarities with the military sexual slavery of the comfort women. The poverty that drives many women into prostitution around army bases today is no different from the poverty that led many to sign up for "jobs" with the Japanese military during World War II. That the Korean military brothels are licensed by the Korean government through an agreement with the United States makes the connection all the clearer.

This is not, however, ultimately a book about victims. All of these women have been victimized, to be sure, but the important message from the 1990s is that women are speaking up, working together—and being heard. The response to them is late in coming and painfully slow in developing, but it

---

27. See, for example, Mark Danner's account of the massacre at El Mozote, El Salvador, where the officer in charge had to bayonet a small child in order to get his men to begin killing the children.

28. Alexandra Stiglmayer interviewed three Serbian perpetrators. All the men reported that they had been ordered to rape and kill Muslim women. One said that the order was supposed to raise their morale and that if he did not do it, they would take away the Muslim house they had given him; another said that the "Chetniks" would have killed him if he had refused to rape and kill. Two of them ran away rather than have to rape or kill anymore. *Mass Rape*, 147–61.

is now irreversible. It is now being embedded in new international laws and court procedures that give women unprecedented power over their lives. That story, surely one of the major accomplishments of women and their allies in recent times, is told in chapter 13.

Throughout the book the reader may look for those forms of violence that are gender-specific. Women suffer not only from torture, kidnapping, and murder, as men do, but also from sexual mutilations and forced pregnancies and sexual slavery, which is the violation of their bodies by rape. It is these crimes that have been invisible during wartime for far too long. The UN special rapporteur on violence against women has observed that "although rape is one of the most widely used types of violation against women and girls, it remains the least condemned war crime."[29]

The authors in this book write with urgency and passion. We are aware that every day women are being tortured, raped, and killed for political reasons. We want to end these atrocities, to stop forever the inhuman and degrading treatment. Because it is a matter of life and death for many, we must all speak up.

---

29. Radhika Coomaraswamy, in *Common Grounds*, ed. I. L. Sajor, 25.

Part One

SEXUAL SLAVERY

Wartime rape is not all of a kind; indeed, three kinds are readily distinguishable. Individual rapes are the sexual assaults that some men commit, whether in civilian or military life; their purpose is almost always to assert power over another. These rapes damage women and can ruin their lives.

Mass rape is used to terrorize communities. This kind of rape, which is described in Part Two, is the outcome of armies and paramilitaries planning sexual attacks on an enemy's women as a strategy of war. Mass rape often takes the form of rape-and-kill; that is, after being assaulted, the victims are murdered as if they were combatants. The results lead to some of the deepest feelings of hatred and revenge that war can produce.

Military sexual slavery is yet another kind of wartime rape. The purpose is to satisfy the sexual desires of an army with maximum efficiency, by supplying women, almost always from a different national group, for the troops. Military sexual slavery, which damages and ruins women's lives and leaves a scar in their communities and in international relations, is not prostitution. To be a prostitute is a voluntary choice, that is, as voluntary as a choice made under extreme economic pressures can be. Women and girls forced into military brothels have not made that choice. They have been tricked or kidnapped into servicing soldiers, and they are confined as if they were prisoners of war.

In World War II Japan organized a massive system of military brothels that extended across the Japanese empire. High officials of the Japanese Imperial Army ordered that women and girls from Japan's colonies, Korea and Taiwan, be "recruited" for the "comfort stations" that were being set up inside or beside all major army, navy, and marine bases. As Japan conquered much of Southeast Asia, women and girls from the newly colonized lands—from China, Malaysia, Indonesia, and the Philippines—were added. Ultimately about 200,000 women were abducted to fill the brothels, but there were never enough: women were forced to service as many as twenty or thirty or more men a day. About half the women died, killed either by disease, the violence of soldiers, or bombings. A number committed suicide.

After the war, although the Allies knew about the system of brothels, they did not prosecute Japan for forcing these tens of thousands of women into sexual slavery. The chapters below document this crime, explore its effects on the women's lives, and introduce the story of what happened when some of the survivors broke silence after fifty years to demand recognition and recompense. In the process, these chapters raise issues of racism, colonialism, imperialism, and militarism, which show what can happen when these forms of oppression are added to the basic crime of sexually exploiting women's bodies.

1

"Your Comfort versus My Death"

Korean Comfort Women

CHUNG HYUN-KYUNG

Her name is Noh Soo-Bock. She was born in a small southern village, Ahn Shim, in Korea in 1921. She was the first daughter of a poor farmer's family. Her father's name was Noh Back-Bong. She cannot remember her mother's name because people never called her mother by her own name.

It was during the time of the Japanese colonial occupation in Korea. Because of severe taxation by the colonial government, Soo-Bock's father, a poor landless farmer, could not feed his family even with his backbreaking work. Soo-Bock's memory of her childhood, therefore, was filled with hunger. She spent many hours a day gathering leaves, wild vegetables, and plant roots in the fields and mountains. It was a difficult time to grow up as a girl-child. She could not even imagine herself attending elementary school. She never learned how to read or write the Korean language. Instead, from her grandfather she learned a few Chinese letters and the Confucian way of womanhood, especially the importance of chastity. In spite of all the hardships of her childhood, however, she still remembers vividly the magnificent colors of spring flowers in the mountains behind her shabby house and the beauty of the calm lake in her village.

When Soo-Bock became fourteen years old, her parents married her off to a family in the next village. Her parents' poverty forced her into this early marriage. One more mouth in the family meant one more bowl of rice that they could not afford. Following the custom of her time, she obeyed her parents and married a man she had never met. Without knowing him, she slept with him in deep darkness on her wedding night, as all Korean women did in her time. The next day she got up and saw her husband's face for the first time. He was a leper, and she fainted.

Reprinted with permission of the publisher from *Women Resisting Violence: Spirituality for Life,* ed. Mary John Mananzan (Maryknoll, N.Y.: Orbis Books, 1996).

It was torture to sleep with her leper husband. Fear and disgust filled her life. Ignoring Soo-Bock's pain, her mother-in-law made her work all the time, but she did not give Soo-Bock enough food to eat. Fear and hunger overwhelmed her, and she decided to run away. As if she were possessed by a ghost, she ran and ran through the mountains and streams and finally arrived at her father's house, the home where she had grown up with her brothers and sister. Her father was so angry with her shaming the family's reputation by running away from her marriage that he chased her away, saying, "If you want to die, go and die in your husband's house. You are not one of our family any longer. You belong to your husband's family."

Weeping, Soo-Bock walked and walked to the nearby big city, Tae-ku, without having any plan or knowing anybody. She became a maid. With the hope that her family might accept her if she had money, she saved all her meager earnings and one year later visited her family again. Her father still did not allow her even to enter the house. Her mother pleaded with him to allow Soo-Bock to stay just one night with her brothers and sister. Her father's response was the same, "Go die in your husband's house," and he chased her away again. Her mother followed her to the edge of the village, weeping and beating her breast in sadness and helplessness.

In despair Soo-Bock went back to the big city and became a maid once more. She moved from house to house and ended in Pu-San, the second largest city in Korea. There she met her second husband. She was now seventeen years old. She visited her family again with her new husband, expecting that her father would accept her now that she had a new husband. But her father was the same. He kept telling her, "What shame you brought upon our family!" She was chased away again. This was the last time she ever saw her home.

It was autumn 1942. Soo-Bock went to the well to wash her clothes. It was dusk. When she tried to draw water from the well, four Japanese policemen appeared. First, they asked her for water; then one policeman tried to grab her. When she escaped his advance, other police joined him and tied her with rope, yelling and threatening to kill her. She resisted them with all her power, but they pulled her by a rope and put her in their vehicle.

Finally Soo-Bock ended up in a police station. There were already five or six young Korean women there. The Japanese policemen said to them that they were chosen to be sent abroad as representatives of the Japanese emperor. Then they gave military uniforms to these women. The Korean women pleaded with them to get a message to their families before leaving Korea, but their requests were denied. If the Korean women talked about or did something that the Japanese police or soldiers did not like, the women were beaten severely.

Soo-Bock and the other Korean women were forced to travel in the bottom level of a Japanese military ship, and they sailed for forty days. Then they arrived on a shore with many palm trees. It was Singapore. Upon their arrival they were transported to a military base. The next morning, when they awoke, they found many Japanese soldiers trying to look into their tent. Seeing the women getting up, the soldiers began to shout and tried to get into their tent. The Korean women held one another tightly and trembled with fear. Then a soldier came in and told them to prepare for the song party.

When evening came, thousands of soldiers filled the military field while Soo-Bock and the other Korean women were forced to go onstage and sing for them. The Japanese soldiers became so excited they began to shout and sing and dance. As soon as the women returned to their tent, a Japanese lieutenant came to Soo-Bock's room and tried to rape her. When she begged him not to, he hit her with his fist and kicked her in the stomach until she fainted. When she regained consciousness, she knew what she had become: she had become a so-called comfort woman for the Japanese soldiers. Soo-Bock saw the other Korean women, to whom the same thing had happened. They burst into tears. They wailed together. Then the soldiers came in and hit them as if the Korean women were their punching bag; they went out, locking the door from the outside. This was the beginning of Soo-Bock's life as a "comfort woman."

Korean women had to clean the Japanese military bases, wash the soldiers' clothing, and carry their bullet boxes in the morning. Starting in the afternoon and lasting through the night, they had to receive Japanese soldiers. Sometimes they received more than sixty soldiers a day. If they resisted, they were stripped and whipped in front of Japanese soldiers in the military field. Japanese soldiers called them "cho-sen-pee," a derogatory term for Korean women (which literally means "Korean pussy").

Many of the women started to die from starvation, exhaustion, venereal diseases, or wounds from being battered by the Japanese soldiers. After many days of despair and crying, Soo-Bock determined that she would survive. She could not die like a dog in this strange land. She started to eat as much as she could, and she also became very obedient. She did everything the soldiers asked her to do. She knew they were ready to kill anybody. Some of them even struck their sword on the *tatami* (Japanese floor) when they raped Korean women. It was better not to provoke them. Soo-Bock was transported from one base to another. On one base in Thailand she saw other Korean women, but they were not allowed to be together. Japanese soldiers were afraid that if Korean women got together, they might make plans to run away.

Early in 1945 Soo-Bock began to hear rumors of Japan's imminent fall. With that rumor more Korean women were gathered from other bases and brought to Soo-Bock's base in order to "comfort" Japanese soldiers. The more they heard about the impending fall of Japan, the more they were raped by nervous soldiers. In June of 1945, Japan surrendered at Singapore, and English soldiers came onto the base. The Korean women were transported to refugee camps. There were many other women from Thailand and Burma. More than two hundred of them lived together, and there they heard the story of Japan's defeat on 15 August. They shouted, "Long live Korea!"; they jumped for joy, embraced one another, and wept together. Finally the day came, the day of returning home. When Soo-Bock heard of the plan, she became very anxious. "How can I go back home and meet my family with this dirty body?" she asked. She became very depressed. Her father's strict face appeared in her dreams again and again. After many days of agony she decided not to go home, and she ran away from the refugee camp.

Soo-Book ran through the jungle and became a beggar in a land where she knew no one and could not speak the language. A man called Mohammed, a devout Muslim, rescued her, and she became a maid in his family. After working in his house in Malaysia and receiving his family's encouragement to work for her own independence, she left for Thailand, landing in Hot Chai, where a new mining business was flourishing. She found a job in a Chinese restaurant there and also met the husband she was to keep for life, a poor old Chinese bachelor, Mr. Chen. He could not marry because he was so poor. It was the first time in her life that Soo-Bock had felt that strange feeling called "love." In the autumn of 1947, she married him in a lotus flower Buddhist temple. For Soo-Bock it was a moment of rebirth. She was determined to bring her own beautiful lotus flower of life to bloom out of her muddy past.

Their restaurant business flourished, but Soo-Bock could not become pregnant because of the many rapes she had endured. She persuaded her husband to take a young second wife to give them children. Although he refused her in the beginning, he later gave in. They took a young Chinese woman, who gave birth to three children. The two women, their three children, and the one husband lived together happily, helping and appreciating one another. Soo-Bock often said, "Korean, Japanese, Chinese, Thai—we are all friends."

Soo-Bock is now seventy-four years old. She misses Korea but is still afraid to go back. She wants to go home at least once before she dies. She asked herself, "Is it really all right to visit home now?" For many days she could not answer that question. Then suddenly peace came into her heart: "Why not? It is my home. What happened to my life was not my fault. Now I am not afraid of anything. I will go home."[1]

---

1. The story comes from Kim Moon-Sook, *Mal Sal Doen Myo Bee-Yeo Cha Chung Shin Dae* (Destroyed tombstone: comfort women) (Seoul: K.W.S.J., 1990), 91–122.

The Comfort Women System

Soo-Bock's story is the story of a Korean woman. It is the kind of story that is both ancient and contemporary for any Korean woman. Women in Korea all know this story both strange and familiar. It haunts each of us every time we hear it because we are Korean women. We are still deep in the story even today.

Every group of women must have their "root story" of what it means to be women in their own specific history and land. African American women remember stories of slavery, brutal kidnappings, rape, forced breeding and labor, and intentional destruction of their family and dignity. Jewish women remember the story of the Holocaust, Nazism, Hitler, German nationalism, Auschwitz, stripping, the gas chambers, and medical experiments with their bodies. European women remember the story of witch-hunting. In the name of holiness so-called witches were captured, tried, tortured, drowned, burned alive. Women from Asia, Africa, Latin America, the Pacific, and former European colonies remember what it means to be "other," "primitive," and "savage" in their own land, slowly losing their language, culture, and memories.

As a Korean feminist liberation theologian who refuses any kind of colonial domination in my life, I have to remember and retell Soo-Bock's story, the Korean women's root story, again and again so that we can exorcise this haunting ghost of debilitating rage, fear, and helplessness to bring our full womanhood to bloom like a lotus flower of wisdom from the mud of suffering. Soo-Bock's story, the story of the comfort women, had been erased from both Korean and Japanese history for the last fifty years until a group of persistent Korean feminists looked for survivors all over Asia and gathered evidence.[2] Neither the Korean nor the Japanese government wanted to talk about what happened to Korean women during World War II. For Korean men it was too shameful for their egos to accept what happened to Korean women, and there were more important things they needed to talk about in relation to Japan. And for Japanese men it was too guilt provoking to confront what really happened. They preferred to deny the whole thing because they did not want uncomfortable guilty feelings, nor did they want to give material reparation. Not surprisingly, Korean churches also kept silence about these women's lives.

According to research by a Korean feminist group, the number of so-called comfort women from Korea was more than 200,000. The exact

2. A group of Korean feminists formed the Korean Council for the Women Drafted for Sexual Slavery by Japan (K.W.S.J.). They are the main women responsible for elevating the "comfort women" issue to a national and international level. For more information, contact them at Room 802, Christian Building 136-46 Yunchi-dong, Chongro-Ku, Seoul, 110-701, Korea. Fax: 822-763-9634.

number is not available because the Japanese government still refuses to release their military documents. The comfort women system was created by the Japanese military in 1932 and maintained until August 1945, when Japan gave in unconditionally to the united army of the West.[3]

Research indicates that comfort women bases were located in China, Hong Kong, Indochina, the Philippines, Malaysia, Singapore, Borneo, the East Indies, Burma, Thailand, Papua New Guinea, Saipan, Guam, the Coral Sea Islands Territory, and Japan.[4] Those who served as comfort women came from Japan, Korea, Taiwan, China, the Philippines, Indonesia, Vietnam, and the Netherlands.[5] These women mainly acted as sexual slaves for the Japanese military. They also worked as cleaning and laundry women, manual laborers, and cooks. The number of soldiers they received a day ranged from one to ninety. "Comfort" bases were established in military tents, in small houses near a base, in the mountains, in small ditches, in halls, etc. One out of three women are thought to have died during their slavery, and there are no records for the women who survived. Only a few women have surfaced as witnesses in several of the involved countries. Most of their recruitment was done by force or deception (a good-paying job, enough food, clothing, education, etc.).

The reasons why the Japanese military needed comfort women were as follows:[6]

1. During the Japan-China War many Japanese soldiers engaged in killing, stealing, burning, and raping. As a result, many Chinese who were victims of these crimes became intensely hostile to the Japanese. Rape especially was most disturbing to them. The Japanese military leaders needed a system of sexual release for their soldiers if they were not to rape women in the occupied land.

2. The Japanese war was a causeless war from the beginning, and there was not much possibility of winning. Many soldiers became restless, and they did not receive the vacations promised them. Therefore, military leaders tried to give them some "comfort" and recreation.

3. Sexual disease was the big concern. Most of the Japanese prostitutes they hired were experienced professionals with a high possibility of

---

3. *Chong Kun We An Bu Moon Che Eui Yeok Sa Hak Chuck Kyu Myung* (A historical research on the comfort women problem) (Seoul: K.W.S.J., 1990), 1.

4. Ibid.

5. In addition, there was a witness that some Australian nurses were forced by the Japanese military to be comfort women.

6. Jin Sung Chung, *Ill Bon Kuk We An Bu Jung Chack Eui Hyung Sung Kwa Byunwha* (The formation and change of comfort women policy in Japanese history) (Seoul: K.W.S.J., 1990), 1–2.

having venereal diseases. The military needed "clean women" who had not been exposed to sexual activity. Therefore they chose "chosun" women (the name of Korea at that time) who were raised in a Confucian ideology of strict chastity. Korean women constituted 90 percent of the entire force of comfort women.

4. In order to preserve military security, authorities needed comfort women based in the military. Otherwise soldiers would visit local brothels and spread military secrets by accident to local people. They needed tight control.

When we critically analyze "military sexual slavery by Japan,"[7] there are four important factors that made this cruel system possible: state, nation, class, and gender. Without looking at the dynamics of these four factors, we cannot clearly name the evil of military sexual slavery by Japan.

Japan's emperor state had been the backbone of sexual slavery since 1889. Japan established a state in which the emperor had absolute power over all people, including the military. What the state required from the people was absolute obedience. This state stabilized a pyramid-shaped, hierarchical society in which discrimination among people of different status was emphasized. In the process of militarization this state began to have the character of fascism. Therefore, young soldiers felt tremendous repression in being only a "yes" man, and they vented their frustration on women with the most raw and cruel forms of violence. For example, kamikaze pilots forced Korean comfort women to commit suicide one day before the pilots themselves left to bomb the united army.[8] Korean women were also forced to say, "Japanese and Korean are one people under the emperor's lordship," before they were raped by Japanese soldiers.[9] Therefore, if kamikaze was a holy, patriotic sacrifice for the emperor's altar, the rape of Korean women by Japanese soldiers was considered holy, patriotic sex at the emperor's temple, which was the military base.

Colonialism, which promoted Japanese supremacy, was also the backbone of the sexual slavery of Korean women. Japan's ambition for expansion was based on its early adaptation of capitalism and its political agenda to assuage the restlessness of the Samurai by attempting domination over other

---

7. This term was developed by K.W.S.J. because they perceived that what happened to Korean women under Japanese militarism was not just being "comfort women" to them. It was systematized, intentional slavery. Therefore, they named it "military sexual slavery by Japan." Young feminists insist on using this term, but old comfort women themselves refuse to use the term "sexual slavery." They prefer the term "comfort women."

8. *Historical Research*, chaps. 5, 11.

9. Witness by a comfort woman; her name cannot be traced.

nations.[10] Since Japanese capitalism was not as well developed as that of Western colonial countries, Japan's colonial policy was most exploitative and violent to accumulate the most capital from the colonies.[11] Japan controlled Korea and Taiwan and tried to destroy peoples' national identities by changing their names, language, religion, and culture into the Japanese style.[12] Using hundreds of thousands of young Korean women, who would become the future mothers of the Korean nation, as sex slaves and making them barren was one of the most effective ways of humiliating, confusing, and finally destroying the Korean people.

The development of capitalism in Japan was state controlled. The expansion of capitalism meant the invasion of more colonies for capital accumulation and the rise of many poor people (a proletariat class) in Japan and its many colonies. The development of capitalism was accompanied by the development of public prostitution. In this system, many poor Japanese women were forced into prostitution, and many young women in the colonies were forced into sexual slavery.

In the patriarchal, or "family," emperor state of Japan the emperor became a national father of all the people. According to Japanese law, a wife was the property of her husband. Because of her gender, she was not allowed any economic activity or ability to make legal decisions. Also she could not act on her own without her husband's permission.[13] On the basis that the establishment of public prostitution would be helpful for two reasons, the emperor state legalized public prostitution, which flourished with the rise of capitalism. One reason was the release of sexual desire, especially for the Samurai caste, because of their own anxiety and psychological instability, which was explosive because of the continued situation of war. A second reason was to protect the maintenance of a strict family system.[14] It was presumed that if men could have access to many sexual adventures in public, they would not leave their wives.

In the process the emperor state used three different gender ideologies for three different classes of women. For upper- or middle-class women who were educated, it was "the ideology of motherhood." The model of female education was the combination of state, family, and motherhood. The state trained women to be the mothers of Japan, the mothers of militarization,

---

10. Masako Fukae, "System of Buying Prostitutes and Emperor System," in *Woman, Emperor System, War*, ed. Yuko Suzuki and Kazuko Hen Kondo (Tokyo: Origin Publishing Center, 1989), 202–5.

11. Chung, *Formation and Change*, 4.

12. See the witnesses in K.W.S.J., *Witnesses of the Victims of Military Sexual Slavery by Japan* (Seoul: K.W.S.J., 1992).

13. Yukiko Tunoda, "Sexual Violence and Emperor System," in *Woman, Emperor System, War*, ed. Y. Suzuki and K. H. Kondo, 197.

14. Chung, *Formation and Change*, 4.

the mothers of warriors, the mothers of a healthy nation, the mothers of the Japanization of Asia, etc. Many lectures and books were published in praise of motherhood.[15] For unmarried middle-class or lower-class women, the state imposed "the ideology of the productive worker." With all kinds of special decrees, the emperor state recruited young unmarried women as workers.[16] Lower-class women excluded from the above two ideologies were given "the ideology of comfort," which proclaimed them to be necessary members of the emperor nation. In this role, the women gave comfort, peace, and stability to the big, abusive, dysfunctional, repressive emperor's family.

A "Root Story" for Korean Women

Why is Soo-Bock's story, which happened fifty years ago, still a "root story" for Korean women? Because it is happening here right now in the everyday lives of Korean women and many other Asian sisters. We still have poor fathers who want to get rid of their daughters. We still have fathers, brothers, and comrades who honor our chastity more than our life itself. We still have our leper husband who thinks his maleness can cover any flaws in his life. Even though prostitution is illegal in Korea and many other Asian countries, we still have a state that sells our women's bodies shamelessly, this time in the name of national progress.[17] We still have colonialists who come to our land and destroy poor women's lives in the name of development, the Uruguay Round, GATT, WTO, MTV, CNN, the peacekeeping army, and tourism. We still have capitalists who commodify everything under the sun: our women, our children, our brides, our workers, our earth. And we still have soldiers who call us "a little brown fucking machine fueled by rice."[18]

After the series of wars in Asia—World War II, the Korean War, and the Vietnam War—Asia became the brothel of the world. Indeed, "bananas, beaches, and bases" went together hand in hand.[19] Where the militaristic state, colonialism, the patriarchal family, and capitalism thrive, modern-day comfort women and sexual slavery flourish.

---

15. Yuko Suzuki, "Mr. Horoshito, 'Showa, and Women'" in *Women, Emperor System, War*, ed. Y. Suzuki and K. H. Kondo, 23–25.

16. Soon-Choo Yeo, "Ill Che Malki Cho Sun In Yeo Cha Keun Ro Chung Shin Dae Ae Kwan Han Yeonku" (Study on Korean women workers in the late stage of Japanese colonialism, master's thesis, Ewha Women's University, Seoul, 1993).

17. Korean Minister of Culture Min Kwan Shik once congratulated Korean prostitutes for bringing foreign currency to the Korean economy. He called them "patriots" who work hard for Korea's economic progress. Similar comments were made by politicians in the Philippines and Thailand.

18. This was a name for Filipino prostitutes used among U.S. soldiers based there.

19. Cf. the excellent research on multinational corporations, tourism, and militarism: Cynthia Enloe, *Bananas, Beaches, and Bases* (London: Pandora, 1989; Berkeley: University of California Press, 1990).

Why Are We Little?

In five hundred years of colonialism we have become little physically and psychologically. Five hundred years of malnutrition, oppression, and repression can make anybody little. The most difficult disease we have in our psyche is five-hundred-year-old internalized colonialism. Come to Korea and see that all the models for the best clothing companies are white Western women and men. Come to Asia. Most of us communicate with one another in English, a colonizer's language. With the CNNization of the world and all the rhetoric of internationalization and globalization, the world became one humongous market. Our young people do not grow up with Tagore, Gandhi, Lao-tzu, or Chang Zu. They grow up with Madonna, Michael Jackson, and Hollywood movies of sex and violence.

Why Are We Brown?

We became a brownized people by the symbolic representation of a graded color system in this racist world. We became brown people who are closer to earth, nature, primitiveness, wildness, and chaos. We are the ultimate oriental mystics, exotic natives, and the "other" by the orientalist formation of world civilization. Orientalism is a form of cultural imperialism, manufactured inside the mind of Westerners.[20] One of the main reasons Western men come to Asia for prostitution or why they buy mail-order brides from Asia is that they want "a real woman," a real feminine woman. Blaming the feminist movement in the West, they say there are no more womanlike women in the West because of feminism. Women have become manlike—no more softness, no more vulnerability, no more obedience! So they come to Asia to find small, brown (more natural), soft, vulnerable, obedient, real women. A San Francisco dating service listed its hottest item as young professional Asian women. Professional white men usually seek Asian women. Asian women also prefer professional white men to upgrade their social status. White men seek psychological and personal happiness by hooking up with Asian women in spite of the downgrading of their social status. They say they are willing to *sacrifice* a little bit of status because they feel happier (feel more like a normal man) being with Asian women because of their femininity, a trait that white women do not have any longer.

Why Are We a Fucking Machine?

We became a fucking machine because we never have been a subject for the soldiers, capitalists, and colonialists. We have been a machine for them. When Western men made the whole earth into a battlefield and became brutally violent warriors as hunters of the world, they began to mechanize

---

20. See Edward W. Said, *Orientalism* (New York: Pantheon Books, 1978).

the whole world, including us. And people who lose subjectivity (the right to act as subjects) become mechanized. "Discover, conquer, dominate, exploit, and manipulate!" Fucking has never been sex. It is not making love. It is violence.

Spirituality for Life

Then where was our subjectivity? Where were our power to resist and our legacy of victory? Are we only the passive victims of complex systems of oppression? Where were Korean men and women when Soo-Bock and her friends were dying in the battlefield? What could the Korean church and Korean Christians have done for so many Soo-Bocks in Korean history?

When Soo-Bock ran away from her leper husband, when she determined not to die and began to eat as much as she could and became extremely obedient to violent soldiers, when she ran away again from the refugee camp in Malaysia and never went home, when she found her work and love in a foreign land, she became an agent, *a subject for her own life.* Her mere survival from sexual slavery to the Japanese military is itself a legacy of victory in the history of Korean women. Like her wish on her wedding day at the lotus flower Buddhist temple, she brought her own lotus flower to bloom out of her suffering.

In her old age she told us, "Korean, Japanese, Chinese, Thai, are not different. We are all friends!" Where did she find this *power of forgiveness?* Why did she choose to forgive the Japanese? Was it her Buddhism with its wisdom, compassion, and loving-kindness? Or was it her experience of being loved by Malaysian, Chinese, and Thai in her new homeland? I do not know. What I know is she cut the vicious cycle of violence and revenge with her power, which I cannot easily name. Then Soo-Bock came home in her heart, the home that starved, deceived, and rejected her. She decided to come home to Korea, saying, "*It is my home.* What happened to my life was not my fault. Now I am not afraid of anything. I will go home." Finally, after fifty years of exile, she knew she had the power to go home, that place of poverty and abandonment. She claimed that place as her home. She accepted her life as it was, seeing that what happened to her life was not her fault. Suddenly she was not afraid of anything, and she came home.

From Soo-Bock we learn her legacy of survival, forgiveness, and acceptance. Her survival was her liberation. Her forgiveness was her best revenge, and her acceptance was her best resistance.

There are many other Korean women who followed the legacy of Soo-Bock, choosing life in their own predicament. Lee Ock-Soon is one of them. Lee Ock-Soon is an ex-prostitute. Now she is an adviser for Magdalena House, a resting place for prostitutes founded by the Maryknoll Sisters.

What Magdalena House does for prostitutes is give them a safe place to rest, talk, share, and just be. It is a ministry of presence. Sisters or volunteers in the house do not teach the Bible or impose worship. They actively are with anybody who comes to see them.

Lee Ock-Soon's life as a prostitute began with rape, too. After retiring from prostitution, she became a big sister to other prostitutes and counsels young prostitutes. If any man treats a prostitute violently or does not pay the fee, she organizes other prostitutes to hit him back, to stop him from abusing women, or to make sure he pays her fee. Therefore, it is clear in her circle of prostitutes that men can buy sexual service, but no violence against women is allowed. She also organized an English class for prostitutes so that they will not be cheated by foreigners, who are their major customers.

While Ock-Soon was doing this kind of "sisterhood work," one man, a taxi driver, joined her group. He helps her by providing the speed and mobility to get her work done. After some years of working together, he confessed his love to her, and she to him. One spring day they were married in the Catholic cathedral in Seoul. Ock-Soon wore a white wedding dress, which is the dream dress for most prostitutes. Prostitutes have an intense longing to marry the one they love while wearing a white wedding dress, the symbol of chastity and purity. Even though they sell their sexual service, they believe they are always keeping their purity and chastity of heart for someone they love.

When Ock-Soon got married, all her friends got together, and we read a poem on Mary Magdalene at her wedding. Everybody cried. For the first time I thought it was good for some theologians in church history to have taught us that Magdalene was a prostitute. That teaching may be wrong, but how wonderful to have that teaching for Korean prostitutes who identify themselves with Mary Magdalene, the beloved disciple of the good news of Nazareth, Jesus.

Many of the prostitutes at Magdalena House became Catholic, inspired by the "presence" they received from the Maryknoll Sisters there. However, they are not the obedient, ordinary Roman Catholic Christians. They have their hermeneutics of suspicion coming from their experience. According to their joke, among their customers the clergy and scholar-professor types are the most stingy and demanding customers, for whom prostitutes do not have much respect. They select what they want to hear from the pastors' sermons, remembering what happened in their workplaces.

I wanted to ask Ock-Soon the same question I put to Soo-Bock: Where did your power of survival, wisdom, and courage come from? What is it in your presence that heals and empowers other prostitutes so much? What is the name or the nature of that power? These are the questions at the root of spirituality for life.

Rita Nakashima Brock has helped us with these questions in her discussion of the importance of innocence and the power of willful nurturing for the empowerment of women.[21] According to Brock, Western Christianity's emphasis on innocent victim and oppositional relationship between good and evil is not helpful to solve the complex problems in women's lives. Rather, it is more empowering to women to lose their childlike innocence and transform it into the willful nurturing of motherhood that embraces the complexity of both good and evil. Brock drops some hints toward new directions for feminist power for problem solving. She observes that the Asian way of problem solving has *aesthetic* direction rather than *ethical* direction. By aesthetic direction she means the longing for harmony and balance. In ethical direction, what is good or evil and what is right or wrong are the main concern. But in aesthetic direction, what restores balance and harmony is the most important concern.

When I look at the present situation of worldwide violence against women, I feel deep despair. Then I become impatient. After all these years of the feminist movement, women's studies, and feminist theology, is the situation of women, especially violence against women, getting any better? Does my work make any difference in women's lives? With all these questions I am searching for that healing power, that life-sustaining, liberating, transforming power that my foremother and sister, Soo-Bock and Ock-Soon, lived out.

What is that power then? More and more I am inclined to Rita's hint of *the power that restores balance and harmony.* Yes, we need feminist social, cultural, political, and economic analysis to name the evil and to see the alternatives. Yes, we need an organized mass movement of women to change laws and customs and to stop the injustice that destroys women's lives. However, we need still more. That "more" might be the energy of raw life: Ki, chi, Shakti, prajna, *ruah,* the Tao, mysterious female, the spirit of the valley that never dries up.[22] How do I really know that power? I am still searching, but I feel something is growing in my womb.

---

21. Rita Nakashima Brock, "Loss of Innocence and Willful Nurturance" (keynote speech given to the Violence against Women Conference organized by the Center for the Prevention of Domestic Violence, Chicago, 1993). Cf. Brock, *Journeys by Heart: A Christology of Erotic Power* (New York: Crossroad, 1988).

22. Lao-Tzu, *Tao Te Ching*, trans. Gia-fu Feng and Jane English (New York: Knopf, 1972), chap. 6.

2

Japanese Women Who Stand with Comfort Women

AIKO OGOSHI and KIYOKO SHIMIZU

At the end of the twentieth century, it is clear that this era has been marked by wars and violence. As such, now is the time that we must recall the crimes of this century against humanity, particularly those of World War II. Of the many atrocities, the ones most often cited are the Nazi Holocaust, the United States' nuclear bombings of Hiroshima and Nagasaki, the Japanese Imperial Army's Rape of Nanking, and Japan's government-sponsored sexual enslavement of women under the euphemism "comfort women."

The latter two issues concern us Japanese, but instead of directly confronting these matters, we have closed our eyes, deceived ourselves, and sought escape in forgetfulness and ignorance. But former comfort women, after many years of great pain and anger, have come forward with their charges. Their appearance has conclusively shaken our self-deception. Through these women, we have had, for the first time, the experience of feeling close at hand to the actual existence of these victims, and in the face of their intense accusation, we have been compelled to see ourselves as victimizers. We have begun to acknowledge our long-denied guilt for a crime in the same category as the Holocaust.

These are issues that our parents' and grandparents' generation have attempted to conceal and erase; however, they are now our problem. Because we neither confronted the actualities of our past nor sought the truth on our own, we have left the former comfort women trapped in a prison of pain and forced silence. We have no choice but to speak out. Should we not face this issue, there is no way we can discuss any ideas of feminist ethics.

Early Japanese feminists made the foolish mistake of agreeing with, and being an active accomplice to, the colonization of Asia and the wars of aggression. We must face the fact that no matter their good intentions, the result of their ignorance and arrogance was the loss of many lives and the rape of countless women. We postwar feminists must make ourselves aware of feminism's complicity in the war: we are in a position where we can no longer allow a single point of deception or concealment.

We are academic women studying and teaching Japanese feminist philosophy and ethics, while we are also activists fighting against sexual harassment and violence in Japanese society. We feel responsible for understanding the appeals of former comfort women. There is a need for a ground-level consideration of this problem, recognizing that this is an issue tied to the basic human rights of contemporary women. We intend to make known the substance of this crime, bring to light its causes, charge those responsible, prosecute the Japanese state for its crime, and demand an apology and financial recompense for each and every one of the victims. Furthermore, we work to understand the roots in Japanese society of these unprecedented crimes: we investigate the environmental and cultural background, sexual mores, power structure, and view of humanity that gave rise to this organized and systematic sexual violence.

Nevertheless, a dangerous tendency to back away from this critical consciousness is manifesting itself. To be specific, the government's development of the "Asian Women's Fund" as a vague, nongovernmental enterprise is yet another cowardly attempt to conceal, misrepresent, and obfuscate the central issue of the comfort women problem. The Asian Women's Fund was established by the Japanese government in July 1995 out of a sense of moral responsibility to the comfort women and is intended to function as a mechanism to support the work of NGOs that address the needs of the comfort women and to collect from private sources "atonement" money for surviving comfort women. The Asian Women's Fund does not, however, satisfy the responsibility of the Japanese government to provide official, legal compensation to individual victims since "atonement" money from the Asian Women's Fund is not intended to acknowledge legal responsibility on the part of the Japanese government for the crime that occurred during World War II.

The baseness of the Japanese state's attitude vividly reveals itself in its persistent efforts to avoid taking governmental responsibility by refusing to face up to the wishes of the former comfort women and reducing their complaints to a matter of money. Further, many more than a few women are being mobilized for such a project, which places Japanese feminism in an exceedingly dangerous position. How should we, as feminists, deal with the state's naked intention—so patently obvious in the "Citizen's Fund"—to use women for its purpose?

Should we women shoulder the responsibility for these crimes in place of the state and the men who committed them and, under the fabricated name of women's solidarity, take part in an enterprise meant only to sweep away the accuser's anger and mortification? Or should we expose the contemptible intention of the state that, in making women its accomplices, is trying to snatch an opportunity for acquittal? Should we resolutely take a stand and act to bare the fullness of the state's sexual violence and crime? We have reached the point where we must decide between the two.

History

To begin with, we would like to report the historical circumstances of this issue. Eight years have already passed since the Japanese military's comfort women became a social issue. At first the Japanese government kept refusing to admit that this systematic violence, this crime against women, was a crime of the state and its military. Then in January 1992, evidence in the archives of the Japanese armed forces was unearthed through the efforts of private citizens. Their discovery clearly showed that the Japanese military had ordered the organizing of the comfort stations.

Nonfiction author Kawada Fumiko first presented evidence that a Korean woman was brought from Korea to Okinawa as a comfort woman. In her book *House of Red Bricks: The Comfort Women Who Came from Korea*, which was published in 1987, she told the story of Pe Pongi.[1] Prior to this publication, the term "comfort woman" had practically become a dead word in Japan. Kawada distributed a small number of pamphlets in Japan, encouraging the former comfort women to speak out after years of silence. In Korea, also, Professors Lee Hyo-Jae and Yun Chung Ok of Ewha Women's University, as well as various Christian women's groups, formed the center of a movement to give aid to these victims who had long been living at the margins of society. Then in May 1990, on the occasion of the Korean president's visit to Japan, these Korean women's groups demanded that the issue of the "women's volunteer corps" be straightforwardly investigated by the Japanese government. They reminded us that:

> The issue of these women is not simply one that must be dealt with historically as the past pain of a colonized people, but has remained a problem to the present, one of sexual violation that has surfaced again and again, as seen in the system of offering prostitutes to the occupying American forces as well as in Japanese sex tours to other parts of Asia. Consequently, we once again urge that the Japanese government and those in charge today investigate this problem with the purpose of resolving it.

---

1. Kawada Fumiko, *House of Red Bricks: The Comfort Women Who Came from Korea* (Tokyo: Chikuma Shobo, 1987), 150; see also her *Gender and War* (Tokyo: Akashi Shoten, 1995), 123.

When Liberal Democratic Party members of the Japanese Diet conducted an investigation to confirm the facts of the matter, the official reply was that women were taken to the comfort stations by "private traders," not by the Japanese military, and that it was impossible to bring to light in detail any more than that. In response to this evasive reply, former comfort woman Kim Hak-Sun came out at a press conference on 14 August 1991. After her, others followed.

In December of the same year, Kim and two other former comfort women came to Japan, along with family members of dead soldiers who were left uncompensated by the Japanese army, for which they fought. The group filed suit against the Japanese government in Tokyo court, demanding compensation. At that time, Yoshimi Yoshiaki, professor of history at Tokyo's Chuo University, received a great shock upon seeing Kim's interview on television and thought, "What can I do about this as a scholar of history?" He recalled having seen documents at the Defense Office Library proving that high Japanese officers had ordered the setting up of comfort stations.

The information that the history professor discovered made the headlines in the *Asahi News* on 13 January 1992, thereby revealing the government's reply as a farce. Immediately thereafter, Prime Minister Miyazawa, visiting Korea, made the first public apology to Korean president Roh concerning the comfort women issue, and the government made public the results of its investigation concerning it. Nevertheless, even though its prime minister had made a public apology, the Japanese government continued to insist that all matters of compensation had been concluded by the Korea-Japan normalization treaty of 1985.

Japanese feminists, who were grappling with issues of sexual discrimination in our own country, were greatly stimulated by the appeal of these elderly victims. Meanwhile, the comfort women's case was strengthened when the UN Commission on Human Rights declared that nine types of crimes directed against civilians were defined as "crimes against humanity." It became clear that the comfort women system was, according to this definition, a war crime in violation of international human rights law.

The UN special rapporteur Radhika Coomaraswamy in her 1996 report on the comfort women issue wrote the following:

> The Special Rapporteur, however, holds that the practice of "comfort women" should be considered a clear case of sexual slavery and a slavery-like practice in accordance with the approach adopted by relevant international human rights bodies and mechanisms. In this connection, the Special Rapporteur wishes to underline that the Sub-Commission on Prevention of Discrimination and Protection of Minorities, in its resolution 1993/24 of 15 August 1993, noting in-

formation transmitted to it by the Working Group on Contemporary Forms of Slavery concerning the sexual exploitation of women and other forms of forced labour during wartime, entrusted one of its experts to undertake an in-depth study on the situation of systematic rape, sexual slavery and slavery-like practices during wartime. The Sub-Commission further requested the expert in the preparation of this study to take into account information, including that on "comfort women," which had been submitted to the Special Rapporteur, on the right to restitution, compensation and rehabilitation of victims of gross violations of human rights.[2]

Here, the relationships between the Japanese and Yugoslavian cases were clearly and strongly acknowledged, and we can take from these statements evidence of a will to search out a solution to the problem of how, from a contemporary vantage point, we might go about building a peacetime order with human rights, including women's human rights, as its basis.

This brings us to the Japanese government's shameful proposal of the Asian Women's Fund. In an attempt to solve the comfort women issue, the government proposed the fund, which was widely publicized to the Japanese people on 15 August 1995. This policy, wherein compensation for the victims was to be collected through civilian donations, effectively shifted the burden of this issue away from the government (the responsible party) and onto the shoulders of the people. The conception behind this fund bore no relationship to the return of humanity and honor that the victims sought and was thus opposed from the outset by victimized women and their supporters throughout Asia. We in Japan who support the pleas of these women also opposed this measure.

Ever since the Asian Women's Fund was enacted, confusion has spread throughout the various groups that had until then been seeking for the Japanese government to take responsibility for actions done in the war. Among these, even men like Wada Haruki, a professor at Tokyo University, who had long supported democratization movements in Korea, came out in support of the fund, saying "This is all that can be done; therefore, let's not go against it," and purposely even went to Korea in search of support. Establishment of the fund marked the beginning of division among the supporters of the victimized women. After this, active work in support of the fund became more intense by the day. Within the next two years, the situation became quite serious indeed.

Japanese feminists and activists formed organizations to overcome the present situation. Among these are the following two groups: VAWW-NET

2. Radhika Coomaraswamy, *Report of the Special Rapporteur on Violence against Women* (Tokyo: Center for Research and Documentation on Japanese War Responsibility, 1996), 3.

Japan and the Association for Research on the Impact of War and Military Bases on Women's Human Rights. VAWW-NET Japan (The Violence against Women in War Network Japan) was formed mainly by feminist journalists and activists in 1997. At the end of that year, VAWW-NET Japan held an international conference on violence against women. Over forty people from twenty different countries attended to talk about violence against women, especially sexual violence, and to support victims. In 2000 the organization plans to open an international tribunal on war crimes against women during World War II.

The other organization is a small one. The Association for Research on the Impact of War and Military Bases on Women's Human Rights was formed by feminist scholars and researchers in May 1997. Both coauthors are involved in it: Kiyoko Shimizu as the representative and Aiko Ogoshi as the secretary-general. The group formed in order to oppose, from a feminist perspective, the activities of the Japanese government and various nationalistic groups within Japan, particularly in regards to the comfort women. The founding message of the group delineates the issue:

With only three years left till the turn of the century, we are acutely reminded that these one hundred years have been characterized by warfare and violence. It cannot be too strongly emphasized that the great majority of victims have been people not directly involved in fighting the wars, such as women, children, and the elderly. This crucial fact has been largely ignored in historical, philosophical and cultural studies dominated by the male point of view, which focuses on issues of politics and power.

In particular, the reality that women have continuously been victims of sexual assault has been concealed by the male attitude of tolerance toward sexual violence. This attitude perpetuates the false assumption that violence against women is a natural consequences of male-female relationships, and that the fault lies with the victim rather than violator. This belief, which serves the assaulting party well, has not only dominated the male perspective, but has also been internalized by women, resulting in a divisive situation whereby some suffer from violence while others take the side of the perpetrators.

The recent surfacing of these realities, which until now had gone unvoiced in this male-dominated society, can be attributed to the succession of shocking testimonies and indictments by women who suffered from acts of violence during wars. For example, the testimonies of the so-called "comfort women," victimized during the Sino-Japanese War and World War II in perhaps the greatest of [Japan's] war crimes sent a shock around the world. This is because the government-instituted system of sexual slavery was a clear indication of how history had been concealing this most fundamental violence against women.

By illuminating the truth behind the sexual violence, we can come face to face with our true history, philosophy, and culture. It is essential to clarify the fact that far from stemming from natural male-female relationships, these acts of violence are the product of a power structure of dominance and submission, a structure that reveals its true colors all the more in extreme situations such as war. Only by acknowledging this will we be able to eradicate the violence that is the source of distrust and hatred. Only then can we embrace the vision of human rights not as an abstract concept, but as a fundamental principle to be actualized in our lives.

To this end, we must thoroughly explore the realities of the past. It is necessary also to decode and criticize the intricate mechanisms which have functioned to legitimize these frightening realities. There is an acute demand for opportunities to discuss this problem from a multi-faceted perspective.

Unfortunately, academic associations currently in existence are unable to sufficiently meet this demand, because they have been dominated by male members who don't want to be engaged in issues of sexual violence. This is why it is necessary to create a new association in which we can discuss issues of "war, women, and human rights." We are endeavoring to create an association that will break through the professional-academic framework, and provide a forum where people who share similar concerns can exchange viewpoints freely.

Japan is presently seeing the emergence of a movement which goes against the world-wide trend toward uncovering the hidden truth behind the violence and national crimes. Claiming the authority of "history," this movement contrives to justify the violators by concealing and distorting the truth, while also trying to silence the victims. It is our responsibility to elucidate, logically and practically, what is behind these violent statements. They regenerate the evils of discrimination against women, racial discrimination, colonialism and cultural imperialism. The new association will endeavor to provide an effective forum for dealing with this task.[3]

After forming our association, we began various kinds of activities to solve the comfort women issue in a proper way. One of them is to promote

---

3. Association for Research on the Impact of War and Military Bases on Women's Human Rights, ed., *Women, War, and Human Rights* (Tokyo, 1998).

our solidarity with victims and supporting groups in Asian countries. For example, we have endorsed reports given by supporting groups from Taiwan, Korea, and the Philippines. At an emergency international meeting held in Tokyo in 1997, these reports considered the effect the Asian Women's Fund has had. The strength of the criticism is shown in one of the report titles: "We Want No Charity, but Dignity: The Demands of Taiwanese War Sexual Slaves."[4]

Speakers from Korea broadened the scope of the movement. One declared that we must "strive against the omission of the facts concerning 'comfort women' from textbooks, and work to prevent any future militarization in Japan." By doing this, she says, "Our efforts will transcend our national borders, bind us together, and bring about true peace in East Asia." Another Korean speaker asserted that many kinds of abuses of women by men all over the world went to extremes in the form of the comfort women system. Women in Asia, including Dutch women who lived in Indonesia at that time, were used as the "public toilet" of Japanese troops. It is a plain example of people suppressing and violating other's rights to live as human beings. The present effort is aimed not only at the restoration of the honor and dignity of each victim but also at the restoration of human rights of women as a whole.

The basis for the Japanese government's resistance to the demands of the comfort women is the rise of postwar nationalism. A part of this is a backlash against the comfort women issue that has occurred among conservative antifeminist people since around 1996. One group, calling itself a "Group to Study the Liberal View of History," started to expand its campaign against the comfort women issue. References to comfort women had finally begun to appear in Japanese textbooks in 1996, thanks to the recommendation of the UN special rapporteur Radhika Coomaraswamy. But the conservative group requested that the education ministry eliminate the references and also declared that it would compile a new textbook based on an ultranationalistic version of history, which denies that the Great East Asia War was a "war of aggression." The group regards it as a war for liberating Asian countries from colonization by the West. Through the media, those revisionists are lavishing all kinds of insulting comments on the victims of military sexual slavery.

Nationalism

Another dangerous tendency exists in present-day Japan. A new nationalism has arisen, one which is a step away from the right-wing statements and ac-

---

4. Yuko Suzuki, ed., *Scrap Asian Women's Fund, Another Disgrace*, 1997.

tions of those who freely interpret our past history to serve Japan's purpose. This new "soft" nationalism tries to reshape the way people understand the war by ambiguously reinterpreting the problem of war responsibility. Let us give a well-known example of this and see how it connects with the comfort women issues.

The book *After Losing the War: A Theory* is being quite warmly received in Japanese intellectual circles. Kato Norihiro, the author and a professor at Meiji Gakuin University, was born in 1948 and was a member of the so-called Zenkyoto (the National Union of Struggle Councils) generation, who entered university in the 1960s and formed a left-wing movement against the Japan–United States Security Treaty. After the protests ended, the Zenkyoto group broke into many sects, which often joined forces to fight together in the 1970s. This generation corresponds to the American postwar baby boomers, who are now in middle age and getting more and more conservative.

Kato explains the heart of Japan's postwar problems in the following way: The subject who is able to accept history responsibly is in a fractured state. He or she is not properly formed because of the manner in which we mourn the war dead. As long as this fractured character is not repaired, there will be in postwar Japan no public space for true intellectual discussion. Consequently, the problem is whether or not this fracture can be overcome. According to Kato, Japanese people had tried to forget the war. They have ignored the dead Japanese soldiers because they died in an unjust war. Against the assertion that Japanese people should mourn the Asian people who were killed by Japanese soldiers, Kato insists that we must first mourn Japanese soldiers because they fought for Japan and were killed in battle.

A newspaper reviewer from the *Asahi News* who thoroughly supported Kato's views had the following things to say:

> We do not say: "We were beaten." Instead we say: "Fighting is bad," shaking our heads. The postwar period starts from this. After being defeated in an unjust war, there is the "twist" of having a Constitution of peace pressed onto one by a victor backed with military might. By thinking that we ourselves wanted this, we force this "twist" outside of our consciousness. It is with this double-layered "twist" that the postwar period began. Complete and total shame always appears together with and opposite to the rationalization of one's purposes...a moral quagmire in which responsibility can never be taken.[5]

---

5. *Asahi News* (Tokyo), 21 September 1997.

Kato's foundational argument recognizes the "hate of shame" at the center of the Japanese national consciousness. We want to place in contrast to this the thoughts of Suzuki Yuko, one of the founding members of our association and one of the most powerful theorists of Japanese feminism. Suzuki says that the Asian Women's Fund policy is but a self-serving attempt to give the greatest priority and weight to Japan's own internal situation.

The ideas of Karl van Wolferen (1941–) in his *To the Japanese Intellectuals* (1995) also shed light on the present-day scenario. Wolferen is a Dutch journalist who has lived in Japan for more than thirty years in a detailed search to understand the Japanese power structure. He states that the Ninth Article of the Japanese Constitution, wherein the Japanese speak of disarmament as the origin of their treasured pacifism, was but one American strategy of governing Japan. This, along with the act of leaving the emperor in place as a means of making the Japanese easier to control, was a means for MacArthur to soothe the fears of those in Washington who feared a revival of the Japanese threat. Thus, the adding of Article 9 effectively rendered the new constitution unrealistic. The Japanese Constitution cannot fulfill the role that a constitution usually must fulfill. Kato's notion of the "twist" accords well with Wolferen's thinking. Both views demand that postwar intellectuals—particularly those who support the constitution—take responsibility.

However, Wolferen is one step ahead. He is saying that advancing a pacifism that claims that all war is bad will always merely be for the Japanese people a means to avoid owning up to World War II as part of their own past history. He then compares the Japanese way of dealing with responsibility for the war with that of the Germans. Whereas Germans are still morally and intellectually taken up with the question of the war, the Japanese are unconcerned. Germany has purposely provided detailed accounts of the war so that young Germans can know what happened in the past. Since intellectual discussions concerning this issue are continuing, it is clear that people are making an effort to explain what it was that made Nazism possible. The situation in Japan is completely opposite. For young people, the past is dead and gone. There is no sincere public debate concerning how this denial has come about. Because historical records are selectively kept and because the wartime actions of the Japanese are often overjustified, the great majority of Japanese people believe that they were indeed the victims in the war. Furthermore, in contrast to the Germans, who are conscious of the fact that they themselves elected Hitler to power, the Japanese feel that they as a people had no influence whatsoever over those things done in the name of the emperor. Wolferen says, "As a result, though being a people with a high level of education, it is extremely difficult for the Japanese to understand the significance of the 20th century's most important event and its result...they have no idea how to take responsibility for the war."[6]

In the claims of both Kato and Wolferen there is a subtle point of agreement. The term twist that Kato uses to express postwar Japan might seem to be an appropriate expression, but we are made to feel uneasy at Kato's use of this concept. We are concerned when we see that his views are drawing the agreement of such a large number of present-day intellectuals. They are those who, rather than engaging in self-criticism, choose simply to defend themselves. They are precisely the upholders of the intellectual status quo whom Wolferen so eloquently criticizes.

According to Kato, the Japanese are subjectively unable to take historical responsibility for the fact that in World War II they sacrificed up to 20 million Asian lives. Will the explanation of this inability with a characteristically Japanese "Oh well, what can you do?" be understood by the rest of the world? Our Japanese feminists must object to such ethnocentric and pessimistic thinking.

We emphasize that Kato's claim is intentionally skirting the comfort women issue. He intends to transform the issue of political and legal responsibility of the Japanese government into the abstract issue of a critique of Japanese identity. He pretends to consider the Japanese war responsibility deeply, but really he tries to cover up the war crimes of the state by identifying the state and its people. In this sense, he is similar to the Asian Women's Fund, which is cleverly taking a pose of offering "goodwill" and "compensation."

What is worse is that Kato has no intention of listening to the testimonies of the former comfort women. He insists that we must mourn Japanese soldiers who were killed but never thinks of women who were raped and killed by them. Kato and many intellectuals who support him are, after all, permissive of sexual violence to women. Under a situation like this, no one can honestly hope that sexual violence by the military will not occur again.

Against the above tendency of Japanese intellectuals, we Japanese feminists are speaking out powerfully. Yayori Matsui, one of the most powerful feminist activists and a representative of VAWW-NET Japan, says:

> We Japanese women have unfolded activities to counter this fascist force. We held a big anti-rightwing rally of women under the motto, "History cannot be erased! Women can no longer be silenced!" in March 1997 in Tokyo. Out of it came a new nationwide network on the issue of comfort women. The Women's struggle against the revisionist force is being conducted in difficult circumstances, and it

---

6. Karl van Wolferen, *To the Japanese Intellectuals* (Toyko, 1995).

is in this context that international support is vitally important. We must have additional pressure to bear on the Japanese government to change its policy in order to help heal the wounds of, and bring justice to, all Asian women victimized by war crimes.[7]

Matsui also points out that the sexual violence against women during World War II was not prosecuted as a war crime at the Tokyo International Tribunal or other war tribunals held in many Asian countries. According to her analysis, Japanese people could not undertake to condemn and prosecute war criminals including the emperor, and war trials were left to the Allied powers. Most of the Allied countries were Western colonial powers, which returned to their colonized territories in Asia. Reflecting their colonial mentality, the Allied powers set up trials that concentrated on war crimes committed by the Japanese military against Allied citizens, mostly war prisoners of the United States, United Kingdom, the Netherlands, and so on. But war crimes committed against Asian victims, who were people of either Western colonies or Japanese colonies, were largely neglected and condoned. No attention was paid to Korean and Taiwanese victims of sexual slavery because they were considered to be subjects of Imperial Japan.

On the basis of the above recognition, Matsui proposed the convening of an international tribunal on violations of the human rights of the comfort women from the feminist viewpoint; the plan is to open it in 2000 in Tokyo. We agree with her idea and want to make not only a practical but also a theoretical contribution to this tribunal. Many Asian feminist activist groups also agree to the convening of an international tribunal.

We think that there is now a worldwide current toward correcting the issues of war crimes from their foundation. The women of the Korean Council for Women Drafted by Japan for Sexual Slavery are at the head of that current. This is seen in the statements of Kim Yun Ok and Yun Chung Ok, which we earlier explained. We will strive to develop our association so that we will be able to make a connection with the world outside of Japan. Through the women's movement, we believe, our feminist solidarity will prove strong enough to overcome national boundaries.

---

7. Yayori Matsui, in *Common Grounds: Violence against Women in War and Armed Conflict Situations*, ed. Indai Lourdes Sajor (Quezon City, Philippines: Asian Center for Women's Human Rights, 1998), 29.

3

Taiwan

"Money Can't Buy Our Youth Back; Apology Can't Make Up for Our Fate"[1]

ANNE LLEWELLYN BARSTOW

Taiwanese ex-comfort women have been few and late in going public. While the records indicate that the Japanese confined at least a thousand Taiwanese in sexual slavery,[2] the restraints on women in Taiwanese society are so strong that few have dared to speak up. On a visit to Taipei in October 1997, I was able to talk with a former comfort woman, hear a radio interview with another, and confer with several of the women who make possible support for comfort women in Taiwan.

When in February 1992 the Taipei Women's Rescue Foundation made a public appeal for comfort women to identify themselves, only three phone calls were received, all from third parties. The pressure on Chinese women not to "shame" their families is so strong that not even knowledge of the Korean and Filipina women's public statements had broken the barrier of silence in Taiwan. Thanks, however, to the persistent encouragement of the Taipei Women's Rescue Foundation, followed by the Taiwanese government, about fifty women eventually spoke up.[3] Their stories confirm the pattern reported in Korea of young, poor women being tricked into sexual slavery and being made to serve far from their homeland. Many did not know where they had been taken, which added to their disorientation and helplessness. Many had incurred debts to the military, which they were forced to work

---

1. Comment of Taiwanese aboriginal women whom the Japanese forced into military prostitution. Comment made in a Taiwanese documentary film.

2. Wang Ching Feng, director of the Taipei Women's Rescue Foundation, interview by author, Taipei, Taiwan, 15 October 1997. My thanks to Lynda Scott of Fu Jen University for arranging the interview.

3. Ibid. Wang Ching Feng and Chiang Mei-Fen, "Taiwanese Comfort Women's Quest for Justice," in *Common Grounds: Violence against Women in War and Armed Conflict Situations*, ed. Indai Lourdes Sajor (Quezon City, Philippines: Asian Center for Women's Human Rights, 1998), 232–43.

38

off. After the war they were abandoned by the retreating Japanese and left to make their way back to Taiwan as best they could. Some attempted suicide, while all suffered physical and psychological damage.

In Taiwan the Japanese rounded up not only ethnic Chinese women but also women from the aboriginal population. The stories of two of the Chinese follow.

SETSUKO

I interviewed "Setsuko" (she would not give her real name) in Taipei on 11 October 1997. Although she had given testimony privately to the Taipei Women's Rescue Foundation, she made this her first public interview. Wang Ching Feng of the foundation provided interpreters.

Now seventy-six, Setsuko had been a twenty-two-year-old seamstress when she signed up with the Japanese to go abroad to work in a hospital, doing laundry and sewing. Sent to Surabaya, Java, she was soon put into a lottery and transferred to a comfort station near Lahad Datu, a Marine base on the island of Borneo. There two groups of Taiwanese women of twenty each, plus Koreans and Indonesians, rotated from camp to camp.

Setsuko's duties seem not to have been as onerous as some: she often serviced officers, who asserted the privilege of having one woman for the entire night, thus sparing her the mass rape by up to twenty or thirty men per night suffered by women assigned to rank-and-file soldiers. The officers would arrive after 4 P.M., the time of day when they would have drinks. She was expected to drink with them on the tatami mat. Sometimes they insulted her, and when she didn't please them, they beat her and called her their "Chinese coolie."

The manager of the brothel, whether a soldier or civilian, sold tickets for access to the women. A ticket for an enlisted man cost only two dollars but carried a time limit and required that the woman be shared. Setsuko was supposed to be paid monthly but actually received money only twice in over two years; in order to pay her expenses, she had to sell the gold she had brought from Taiwan.

When I asked if she ever tried to escape, she did not reply. When I asked if any of the soldiers were Taiwanese, she replied yes but would say no more. When the war was over, she was helped by a local association of Taiwanese in Indonesia to make the trip home. She came home on a military ship with twenty-two other Taiwanese women. Many were left behind in graves: they had been killed in the bombings or had died from illnesses. Two had simply disappeared.

On the surface it would seem that Setsuko came through the ordeal not too badly. She had weekly medical checkups, was never sick, and did not become pregnant. But much of the scarring of these women is emotional, and there she did not escape. Setsuko internalized guilt for the "bad things" she had done. On her return to Taiwan, she spent a period of years doing penance, living in the compound of a Buddhist temple, sweeping the grounds, doing the most humble work. She studied the scriptures and adopted a little girl whom she found there. "I worshiped a lot in the temple," she said with a sigh. "For years I repented of the bad things I had done." Finally she married "a country man" and was able to bear a son. She is now widowed and thus is free to claim a little space for herself and to tell her story to persons whom she trusts.

The third time she told me what a bad person she was, I broke in and said, "The men who made you do these things are the evil ones." She looked startled. Apparently she still accepts her society's view that the woman is responsible for sexual sin, no matter what the situation. Sometimes she denigrates herself. When my husband was adjusting the tape recorder before the interview and asked her to speak into it, she demurred, "My voice doesn't matter." And yet it was she who was being interviewed.

Another clue to her inner torment came when she suddenly fell asleep. The interview was over, and we were all sitting around the table, relaxing and getting better acquainted. It was not yet noon. Setsuko had been talking animatedly a few moments before, yet now she was sound asleep. I had read that many comfort women suffer all their lives from anxiety, sleep disorders, chronic drowsiness, depression, and psychological problems such as fear of men or of being alone. While Setsuko did not suffer from the latter, she clearly had the former afflictions.

And Setsuko lives in dread of being "discovered." Perhaps this is the greatest burden of all for these women. Even though she receives a government pension for having suffered from war crimes, she still believes that her son knows nothing about her past. Her daughter does know, having learned about it from Setsuko's women friends from the comfort station days. Much of her energy continues to go into covering up her life as a comfort woman. It was clear that she cannot imagine Taiwanese society accepting her or seeing her as an innocent victim.

A pious Buddhist, Setsuko prays for long hours. She considers herself fortunate to have a wonderful family. Now she is holding out for a big settlement and an official apology from the Japanese government (she specified "not from the Japanese people"). Yet she does not accept invitations to attend international meetings where other comfort women make the same demands. She maintains that she will *never* go public with her story. Indeed, although the Taipei Women's Rescue Foundation urges the women to travel and to join in the international movement for recompense, only one had done so by 1997.

LI-CHUN

While in Taipei I was able to hear a radio interview with another comfort woman, a program taped while I was there.[4] Li-Chun's story had many parallels with Setsuko's, but her attitude was somewhat more open. She used her own name and seemed to welcome the chance to talk about the terrible war years.

Approached by a Japanese businessman who owned a restaurant in the Philippines, Li-Chun had signed up for work. The job would have been a step up for her. But when she reached the Philippines, she was placed in a military brothel. She recounted, "I knew that I had been tricked." Although she was devastated and wept, there was no way out for her. She was far from home and was indeed in slavery.

Once there Li-Chun was forced to service soldiers every day; they came in especially large numbers on weekends. They were "very mean, abusive, drunk. They showed me no respect. Even when I tried to be nice and said, 'Good morning,' to them, they hit me. One permanently damaged my ear; another nearly killed me. They treated us like dogs." All of the men used condoms, but still some of the women became pregnant. Some had miscarriages; others had to bear their babies.

Li-Chun had had a child out of wedlock before going to the Philippines, but after her experiences there, she never married. She reported that "because of the way their sex organs were abused ... 60 percent of [comfort women] cannot have children—or normal marriages." She had to raise her child as a single mother. Some women settled for becoming "second wives" of married men.

Li-Chun regrets that only forty or so Taiwanese comfort women have made themselves known. Many died during the war, and many of the survivors are too ashamed. But Li-Chun shares some of that shame: she too referred to the "dirty, bad girls." She explained, "Many of us have lost hope in ourselves."

A man who called in during the interview made me question if the Taiwanese public is as hostile to the comfort women as they fear. Clearly sympathetic to them, he deplored the brutality they had been subjected to. He said, "Japan ruined their lives. It should do more than pay; it should apologize." He urged the Taiwanese government to join with other affected nations to put pressure on the Japanese for a full public apology.

Li-Chun was well informed about international efforts to gain recompense for the women. She reported that a major conference would be held in Tokyo at the end of that month.

•

---

4. Radio IRCT, 11 October 1997. The interviewer was "Natalie"; the translator was Chiang Mei Fen of the Taipei Women's Rescue Foundation. My thanks to Sue Babcock for providing me with this tape.

Setsuko and Li-Chun, like almost all Taiwanese comfort women, served far from Taiwan. We know that the Japanese had many military brothels on the island itself, but the history of Japanese sexual exploitation on Taiwan has not been researched. The Japanese filled their Taiwanese brothels almost entirely with foreign women, mostly Korean.[5] The only Taiwanese women whom they used on Taiwan were seventy aboriginal women from the tribes who still live in the mountainous areas of the island. These facts raise an important question about the nature of Japanese racism: Why were ethnic Chinese women used in one way and Korean and aboriginal women in another? It is imperative that the history of comfort stations on Taiwan be investigated—even if doing so implicates Taiwanese men as well as Japanese.

The ending of the war brought little relief for any of these women. When the Japanese surrendered on northern Borneo, Taiwanese and Japanese nurses ("nurse" was often a euphemism for "comfort woman" in Japanese records) were raped by the conquerors: the U.S. and other Allied soldiers.[6] The victors turned out to be no different from the vanquished in their disrespect for women. On return to Taiwan, out of shame many women could not go back to their families, who were in most cases very poor themselves. Most of the women had no education or training; in order to support themselves, many of the women did the only job they knew—they became prostitutes in the big cities such as Taipei.[7]

According to Mrs. Wang, the women had insuperable obstacles to overcome: physical damage, infertility, societal condemnation, poverty, psychological scars. Of them all, the worst is the emotional damage. The women think of themselves as "dirty" and shameful. Many have considered themselves unworthy of marriage. Some of them carry the mark of Cain—in their case, the word "comfort" tattooed on their arms.[8] Some have even killed themselves. They know a kind of suffering for which there is no end.

The struggle for women's rights in Taiwan is an uphill battle. It could not officially begin until 1987, when martial law was finally lifted and nongovernmental groups could begin to meet in public. Since then the civil code has been amended to give wives equal rights to property and custody of children in divorce cases. But a horrifying murder that occurred in 1996

---

5. George Hicks, *The Comfort Women: Japan's Brutal Regime of Enforced Prostitution in the Second World War* (New York: W. W. Norton, 1995), 112–15. See the account of the very young Korean girl, Yi Ok Bun, who was taken to Taiwan when she was twelve. She estimated that there were about seven thousand comfort women on Taiwan. When the war ended, many of them were killed by Taiwanese.

6. Ibid., 167.

7. As of 1998, there were tens of thousand of prostitutes in Taiwan, including 364 who work in the fifty-five licensed brothels: Edward A. Gargan, "The Mayor Won't Abide Licensed Licentiousness," *New York Times*, 30 March 1998.

8. Hicks, *The Comfort Women*, 239.

indicates how far Taiwanese women have to go to claim even basic rights to life and security. On 1 December the Democratic Progressive Party enacted a rule to require that one fourth of the party's candidates be female. The next day, the director of the party's women's department, Peng Wan-ju, was missing. She had been last seen late the night before, lobbying for the rule. Two days later her body was found in a vacant lot. She had been stabbed to death. In Taiwan, the forces of patriarchy do not play around.[9]

---

9. Anita Huang, "Women Wronged," *Free China Review*, February 1997, 4–10.

Part Two

RAPE AS A WEAPON OF ARMED CONFLICT

Mass rape has long been a deliberate strategy of military leaders. By marking the raped women as "polluted," mass rape destroys families and weakens communal life. And no act of war better flaunts the power of the victor than the ability to defile the women of the conquered. It settles scores among men, as it did in recent internal conflicts in Haiti, Kenya, and Nicaragua. But these results refer only to the damage to the honor of the defeated men. What mass rape means to the women of a society can be observed in the accounts that follow from China, Bosnia, Rwanda, Guatemala, and Haiti.

Rape is never "just rape," a statement never more true than during war. Mass rape has the power to effect changes far beyond the chaos of the particular attack. As a political weapon, it can change the balance between ethnic, racial, or religious groups. In establishing the racial superiority of one group over another, as in Bosnia, it can alter regional balance.

Mass rape has further uses. When it is combined with a deliberate policy of forced impregnation, as by the Serbs in Bosnia and the Hutus in Rwanda, it aims at the destruction of an ethnic group. It becomes a technique of genocide: to so defile the enemy's women that they will no longer be considered as future mothers for their own people. When used with this intention, systematic mass rape is as powerful a weapon of destruction as massacre.

In the last sixty years we have invented the most sophisticated weapons ever known—nuclear missiles, "smart" bombs. Yet in recent years armies have increasingly turned back to the oldest forms of attack—rape and sexual torture. We have developed elaborate international curbs on nuclear proliferation but have been scarcely aware of the increase in attacks on women. We have not realized that women's bodies are now a common factor in warfare. All of the following chapters speak to that one unspeakable fact.

4

The Rape of Nanking

IRIS CHANG

Editor's Foreword to Iris Chang's
The Rape of Nanking

On 13 December 1937, Nanking, the capital of China, surrendered to the Japanese Imperial Army. In the ensuing eight weeks or so, Japanese soldiers carried out a bloodbath of enormous proportions: a death toll of over 300,000, both civilian and military, including an untold number of women who were first raped, estimated at between twenty thousand and eighty thousand. The extent of the torture was extraordinary; it included live burials, burnings, killing for sport, and gruesome sexual mutilations.

Although these atrocities were quickly reported around the world, they are now little known. At the Tokyo War Crimes Trial the rape of tens of thousands of Nanking women was known but was not dealt with. Now Japan has removed many references to the massacre from its history texts, and much of the world has forgotten about it. Yet it was one of the major atrocities in a century known for mass exterminations. It was in order that this holocaust not drop entirely from memory that Iris Chang published the first full-length account of it in English.

Ironically, the destruction of Nanking led to a further, even greater disaster for women: the setting up of the comfort stations throughout the Japanese empire. World opinion condemned Japan so severely for the Rape of Nanking that the imperial government adopted an unusual strategy to protect its public image. The army had set up brothels for their troops in Manchuria and Shanghai beginning in 1932, but it was after the orgy of rape at Nanking that the Japanese high command organized the vast network of comfort stations that eventually stretched across East Asia. By this strategy Japan would prevent further mass rape of conquered populations with the ensuing world condemnation and control the spread of venereal disease through the troops as well. That this plan, which we now recognize as military sexual slavery, would ruin the lives of some 200,000 comfort women was not considered.

46

Chang asks the hard question about these atrocities: How could young men who led "normal" lives at home engage in such barbaric behavior? Her research points to the high level of militarization in Japanese education and culture at that time, the brutality of military training, and the new attitude toward the Chinese, previously admired but now looked down upon. She also describes the deeply ingrained contempt for women within Japanese military culture but does not explore how general attitudes toward women might have led to the specifically sexual tortures; this research, she believes, should be pursued.

Chang's book is a powerful call not to allow a second Rape of Nanking by forgetting the victims. She calls on Japan to acknowledge these crimes and on the world to remember.

•

Next, the Japanese turned their attention to the women.

"Women suffered most," Takokoro Kozo, a former soldier in the 114th Division of the Japanese army in Nanking, recalled. "No matter how young or old, they all could not escape the fate of being raped. We sent out coal trucks from Hsiakwan to the city streets and villages to seize a lot of women. And then each of them was allocated to fifteen to twenty soldiers for sexual intercourse and abuse."

Surviving Japanese veterans claim that the army had officially outlawed the rape of enemy women. But rape remained so deeply embedded in Japanese military culture and superstition that no one took the rule seriously. Many believed that raping virgins would make them more powerful in battle. Soldiers were even known to wear amulets made from the pubic hair of such victims, believing that they possessed magical powers against injury.

The military policy forbidding rape only encouraged soldiers to kill their victims afterward. During an interview for the documentary *In the Name of the Emperor*, Azuma Shiro, a former Japanese soldier, spoke candidly about the process of rape and murder in Nanking:

> At first we used some kinky words like *Pikankan. Pi* means "hip," *kankan* means "look." *Pikankan* means, "Let's see a woman open up her legs." Chinese women didn't wear underpants. Instead, they wore trousers tied with a string. There was no belt. As we pulled the string, the buttocks were exposed. We "pikankan." We looked. After a while we would say something like, "It's my day to take a bath," and we took turns raping them. It would be all right if we only raped them. I shouldn't say all right. But we always stabbed and killed them. Because dead bodies don't talk.

This selection is excerpted from *The Rape of Nanking: The Forgotten Holocaust of World War II*, Penguin Books, 1997, pp. 49–50, 89–99, by permission of the author, Iris Chang.

Takokoro Kozo shared Azuma's bluntness in discussing the issue. "After raping, we would also kill them," he recalled. "Those women would start to flee once we let them go. Then we would 'bang!' shoot them in the back to finish them up." According to surviving veterans, many of the soldiers felt remarkably little guilt about this. "Perhaps when we were raping her, we looked at her as a woman," Azuma wrote, "but when we killed her, we just thought of her as something like a pig."

This behavior was not restricted to soldiers. Officers at all levels indulged in the orgy. (Even Tani Hisao, the senior general and commander of the Japanese 6th Division, was later found guilty of raping some twenty women in Nanking.) Some not only urged soldiers to commit gang rape in the city but warned them to dispose of the women afterward to eliminate evidence of the crime. "Either pay them money or kill them in some out-of-the-way place after you have finished," one officer told his underlings....

The Rapes

If the scale and nature of the executions in Nanking are difficult for us to comprehend, so are the scale and nature of the rapes.

Certainly it was one of the greatest mass rapes in world history. Susan Brownmiller, author of the landmark book *Against Our Will: Men, Women and Rape* believes that the Rape of Nanking was probably the single worst instance of wartime rape inflicted on a civilian population with the sole exception of the treatment of Bengali women by Pakistani soldiers in 1971. (An estimated 200,000–400,000 women were raped in Bangladesh during a nine-month reign of terror following a failed rebellion.) Brownmiller suspects that the Rape of Nanking surpasses in scale even the raping of women in the former Yugoslavia, though it is difficult for her to say for certain because of the unreliability of Bosnian rape statistics.

It is impossible to determine the exact number of women raped in Nanking. Estimates range from as low as twenty thousand to as high as eighty thousand. But what the Japanese did to the women of Nanking cannot be computed in a tally sheet of statistics. We will never know the full psychic toll, because many of the women who survived the ordeal found themselves pregnant, and the subject of Chinese women impregnated by Japanese rapists in Nanking is so sensitive that it has never been completely studied. To my knowledge and to the knowledge of the Chinese historians and officials at the memorial hall erected in memory of the Nanking massacre, not a single Chinese woman has to this day come forward to admit that her child was the result of rape. Many such children were secretly killed; according to an American sociologist in the city at the time of the massacre, numerous half-Japanese children were choked or drowned at birth. One can only guess at the guilt, shame, and self-loathing that Chinese women endured when they faced the choice of raising a child they could not love or committing infanticide. No doubt many women could not make that choice. Between 1937 and 1938 a German diplomat reported that "uncounted" Chinese women were taking their own lives by flinging themselves into the Yangtze River.

We do know, however, that it was very easy to be a rape victim in Nanking. The Japanese raped Nanking women from all classes: farm wives, students, teachers, white-collar and blue-collar workers, wives of YMCA employees, university professors, even Buddhist nuns, some of whom were gang-raped to death. And they were systematic in their recruitment of women. In Nanking Japanese soldiers searched for them constantly as they looted homes and dragged men off for execution. Some actually conducted door-to-door searches, demanding money and *hua gu niang*—young girls.

This posed a terrible dilemma for the city's young women, who were not sure whether to remain at home or to seek refuge in the International Safety Zone—the neutral territory guarded by Americans and Europeans. If they stayed in their houses, they ran the risk of being raped in front of their families. But if they left home in search of the Safety Zone, they ran the risk of being captured by the Japanese in the streets. Traps lay everywhere for the Nanking women. For instance, the Japanese army fabricated stories about markets where women could exchange bags of rice and flour for chickens and ducks. But when women arrived on the scene prepared to trade, they found platoons of soldiers waiting for them. Some soldiers employed Chinese traitors to seek out prospective candidates for rape. Even in the Safety Zone, the Japanese staged incidents to lure foreigners away from the refugee camps, leaving women vulnerable to kidnapping raids.

Chinese women were raped in all locations and at all hours. An estimated one third of all rapes occurred during the day. Survivors even remember soldiers prying open the legs of victims to rape them in broad daylight, in the middle of the street, and in front of crowds of witnesses. No place was too sacred for rape. The Japanese attacked women in nunneries, churches, and Bible training schools. Seventeen soldiers raped one woman in succession in a seminary compound. "Every day, twenty-four hours a day," the *Dagong Daily* newspaper testified of the great Rape of Nanking, "there was not one hour when an innocent woman was not being dragged off somewhere by a Japanese soldier."

Old age was no concern to the Japanese. Matrons, grandmothers, and great-grandmothers endured repeated sexual assaults. A Japanese soldier who raped a woman of sixty was ordered to "clean the penis by her mouth." When a woman of sixty-two protested to soldiers that she was too old for sex, they "rammed a stick up her instead." Many women in their eighties were raped to death, and at least one woman in that age group was shot and killed because she refused a Japanese soldier's advances.

If the Japanese treatment of old women was terrible, their treatment of young children was unthinkable. Little girls were raped so brutally that some could not walk for weeks afterward. Many required surgery; others died. Chinese witnesses saw Japanese rape girls under ten years of age in the streets and then slash them in half by sword. In some cases, the Japanese sliced open the vaginas of preteen girls in order to ravish them more effectively.

Even advanced stages of pregnancy did not render women immune to assault. The Japanese violated many who were about to go into labor, were in labor, or who had given birth only a few days earlier. One victim who was nine months pregnant when raped suffered not only stillbirth but a complete mental collapse. At least one pregnant woman was kicked to death. Still more gruesome was the treatment allotted to some of the unborn children of these women. After gang rape, Japanese soldiers sometimes slashed open the bellies of pregnant women and ripped out the fetuses for amusement.

The rape of women frequently accompanied the slaughter of entire families. One of the most notorious stories of such a slaughter was recorded in detail by American and European missionaries in Nanking. On 13 December 1937, thirty Japanese soldiers came to the Chinese home at 5 Hsing Lu Kao in the southeastern part of Nanking. They killed the landlord when he opened the door, and then Mr. Hsia, a tenant who had fallen to his knees to beg them not to kill anyone else. When the landlord's wife asked why they murdered her husband, they shot her dead. The Japanese then dragged Mrs. Hsia from under a table in the guest hall where she had tried to hide with her one-year-old baby. They stripped her, raped her, then bayoneted her in the chest when they were finished. The soldiers thrust a perfume bottle in her vagina and also killed the baby by bayonet. Then they went into the next room, where they found Mrs. Hsia's parents and two teenage daughters. The grandmother, who tried to protect the girls from rape, was shot by revolver; the grandfather clasped the body of his wife and was killed immediately.

The soldiers then stripped the girls and took turns raping them: the sixteen-year-old by two or three men, the fourteen-year-old by three. The Japanese not only stabbed the older girl to death after raping her but rammed a bamboo cane into her vagina. The younger one was simply bayoneted and "spared the horrible treatment meted out to her sister and mother," a foreigner later wrote of the scene. The soldiers also bayoneted another sister, aged eight, when she hid with her four-year-old sister under the blankets of a bed. The four-year-old remained under the blankets so long she nearly suffocated. She was to endure brain damage for the rest of her life from the lack of oxygen.

Before leaving, the soldiers murdered the landlord's two children, aged four and two; they bayoneted the older child and split the head of the younger one with a sword. When it was safe to emerge, the eight-year-old survivor, who had been hiding under the blankets, crawled to the next room where she lay beside the body of her mother. Together with her four-year-old sister, they lived for fourteen days on rice crusts that their mother had prepared before the siege. When a member of the International Committee arrived at the house weeks after the slaughter, he saw that one young girl had been raped on the table. "While I was there," he testified later, "the blood on the table [was] not all dry yet."

A similar story, no less grisly, involves a fifteen-year-old Chinese girl whose family was murdered before her eyes. The Japanese first killed her brother, whom they wrongly accused of being a Chinese soldier, then her brother's wife and her older sister because they both resisted rape, and finally her mother and father, who knelt on the floor begging the Japanese to spare the lives of their children. Before they died under the thrusts of Japanese bayonets, their last words urged the young girl to do whatever the enemy soldiers wanted from her.

The girl fainted. She revived to find herself naked on the floor in a strange, locked room. Someone had raped her while she had been unconscious. Her clothes had been taken from her, as they had been taken from other girls in the building. Her room was on the second floor of a building converted into barracks for two hundred Japanese soldiers. The women inside consisted of two groups: prostitutes, who were given their freedom and treated well, and respectable girls who had been kidnapped into sexual slavery. Of the latter group, at least one girl attempted suicide. For a month and a half the fifteen-year-old was raped two or three times a day. Eventually she became so diseased the Japanese left her alone. One day a kind Japanese officer who spoke Chinese approached her and asked why she was weeping. After hearing her story, he took her to Nanking by car, set her free inside the South Gate, and wrote down the name of Ginling College for her on a piece of paper. The girl was too sick to walk to Ginling the first day and took refuge in a Chinese house. Only on the second day did she reach Ginling, where International Committee members immediately rushed her to the hospital.

That girl was considered fortunate. Many other girls, tied naked to chairs, beds, or poles as permanent fixtures for rape, did not survive such treatment. Chinese witnesses described the body of an eleven-year-old girl who died after she was raped continuously for two days: "According to eyewitness reports, the blood-stained, swollen and ruptured area between the girl's legs created a disgusting scene difficult for anyone to look at directly."

During the mass rape the Japanese destroyed children and infants, often because they were in the way. Eyewitness reports describe children and babies suffocating from clothes stuffed in their mouths or bayoneted to death because they wept as their mothers were being raped. American and European observers of the Rape of Nanking recorded numerous entries like this one: "415. February 3, about 5 P.M. at Chang Su Hsiang (near Ta Chung Chiao) three soldiers came and forced a woman to throw away her baby and after raping her they went away laughing."

Countless men died trying to protect their loved ones from rape. When the Japanese dragged away one woman from a mat shed and her husband intervened, they "stuck a wire through his nose and tied the other end of the wire to a tree just like one would tie up a bull." There they bayoneted him repeatedly despite the pleas of his mother, who rolled around on the ground, crying hysterically. The Japanese ordered the mother to go into the house or they would kill her. The son died from the wounds on the spot.

There seemed to be no limit to the Japanese capacity for human degradation and sexual perversion in Nanking. Just as some soldiers invented killing contests to break the monotony of murder, so did some invent games of recreational rape and torture when wearied by the glut of sex.

Perhaps one of the most brutal forms of Japanese entertainment was the impalement of vaginas. In the streets of Nanking, corpses of women lay with their legs splayed open, their orifices pierced by wooden rods, twigs, and weeds. It is painful, almost mind-numbing, to contemplate some of the other objects that were used to torment the Nanking women, who suffered almost unendurable ordeals. For instance, one Japanese soldier who raped a young woman thrust a beer bottle into her and shot her. Another rape victim was found with a golf stick rammed into her. And on December 22, in a neighborhood near the gate of Tongjimen, the Japanese raped a barber's wife and then stuck a firecracker in her vagina. It blew up and killed her.

But not all of the victims were women. Chinese men were often sodomized or forced to perform a variety of repulsive sexual acts in front of laughing Japanese soldiers. At least one Chinese man was murdered because he refused to commit necrophilia with the corpse of a woman in the snow. The Japanese also delighted in trying to coerce men who had taken lifetime vows of celibacy to engage in sexual intercourse. A Chinese woman had tried to disguise herself as a man to pass through one of the gates of Nanking, but Japanese guards, who systematically searched all passing pedestrians by groping at their crotches, discovered her true sex. Gang rape followed, at which time a Buddhist monk had the misfortune to venture near the scene. The Japanese tried to force him to have sex with the woman they had just raped. When the monk protested, they castrated him, causing the poor man to bleed to death.

Some of the most sordid instances of sexual torture involved the degradation of entire families. The Japanese drew sadistic pleasure in forcing Chinese men to commit incest—fathers to rape their own daughters, brothers their sisters, sons their mothers. Guo Qi, a Chinese battalion commander stranded in Nanking for three months after the city fell, saw or heard of at least four or five instances in which the Japanese ordered sons to rape their mothers; those who refused were killed on the spot. His report is substantiated by the testimony of a German diplomat, who reported that one Chinese man who refused to rape his own mother was killed with saber strokes and that his mother committed suicide shortly afterward.

Some families openly embraced death rather than participate in their own destruction. One such family was crossing the Yangtze River when two Japanese soldiers stopped them and demanded an inspection. Upon seeing the young women and girls in the boat, the soldiers raped them right in front of their parents and husbands. This was horrifying enough, but what the soldiers demanded next of the family devastated them. The soldiers wanted the old man of the family to rape the women as well. Rather than obey, the entire family jumped into the river and drowned.

Once women were caught by Japanese soldiers, there was little hope for them, for most were killed immediately after rape.

But not all women submitted easily. Many were able to hide from the Japanese for months—in fuel stacks, under piles of grass or straw, in pig pens, on boats, in deserted houses. In the countryside women hid in covered holes in the earth—holes that Japanese soldiers tried to discover by stamping on the ground. One Buddhist nun and a little girl avoided rape and murder because they lay still in a ditch filled with bodies and feigned death for five days.

Women eluded rape using a variety of methods. Some used disguise—rubbing soot on their faces to appear old and diseased or shaving their heads to pass themselves off as men. (One clever young woman disguised herself as an old woman, hobbling about on a cane and even borrowing a little boy of six to carry on her back until she safely entered the Safety Zone at Ginling College.) Others feigned sickness, such as the woman who told Japanese soldiers she had given birth to a dead child four days before. Another woman took the advice of a Chinese captive to force her finger down her throat and vomit several times. (Her Japanese captors hastily expelled her from the building.) Some escaped by sheer quickness, ducking in and out of crowds, climbing over walls, with the Japanese in hot pursuit. One girl barely avoided assault by tripping up a Japanese soldier on the third floor of a house and sliding down a bamboo pole that a Chinese man propped up for her from the garden.

Once caught, women who struggled faced the possibility of torture as a warning to others who dared to resist the Japanese. Those who defied the Japanese were often found later with their eyes torn out, or their noses, ears, or breasts cut off. Few women dared fight their assailants, but there were scattered accounts of resistance. A schoolteacher gunned down five Japanese soldiers before being shot to death. The most famous story involves Li Xouying, a woman who not only suffered thirty-seven bayonet wounds during her struggle against the Japanese but survived and remained robust enough to narrate and playact the story almost sixty years later.

In 1937, eighteen-year-old Li Xouying was the bride of a military technician. When the government evacuated the capital, her husband left Nanking on the top of a train packed with Chinese soldiers. Li stayed behind because she was six to seven months pregnant and believed it was dangerous in her condition to board a crowded train.

Like many other Chinese civilians in Nanking, Li and her father fled into the foreign-run Safety Zone. They hid in the basement of an elementary school that had been converted into a refugee camp. But this camp, like others in the zone, was subject to repeated Japanese inspections and invasions. On December 18, a group of Japanese soldiers broke in and dragged the young men out of the school. The following morning they returned for the women. Fearful of what the Japanese would do to a pregnant housewife, Li made an impulsive decision. She tried to kill herself by slamming her head against the basement wall.

When she regained consciousness, she found herself lying on a small canvas cot on the floor of the basement. The Japanese were gone, but they had taken several young women with them. Wild thoughts raced through Li's head while she lay in a daze on the cot. If she ran out of the building, she might be throwing herself at Japanese rapists. But if she did nothing and waited, they would probably come back for her. Li decided to stay. If the Japanese did not return, all would be well and good, but if they did, she would fight them to the death. She would rather die, she told herself, than be raped by the Japanese.

Soon she heard the heavy footsteps of three Japanese soldiers coming down the stairs. Two of them seized a couple of women and dragged them screaming out of the room. The one who remained eyed Li intently as she lay immobile on the cot. Someone told him Li was sick, and he responded by kicking all the other people out of the room into the corridor.

Slowly the soldier walked back and forth, appraising her, Suddenly— before he quite realized what was happening—she made her move. She jumped from the cot, snatched his bayonet from his belt, and flung her back against the wall. "He panicked," Li recalled. "He never thought a woman would fight back." He seized her wrist that held the bayonet, but Li clutched his collar with her free hand and bit his arms with all her might. Even though the soldier wore full battle gear and Li wore only a cotton *chipao*, which impeded movement, she put up a good fight. The two of them grappled and kicked until the soldier found himself overwhelmed and screamed for help.

The other soldiers ran in, no doubt incredulous at what they saw. They lunged toward her with their bayonets but failed to stab her effectively because their comrade was in the way. Because her opponent was so short and small, Li was able to jerk him completely off his feet and use him like a shield to parry their thrusts. But then the soldiers aimed their bayonets at her head, slashing her face with their blades and knocking out her teeth. Her mouth filled with blood, which she spit into their eyes. "Blood was on the walls, on the bed, on the floor, everywhere," Li remembered. "I had no fear in my mind. I was furious. My only thought was to fight and kill them." Finally a soldier plunged his bayonet into her belly and everything went black for her.

The soldiers left her for dead. When Li's body was brought before her father, he could not sense any breath coming from her and assumed the worst. He asked someone to carry her behind the school and to dig a pit for her grave. Fortunately, someone noticed before the burial that Li was still breathing and that bubbles of blood foamed from her mouth. Friends immediately rushed Li to Nanking University Hospital, where doctors stitched up her thirty-seven bayonet wounds. While unconscious, she miscarried that evening.

Word of Li's fight somehow reached her husband, who immediately asked the military for three months' leave and borrowed money to get back to Nanking. In August 1938, he returned and found his wife with her face swollen and crosshatched with scars and her newly shorn hair growing from her head like bristles.

Li would suffer both pain and embarrassment from her wounds for the rest of her life. Mucus leaked from a gaping hole on the side of her nose, and tears ran down her eyes during bad weather or bouts of illness. (Miraculously, although the Japanese had stabbed the whites of her eyes with their bayonets, Li did not go blind.) Every time she looked in a mirror, she saw the scars that reminded her of that terrible day, 19 December 1938. "Now, after fifty-eight years, the wrinkles have covered the scars," she told me during my visit to her apartment in Nanking. "But when I was young, the scars on my face were obvious and terrible."

Li believes it was the combination of her personality and unique family background that gave her the will to fight back. Unlike other Chinese women, typically taught at an early age to be submissive, she came from a family completely devoid of feminine influence. Her mother died when she was only thirteen, forcing Li to grow up among men in a tough military family. Her father, brother, and uncles were either soldiers or policemen, and under their influence she became a tomboy. As a young girl, she also possessed a temper so short that her father dared not teach her kung fu, no doubt out of fear that she would terrorize the other kids on the block. Almost sixty years later, surrounded by her numerous children and grandchildren, Li had retained her health and passion for life—even her reputation for being ill-tempered. Her one regret, she said, was not learning kung fu from her father; otherwise, she might have enjoyed the pleasure of killing all three of the Japanese soldiers that day.

5

Former Yugoslavia

Women Speak

MARICA

Marica, thirty, lived in an underground shelter for three months while Vukovar was bombed.

There were hundreds of us, from the building and surrounding [streets]. Every day JNA (Serbian) planes bombed the city. Occasionally, we went out of the shelter to see what was going on outside. After a few days most of the stores were closed, and the last time I bought food was at the end of September. Besides bombs and shells, you could die from the snipers. You couldn't leave the shelter without hearing the bullets whistling.

We had food; only we lacked bread. We cooked on a gas stove. We had no electricity. At the beginning we had water, brought to us in cisterns. We had to boil it to avoid infectious diseases. Later, they didn't come any more, and we had to go to the river Danube or collect rainwater. But the rainwater wasn't drinkable because the Chetniks kept using war gases and blister gases. When we had soap, we washed our clothes but later there was no soap.

In the shelter we were all united and helped each other. [Then] a man came—later we discovered he was a Serb—to spy on us. This building used to be a post office, so information could be sent [out from it]. We watched that man. We didn't want him to send certain messages. As time passed, it became more and more unbearable in the shelter. Autumn was approaching and it was growing colder. We went out in pairs to collect firewood.

"How would you feel?"

[After the fall of Vukovar, the Serbs] started to take away our people, threatening us with machine guns. They took us to barracks where we were imprisoned for ten days. I was raped there. They ordered me to take off my clothes. I refused [but] they threatened me with a knife. One by one, they raped me

These accounts are taken from Olivia Bennett, Jo Bexley, and Kitty Warnock, eds., *Arms to Fight, Arms to Protect: Women Speak Out about Conflict* (London: Panos, 1995), 235–51. The events took place between 1992 and 1994.

57

on the floor. There were always two men always holding me down. When the fifth came, I asked him: "How would you feel if someone treated your mother, sister, or daughter like this?" He hesitated, as if he had lost the desire, and opened the door. He asked the others if there was anyone else nearby who would like to do it too. There was nobody, so they left.

Hopes of healing

Of course I want to go back. I love my town because it's a very special town. I love the people that I grew up with. I left everything in Vukovar. I know I would often be reminded of having been raped, but the love toward my town is stronger and it would be possible to overcome it. Besides, I have two kids. I think that taking care of them could help me not to think about it. We can rebuild the town. We can do it, if only we can get back.

The blame [for the mass rapes] can be equally placed on individuals and on the politics in general. I think it was the will of individuals but also the strategy of Serbian politics to perform "ethnic cleansing" of the non-Serbian population in Croatia.

Some [women] can talk about [their ordeal] while others find it hard. The reasons are numerous and I can understand them. For women who were mothers and who, up till then, lived in harmonious families, it is hard to stand because of their hurt husbands and because of their children. And young, unmarried girls try to hide it because they hope to have a family in the future.

Although our people are very conservative, these [raped] women are accepted and understood. [The scale of] rape in this war has been so massive that it ceased to be a taboo. And, besides rape, other very serious crimes happened...massacres, torture. The most important thing for women is to be well accepted in their families. Unfortunately, I know of some cases of women who got pregnant after being raped and were imprisoned until it was too late to perform an abortion. They had to give birth to those poor babies. Their husbands' reactions varied. Most of [the women] gave away the child for adoption and continued to live within the family. But a few of the husbands didn't want to accept them after [what had happened].

RABIJA

A twenty-five-year-old Bosnian Muslim, Rabija now lives in a Zagreb refugee camp.

I learned to write first in Cyrillic script and not until three years later in Roman script. In the fourth grade of elementary school, we Muslims were forced to learn Russian although nobody wanted it. Non-Serbian kids who had problems with learning were treated as if they were retarded, expelled from everyday tuition and put in "special" classes. When the war was declared, first in Croatia, then in Bosnia-Herzegovina, the situation rapidly became tense. Muslim and Croatian kids went to school frightened and came back in tears because they were threatened by Serbian children, and even by Serbian teachers. Some Muslim kids were beaten all over. Little by little, the kids started to drop out of classes. Employed adults were dismissed on a massive scale, [many] without being given their salary. Serbian neighbors constantly threatened to burn our houses, mosques... to kill us all. We lived in constant fear.

"A living hell"

The attack [on our village] began with houses being set on fire, starting from the outskirts [and moving] toward the center. People were running in all directions. We were looking through the window and saw clouds of thick, black smoke. The heat was unbearable, but we sat helplessly inside the house, awaiting the worst. It was senseless trying to run away because the living hell was everywhere.

I saw tanks near the house. The soldiers were wearing masked uniforms, boots, cockades. They were armed, hundreds of them crawling in all directions. My mother-in-law asked me what was happening. I looked at her without saying a word and took the baby in my arms. Chetniks were drinking, smashing bottles, battering on doors, firing machine-guns, breaking into houses. I heard them singing songs. I remember one in particular—I have heard it a hundred times since: "Who is saying, who is lying: Serbia is small? It is not, it is not. We made war three times before. We shall make it again and defeat them all."

They were shouting: "Is anybody in the house?" We did not dare respond. They shouted again, demanding the men in the house. I went out and stood at the door but did not say that my father-in-law was inside. I saw another group of Chetniks on the road. They were dragging an old man, a neighbor. He could hardly walk or breathe. They were forcing him to walk faster and kept kicking him, beating him with gun barrels and sticks on the head and on the body. Then the old man fell. The soldiers lost patience and fired at him. I turned my head. I could not watch. He was left lying on the road. I started to walk toward him but two Chetniks held me back. They stepped inside [our house]. We were ordered to hand over all our jewelry and money. They left with my father-in-law.

They stopped in front of the next-door house and took the neighbor out. Both men had to lie down. For about half an hour five Chetniks beat them all over. They were laughing and, in between the kicks, "offering" them cigarettes. Then they ordered them to move on. About fifteen minutes later we saw our neighbor coming back with a Chetnik. In front of his house, the poor man was ordered to kneel down and they shot him in the head. We heard screams from the house. His wife and daughters buried him in the garden. Three days later we heard that my father-in-law had been killed. Some acquaintances had buried his body in the forest and brought us his ID card covered in blood. I still keep it.

[Later] when I ended up in the camp at Trnopolje I heard from a boy who knew my husband that he had seen three dead bodies, in the woods next to the brook, beaten and disfigured. He thought one of them might have been my husband, but he wasn't sure.

"No strength to talk about it"

I was raped almost every day, by groups. And many other girls and women were raped in that house. We were imprisoned; we couldn't go out. There was never enough food. I was always hungry, I could not feed my baby. They even forbade us to drink water and, besides that, the summer heat was unbearable.

They came almost every evening, sometimes at night. They boozed all night long, singing, celebrating the "victory," and then, dead drunk, used to take us one by one into the next room or sometimes into one of the empty houses in the vicinity. They raped us, always in groups, all night long. Always the same ones, ten of them or so. When I was forced to go, I left my baby with my mother-in-law. She watched helplessly as they dragged me off. The hardest thing for me was the fact that she knew about it all.

We've never talked about it. Besides that, she is suffering anyway because she doesn't know if her son, my husband, is alive. We are wondering if it's true that he was killed. It is hard to live with her. We went through hell together but the worst thing is that neither of us has enough strength to talk about it. [It's] as if this situation makes me feel guilty for all the bad things that have happened to us. I presume that to some extent she feels pity for me, but also that her sorrow over the son she has lost is far stronger. She will never understand my situation, all I've lived through and what I'm feeling now. We don't talk much [at all]. She mainly looks after my child. My sister-in-law, who also lives with us in the refugee camp, experienced the same [ordeal] though she wasn't with us. I think she is able to understand me better although I rarely talk with her about it.

SABINA

Sabina, twenty-four, is from Bosnia but is now in a refugee camp in Zagreb.

About four thousand people lived in [my village], mostly Muslims, a smaller number of Serbs and even fewer Croats. Around our village there were a few

Serbian villages. Relationships between us were good. We associated with each other, celebrated holidays together, often married each other. There was no evidence of misunderstandings or hate.

It was obvious that Serbs had always been more involved in political [and public] life, especially in state services, while male Muslims and Croats were often forced to take temporary work in foreign countries because they couldn't find jobs here. Nobody ever spoke about it. [It was as] if everyone was aware of it but no one dared to expose it in public.

The outbreak of war

The situation changed rapidly when Croatia went to war. We all knew that the war would reach us, too, but nobody foresaw its magnitude. I remember, when the fighting was going on in Croatia, the Chetniks were coming in their uniforms and walking around the village saying they were going to "free Croatia from its enemies." They were looting there, and their wives came to resell the stolen goods. Nobody wanted to buy [the plunder] because we knew where it came from.

On 22 May 1992, the Chetniks' infantry, tanks and army carriers reached our village. They broke into houses in groups. They all wore masks, army uniforms, army boots, cockades on their heads. Males between fourteen and sixteen were killed instantly. Kids were asked about their older brothers and fathers, and they were beaten. I saw them pulling one young man; they made him imitate a sheep. They struck him and then killed him. I saw how they tortured a group of four men and then showered them with bullets.

"I wanted to be dead"

Two Chetniks forced my younger sister [aged seventeen] to enter the house, took her to the basement, and raped her. I could only listen to her screams. Then they went to the neighbor's house, and came back after thirty minutes, this time with a girl from the neighborhood [aged fourteen] and one from another village. They ordered me, my sister, and those two girls to go to the basement with them, and three men took turns to rape us. When I tried to fight them, one man slashed my lower leg. You can see the scar. Two men held me down while the third raped me. And then they swapped over. I don't know how long they were doing it because I almost fainted. I don't want to talk about it anymore.

When they were done with me, it was my sister's turn. She had watched what they did to me, but I was told to leave. It was even harder listening [to the screams] because I couldn't help. For the first time in my life I wanted to be dead.

In the evening the Chetniks left the village. We went out of the house. Everywhere, around the houses, in the yards, in the gardens, on the fields, on

the road, there were dead bodies. I knew them all. They were my relatives, .
cousins, friends, neighbors, acquaintances. I felt the ground moving under
me. It was summer...strong heat. The smell of blood filled the place.

For five days the Chetniks forbade us to bury the bodies. After that it took
us, the survivors, two days to bury them. They were stinking; worms were
crawling over them, and flies buzzing around them. On 29 June the Chetniks
came again. They ordered us to leave our homes.

"Destroying the soul of a nation"

About three hundred of us ended up in the concentration camp called
Trnopolje. Thousands of people were already there. Women and children
were separated from the men. The living conditions were terrible. During the
day [things] seemed to be calm, but at night we heard shooting. And they
used to take dozens of young girls and women and rape them all night long.
They were killing kids and adults with electric shocks. Nobody was allowed to
talk, move, cry, not even mourn over somebody. I was surrounded by blank
faces, faces like masks.

I have no explanation for [the massive incidence of rape]. I don't know
why. [But] I think it was planned in advance and intended to destroy the soul
of a nation. At first, talking [about it] gave me some relief. But, as time passes
by, I feel less and less like talking. I think it would be the best for me to try
to forget it all...well, as much as I can. I know that is going to be very hard.
Life goes on. I am still very young and I have to think about my future.

ANONYMOUS

A Bosnian refugee whose husband went missing in 1992.

The children were asking for their father, getting up at night and crying. Everyone was crying. I was living in a classroom with forty-five people—women,
children, the wounded. My younger daughter used to want to open the door,
saying that her dad was coming to us. The older one made drawings of him,
bending her head over the paper, hiding it from me. I just cried and cried.
The advice given by women who had been through the same experience did
not help me. It seemed that they bore it more easily, or it only appeared like
that to me. They were telling me that I must fight, that I must be strong, that
I was not the only one who had experienced this. But in vain. They did not
calm me down.

"Rape Camps," Forced Impregnation, and Ethnic Cleansing

Religious, Cultural, and Ethical Responses to Rape Victims in the Former Yugoslavia

TODD SALZMAN

Introduction

The International War Crimes Tribunal in The Hague, Netherlands, continues its proceedings against indicted war criminals in the Bosnia-Herzegovina war. What has come to light throughout these trials, and what was suspected and documented by the United Nations and NGOs (nongovernmental organizations) during the conflict itself, is the extensive sexual abuse and rape of women on all sides of the warring factions. Estimates reveal that twenty thousand women were tortured and raped in this conflict.[1] By and large the perpetrators of these crimes were Serbs,[2] who targeted primarily Muslim women, though Catholic Croats were victimized as well.[3] While rape and sexual assault have frequently accompanied wars, the Bosnia-Herzegovina conflict has utilized this atrocity to attain the objective of the conflict itself, ethnic cleansing. In and through rape, and in particular rape for the purpose of impregnation, Serbs utilized the female gender violating her body

---

A similar version of this article first appeared in *Human Rights Quarterly* 20 (May 1998): 348–78.

1. UN Economic and Social Council, *Contemporary Forms of Slavery* (Document E/CN.4/Sub.2/1995/38 [13 July 1995]), §4. M. Cherif Bassiouni and Marcia McCormick, *Sexual Violence: An Invisible Weapon of War in the Former Yugoslavia* (Chicago: International Human Rights Law Institute, DePaul University, 1996), 3 (hereinafter *Sexual Violence*), distinguish between rape, sexual assault, and sexual violence: "*Rape* denotes vaginal, oral, or anal sexual intercourse without the consent of one of the people involved. *Sexual assault* is a broader term, which includes rape and other forced or coerced sexual acts, as well as mutilation of the genitals. *Sexual violence* is the most general term, used to describe any kind of violence carried out through sexual means or by targeting sexuality."

2. Clearly many Serbs were appalled at the atrocities that took place during the Bosnian war. In this article, "Serbs" refers to those who were politically and militarily responsible for the policy of ethnic cleansing and the atrocities committed against non-Serbs.

3. Bassiouni and McCormick, *Sexual Violence*, 10–11.

and its reproductive capabilities as a "weapon of war." This policy was systematically planned by Serbian political and military leaders and strategically executed with the support of the Serbian and Bosnian Serb armies and paramilitary groups as a policy of ethnic cleansing or genocide in order to create a "greater Serbia," that is, a religiously, culturally, linguistically homogenous Serbian nation.[4]

In this paper we will examine two main issues. First, we will investigate the systematic use of rape camps by the Serbs, particularly with the intention of impregnating their victims, as a form of ethnic cleansing or genocide and the cultural, political, and even religious foundations that support this usurpation of the female body. Secondly, we will investigate the various responses to these women rape victims, which often lead to "secondary victimization" and implicitly support the Serbian practice and objective.

The Serbian Usurpation of the Female Body

In a traditionally patriarchal society, the Serbian government, military, and Orthodox Church have explicitly formulated a perception of the female gender and its role and function within society. Essentially, the female is reduced to her reproductive capacities in order to fulfill the overall objective of Serbian nationalism by producing more citizens to populate the nation. Limiting womanhood to a single physiological quality in this way proves nondiscriminatory in that not only are Serbian women thus perceived, but non-Serbian women are as well. This attitude has certainly had an impact, conscious or unconscious, on the overall perception and treatment of women, playing a part in the establishment of rape camps and the usurpation of women's bodies to achieve ethnic cleansing.

Serbian Usurpation of the Serbian Female Body

Perhaps the traditional role of the Serbian woman is most clearly depicted by the Mother of the Jugovici, the epic heroine from the Battle of Kosovo in 1389, who, in spite of the death of her nine sons in the battle with the Turks, did not weep.[5] Her courage, self-sacrifice, altruism, and, most of all, her fertility have been utilized to inspire and serve as a paradigm for Serbian women and their responsibility as mothers of the nation. According to this twisted reasoning, the necessity of reproduction guarantees Serbian perseverance against aggressors and establishes a greater Serbia, "Mother-Homeland." To shirk one's duty of reproduction amounts to antipatriotism and treason. The assertion of a Sarajevo woman who claimed that she planned to "fire

---

4. Ibid., 5.
5. Wendy Bracewell, "Mothers of the Nation," *Warreport* 36 (September 1995): 28.

off one baby every year to spite the aggressors" reflects the power of this myth and its message.[6] Serbians have waged this propaganda campaign of women's national and social reproductive responsibility on both political and religious fronts with remarkable success, as is evidenced in legislation "encouraging" women's reproductive responsibilities.

Government Policy and Demography

In October 1992, powerful organs in Serbian society published a document entitled "Warning," which focused on demographic issues.[7] Signed by the Serbian ruling party, the Serbian Socialist Party (SPS), the Serbian Academy of Arts and Sciences, and the Serbian Orthodox Church, this document highlighted the imbalance in terms of growth and renewal of various ethnic groups. In particular, "Albanians, Muslims and Romans [*sic*], with their high birth rate, are beyond rational and human reproduction."[8] The SPS conference adopted this document, and the Serbian Parliament enacted a resolution promoting "population renewal," seeking to stimulate the birthrate in some areas while suppressing it in others.[9] Perhaps it is by no means coincidental that those areas designated for an increase in birthrates were predominantly developed Serbian areas, whereas the suppression of birthrates was encouraged in predominantly undeveloped Albanian and Muslim areas. In fact, statistics in many areas of the Balkans do reveal higher reproduction rates among non-Serbs,[10] but the reasons given for this difference vary depending on the source.

While numerous sociological, cultural, and historical factors may account for the differences in population growth among the different cultural and religious groups, the Serbian government has focused on ideological and naturalist reasons. Ideologically, non-Serbs reproduce as a political strategy to outgrow the Serbian nation. The naturalist reason asserts that non-Serbs are intrinsically primitive in their ethnic reasoning and will not adjust or adapt to the Serbian mentality.[11] Such political rhetoric instills the fear that the subtle, though very real, means of a shift in demography and population growth threatens the Serbian nation and thus promotes a nationalist sentiment. It singles out Serbian women and their responsibility to serve the nation through reproduction to insure population expansion and to provide

---

6. Ibid.
7. Zarana Papic, "How to Become a 'Real' Serbian Woman?" *Warreport* 36 (September 1995): 41.
8. Ibid.
9. Ibid.
10. See Vatro Murvar, *Nation and Religion in Central Europe and the Western Balkans— The Muslims in Bosnia-Herzegovina and Sandzak: A Sociological Analysis* (Madison: University of Wisconsin Press, 1989).
11. Papic, "How to Become a 'Real' Serbian Woman?" 41.

future soldiers to defend the nation in times of war.[12] Furthermore, governmental legislation supporting reproduction found ecclesiological support from the Serbian Orthodox Church.

The Serbian Orthodox Church: Reproduction and Religious Sanctions

In December 1994, Patriarch Pavle, leader of the Serbian Orthodox Church, delivered a Christmas message denouncing the "White Plague," that is, the low birthrate among Serbian women.[13] The plague results from infanticide "committed by women who choose not to give birth because of their 'contentment.'"[14] The "disease" can only be cured by making Serbian women want to bear children. Accomplishing this objective mandates religious sanctions to stigmatize a woman for not wanting to procreate and declares such an attitude to be a threefold sin: against themselves, the Serbian nation, and God Himself.[15] The women sin against themselves because "many mothers who did not want more than one child, today bitterly cry and pull their hair in despair over the loss of the only son in the war...why did they not give birth to more children and have them as consolation."[16] They sin against the Serbian nation because "in twenty years, the Serbs will, if such a birth-rate remains, become an ethnic minority in their own country."[17] Finally, they sin against God because "when they come to meet God, those mothers who never allowed their children to be born will meet their children who will sadly ask: why did you kill me? Why did you not let me live?"[18] In a passionate plea, Pavle appealed to the nationalistic sentiment of Serbian women to willfully reproduce for the betterment of the country. In his speech, Pavle drew certain parallels between women, their bodies, the survival of the nation, and the war effort. By not giving birth to more children, women have placed the survival of the nation in jeopardy. Therefore, Serbian woman must heed the battle call and respond by offering their bodies as incubators, preferably to male children. This attitude is reflected in the frequently cited aphorism that "for every Serbian soldier dead in battle in Slovenia, Serbian mothers must bear 100 more fighters!"[19]

Serbian reproduction then has served two particular objectives: to create more Serbs to further the Serbian nationalist ideology and to create more soldiers to defend the country. The obvious irony of the nationalistic appeal

---

12. See Norman Cigar, *Genocide in Bosnia: The Policy of "Ethnic Cleansing"* (College Station: Texas A & M University Press, 1995), 78–80.
13. Papic, "How to Become a 'Real' Serbian Woman?" 40 (quoting Pavle's speech).
14. Ibid.
15. Ibid., 40–41.
16. Ibid., 40.
17. Ibid.
18. Ibid.
19. Bracewell, "Mothers of the Nation," 28.

for Serbian women to reproduce so that their (male) children can die for the country is that it somewhat defeats the purpose of the first objective. This irony notwithstanding, the attitude limits women's potential as human beings to their reproductive faculties; they are a means of attaining the end of a "greater Serbia." In a very real sense, Serbian women have served as a "weapon of war" for the military agenda of their own country. This attitude and perception of women and their bodies had much broader implications, however.

Serbian Usurpation of Non-Serbian Women: Rape Camps as a Weapon of War

Serbian Propaganda: Muslims Raping Serbian Women

Propaganda has played a major role in conflicts of the twentieth century both to instill feelings of compassion, sympathy, and solidarity among a people and to incite and justify violence toward a real or perceived enemy. Serbia is no exception. As early as 1981, the media reinforced and exploited Serbian nationalism in its depiction of the uprising of the Kosovo Albanians seeking autonomy from Serbia.[20] Though Serbian forces immediately suppressed the uprising, the Serbian people heard of an Albanian genocidal plot against ethnic Serbs involving various atrocities, including mass rapes committed against the local Serbian population in Kosovo.[21]

Even though these accusations were highly exaggerated, they accomplished their objective by stirring nationalistic Serbian feelings, uniting the country in solidarity against Albanians initially and, later, against all non-Serbs, and bringing Slobodan Milosevic, the "most zealous advocate of the thesis of 'genocidal Kosovo Albanians,'" into power.[22] Milosevic rapidly developed the plan for a "greater Serbia" through the calculated use and manipulation of the media to foster popular support. In fact, Milosevic immediately took over the press and national television.[23] Already having successfully roused national Serbian sentiment against the Albanians, the Serbian propaganda machine went into full force when the Muslims and Croats of Bosnia-Herzegovina declared independence on 3 March 1992.

---

20. Alexandra Stiglmayer, "The War in the Former Yugoslavia," in *Mass Rape: The War against Women in Bosnia-Herzegovina*, ed. Alexandra Stiglmayer, trans. Marion Faber (Lincoln: University of Nebraska Press, 1994), 14 (hereinafter "War"; and *Mass Rape*).

21. See Srdjan Vrcan, "Faith under Challenge," *Warreport* 40 (April 1996): 26. One of the leading papers spreading the alleged persecutions of Serbs in Kosovo was the religious Serbian newspaper *Pravoslavlje*. In 1982, twenty-one Orthodox priests openly appealed to Serbian political leaders for better protection of the remaining Serbs in Kosovo. This request religiously legitimated these accusations and gave almost unanimous support to the Serbian national political strategy. See ibid.

22. Stiglmayer, "War," 14.

23. Ibid., 14–15.

National television aired what appeared to be Muslims or Croats raping Serbian women when, in actuality, the scenes showed Serbs raping Muslim or Croat women.[24] Roy Gutman, the Pulitzer Prize–winning reporter on the ethnic cleansing in Bosnia, depicted another case of the blatant use of propaganda to incite the Serbian people when he recounted an interview with Major Milovan Milutinovic.[25] When Gutman met with him, Milutinovic was working on a text, "Lying [*sic*] Violent Hands on the Serbian Woman."[26] This document maintained that Muslims and Croats were committing genocide against the Serbian people.[27] One of the most telling citations from this document deals with the alleged atrocities committed by Muslims against Serbian women:

> By order of the Islamic fundamentalists from Sarajevo, healthy Serbian women from 17 to 40 years of age are being separated out and subjected to special treatment. According to their sick plans going back many years, these women have to be impregnated by orthodox Islamic seeds in order to raise a generation of janissaries [i.e., Turkish military elite composed of Christian youth forced to convert to Islam in the middle ages] on the territories they surely consider to be theirs, the Islamic republic. In other words, a fourfold crime is to be committed against the Serbian woman: to remove her from her own family, to impregnate her by undesirable seeds, to make her bear a stranger and then to take even him away from her.[28]

What Gutman, the UN Security Council, and the world have come to discover is that this is, indeed, an accurate portrayal of what was taking place, with one minor exception: the perpetrators were primarily Serbs, and the victims were primarily Muslim women and children.

Ethnic Cleansing and Genocide

Serbian governmental and military powers appear to have utilized systematic rape as a weapon of war[29] to serve their overall objective of "ethnic cleansing," a euphemism for genocide. According to the Commission of Experts appointed by the UN Secretary-General Boutros Boutros-Ghali, the expres-

---

24. See Catharine A. MacKinnon, "Rape, Genocide, and Women's Human Rights," in *Mass Rape,* ed. A. Stiglmayer, 190.
25. Roy Gutman, *A Witness to Genocide* (London: Element, 1993), x.
26. Ibid., ix.
27. Ibid.
28. Ibid., x.
29. See Bassiouni and McCormick, *Sexual Violence,* 21. While the policy of systematic rape by the Serbian military remains to be definitively proven, there is substantial evidence to support that such a policy existed.

sion "ethnic cleansing" is relatively new.[30] "Considered in the context of the conflicts in the former Yugoslavia, 'ethnic cleansing' means rendering an area ethnically homogenous by using force or intimidation to remove persons of given groups from the area."[31] Ethnic cleansing is accomplished through the use of "concentration camps, torture, sexual violence, mass killings, forced deportations, destruction of private and cultural property, pillage and theft, and the blocking of humanitarian aid."[32]

In 1944, Raphaël Lemkin coined the term "genocide," from the Greek word *genos* (race or tribe) and the Latin suffix *cide* (to kill), to depict the Nazi atrocities against the Jews.[33] He described genocide as the destruction of a nation or ethnic group, although not its total extermination.[34] The UN legal definition of genocide likewise reflects this qualification by declaring that genocide is the intent "to destroy *in whole or in part* a national, ethnic, racial or religious group as such."[35] The early formulators of this definition included the phrase "in whole or in part" to emphasize the fact that genocide does not require the aim of killing all the members of a group.[36] Some scholars have argued that the Serbian policy toward Muslims cannot be considered genocide because it was concerned primarily with control over territory rather than inhabitants, and the Serbian "intention was to get rid of the Moslems not to exterminate them."[37] Nevertheless, several acts committed by the Serbian military constitute genocide as enumerated in article II of *The 1948 Convention on the Prevention and Punishment of the Crime of Genocide.* [38] These acts include killing members of another group on the basis of their religion, physical and mental torture, using measures whose aim is to prevent births within the group, and forcibly transferring children from one group to another.[39] Evidence suggests that all of these acts were

---

30. See ibid., 7. On 6 October 1992, the UN Security Council adopted Resolution 780 establishing the Commission of Experts to investigate allegations of violations of international humanitarian law in the former Yugoslavia.

31. UN Security Council, *Final Report of the Commission of Experts Established pursuant to Security Council Resolution 780 (1992)* (Chair, Commission of Experts, Cherif Bassiouni; General Document S/1994/674; 27 May 1994), §55 (hereinafter *Final Report*).

32. Bassiouni and McCormick, *Sexual Violence*, 5.

33. Raphaël Lemkin, *Axis Rule in Occupied Europe* (Washington, D.C.: Carnegie Endowment for International Peace, 1944), 79–80.

34. Ibid., 79.

35. UN General Assembly, *The 1948 Convention on the Prevention and Punishment of the Crime of Genocide* (12 January 1951), art. II (emphasis added) (hereinafter *Genocide Convention*).

36. UN Security Council, *Final Report*, 93.

37. Alain Destexhe, *Rwanda and Genocide in the Twentieth Century* (New York: New York University Press, 1994), 19. For a critique of his position, see David Rieff, "An Age of Genocide: The Far-Reaching Lessons of Rwanda," *The New Republic*, 29 January 1996, 34–36.

38. UN General Assembly, *Genocide Convention*, art. II.

39. UN Security Council, *Final Report*, §98.

committed according to a logistically coordinated policy that unequivocally constituted genocide.

In essence, genocide and ethnic cleansing coincided, the goal being the establishment of a "greater Serbia"—that is, a Serb-inhabited region purged of all non-Serbs throughout Serbia, Bosnia-Herzegovina, and Croatia. Within the Bosnian, Muslim, and Catholic communities, sexual assault and rape served as particularly effective means of achieving this goal.

Rape and Sexual Assault: Evidence of a Policy

According to Ruth Seifert, "[a] violent invasion into the interior of one's body represents the most severe attack imaginable upon the intimate self and the dignity of a human being: by any measure it is a mark of severe torture."[40] This violent invasion has occurred against the women on all sides of the conflict in Bosnia: Serbs, Croats, and Muslims. What differentiates the Serbian practice of rape and sexual assault from other assaults is that it is a systematic military policy conceived and planned before the outbreak of the war to affect the ethnic cleansing of Muslims from Serbian territory. On the subject of rape and sexual assault, the UN Commission of Experts concluded that "the practices of 'ethnic cleansing,' sexual assault and rape have been carried out by some of the parties so systematically that they strongly appear to be the product of policy."[41] In a follow-up report, the UN General Assembly asserted that it was "*[c]onvinced* that this heinous practice [rape and abuse of women] constitutes a deliberate weapon of war in fulfilling the policy of ethnic cleansing carried out by Serbian forces in Bosnia and Herzegovina, and...that the abhorrent policy of ethnic cleansing was a form of genocide."[42] Several factors support this allegation of a Serbian rape policy.

The RAM Plan.   First, and most importantly, documentation exists substantiating the claim of a Serbian military policy to ethnically cleanse Bosnia-Herzegovina, and designating rape as a specific means of attaining this goal. This policy is clearly spelled out in the so-called RAM plan written by Serb army officers around the end of August 1991.[43]

---

40. Ruth Seifert, "War and Rape: A Preliminary Analysis," in *Mass Rape*, ed. A. Stiglmayer, 55.

41. UN Security Council, *Final Report*, §313.

42. UN General Assembly, *Resolution Adopted by the General Assembly* (Document A/RES/49/205; 6 March 1995), 2. See also UN Economic and Social Council, *Preliminary Report Submitted by the Special Rapporteur on Violence against Women, Its Causes and Consequences, Ms. Radhika Coomaraswamy, in accordance with Commission on Human Rights Resolution 1994/45* (Document E/CN.4/1995/42; 22 November 1994), §268 (hereinafter *Preliminary Report*).

43. Bassiouni and McCormick, *Sexual Violence*, 21, n. 4; see also Beverly Allen, *Rape Warfare: The Hidden Genocide in Bosnia-Herzegovina and Croatia* (Minneapolis and London: University of Minnesota Press, 1996), 56–60 (hereinafter *Rape Warfare*).

An Italian journalist and the Ljubljana newspaper *DELO* both confirm the existence of this plan and its policy to target "women, especially adolescents, and . . . children" in order to cause fear and panic among the Muslims and bring about a Muslim retreat from the designated territories.[44] *DELO* reports that the Yugoslav National Army (JNA) Psychological Operations Department in Belgrade developed a plan to drive Muslims out of Bosnia based on an analysis of Muslim behavior which "showed that their morale, desire for battle, and will could be crushed more easily by raping women, especially minors and even children, and by killing members of the Muslim nationality inside their religious facilities."[45] Concrete evidence accumulated by various humanitarian organizations, including the United Nations and Human Rights Watch, supports the existence of such a practice. These organizations' reports indicate that the research, planning, and coordination of rape camps was a systematic policy of the Serbian government and military forces with the explicit intention of creating an ethnically pure state.

Official Toleration of Rape. In their final report, the Commission of Experts appointed by the United Nations to investigate allegations of rape and sexual assault in the former Yugoslavia speculated that camp commanders had direct control over those who committed rapes within these camps, indicating that the commanders could have halted the practice and punished the perpetrators if they chose.[46] The commission cited as evidence the fact that during the height of the reported rapes (April to November 1992) the media attention gradually grew from a few reports in March 1992 to a high of 535 stories in January 1993 and 529 in February 1993.[47] In the months following these media reports, the number of reported cases dropped dramatically. The correlation between increased media attention and the decrease in reported cases of rape, the commission speculated, "would indicate that the commanders could control the alleged perpetrators if they wanted to. This could lead to the conclusion that there was an overriding policy advocating the use of rape as a method of 'ethnic cleansing,' rather than a policy of omission, tolerating the widespread commission of rape."[48]

---

44. See Allen, *Rape Warfare*, 57.

45. Bassiouni and McCormick, *Sexual Violence*, 21 n. 4.

46. UN Security Council, *Final Report*, §253. See also Bassiouni and McCormick, *Sexual Violence*, 21–22.

47. UN Security Council, *Final Report*, §237.

48. Ibid. The commission's tentative conclusion, however, though it implicates those in authority and points to an official policy of tolerating rape, does not necessarily reflect a decreased number of rapes after international media coverage. We need only to consider, for example, the rampant spread of AIDS throughout the world and the relatively sparse media coverage of this disease to realize that the media is by no means an accurate representation of what is occurring in reality. Beverly Allen notes that in October 1994 she spoke with Dr. Kozaric-Kovacic who reported that pregnant survivors from rape/death camps continued to arrive in Zagreb and yet

Patterns of Rape and Sexual Assault.   Perhaps the strongest indication of a
Serbian systematic policy is reflected in the five patterns of rape documented
by the UN Commission of Experts.[49] These patterns required logistical coordination, especially within rape camps where rape was used to impregnate
Muslim and Catholic Croat women.

In the first pattern, sexual violence occurred with looting and intimidation before widespread fighting broke out in a particular region.[50] As ethnic
tensions grew, those in control of the local government would encourage
paramilitaries, individuals, or gangs of men to initiate a policy of terror-
izing local residents. These people would break into homes, steal property,
and torture and sexually assault the inhabitants, oftentimes in front of other
family members or in public.[51]

The second pattern of sexual violence occurred during fighting. In the process of attacking a town or village, the forces would rape or sexually assault
some women in their homes.[52] Once the town was secured, the forces would
gather the surviving population and divide them according to sex and age,
selecting some women for rape or sexual assaults.[53] The forces then transported the remaining population to detention facilities. The psychological

---

there was nothing or next to nothing in the international media acknowledging these events.
The decline in reports of rapes, then, could be a result of the media's loss of infatuation with the
topic. It could also be associated with a silencing of the victims by the perpetrators, who feared
that they would be called to justice as news of an international war crimes tribunal spread
in early 1993. On 22 February 1993 the UN Security Council established the International
Tribunal for the Prosecution of Persons Responsible for Serious Violations of International
Humanitarian Law Committed in the Territory of the Former Yugoslavia since 1991 (Security
Council Resolution 808, §1; UN Doc. S/RES/808 [1993]). Cited in Catherine N. Niarchos,
"Women, War, and Rape: Challenges Facing the International Tribunal for the Former Yugoslavia," *Human Rights Quarterly* 17 (1995): 651 n. 9. In interviews with women who were
raped, the perpetrators frequently threatened these women that if they told anyone of the incident, either themselves or their family members would be hunted down and murdered. Thus,
a possible interpretation of the decline in rape cases reported by the media is that while the
number of rapes did not decrease significantly in conjunction with increased media attention,
the tendency for victims to publicly reveal such events decreased because of the perpetrator's
threats of reprisal for fear of being called to justice by the War Crimes Tribunal. These are
tentative conclusions, the truth of which is difficult to establish.

49. The *Final Report* of the Commission of Experts states that "[f]ive patterns emerge from
the reported cases, regardless of the ethnicity of the perpetrators or the victims" (UN Security
Council, *Final Report*, §244). This indicates that all sides utilized rape as a systematic policy.
However, in a later paper written by Professor Cherif Bassiouni, who chaired the Commission
of Experts, he emphasizes that the Serbs ran most of the detention camps where sexual violence
occurred (Bassiouni and McCormick, *Sexual Violence*, 16). Furthermore, ethnic cleansing to
create a "greater Serbia" was a specific political and military objective unique to the Serbs.
While all sides may have utilized sexual violence to oppress the enemy, and in particular the
women of the enemy, it was the Serbian overall objective that utilized sexual violence as a form
of ethnic cleansing that has received the greatest attention and provoked the greatest outcry.

50. UN Security Council, *Final Report*, §245.

51. See ibid.

52. See ibid., §246.

53. See ibid.

impact of such atrocities is evident. Through fear and intimidation, victims and witnesses would be hesitant to return to the scene of such events.

The third pattern of sexual violence occurred in detention facilities or other sites referred to as refugee "collection centers."[54] After the population had been divided, men of fighting age were either tortured and executed or sent off to work camps while women were generally sent to separate camps. There, soldiers, camp guards, paramilitaries, and civilians raped or sexually assaulted many of the women.[55] Generally, these sexual assaults occurred in one of two ways. The most common practice involved selecting women from crowded rooms, taking them to another location, raping them, and either murdering them or returning them to the collection center. Another, though less frequent, practice entailed raping and sexually assaulting women in front of other detainees, or forcing detainees to rape and assault one another, thus humiliating the victims and instilling terror in the witnesses.[56] In this setting, gang rapes were frequently reported as being accompanied by beatings, torture, and other forms of humiliation.[57]

A fourth pattern of sexual violence occurred in rape camps established in buildings such as hotels, schools, restaurants, hospitals, factories, peacetime brothels, or even animal stalls in barns, fenced pens, and auditoriums.[58] The purpose of these camps was to punish women through sexual assault and other forms of torture. No one was exempt from this treatment in the camps. Frequently, the Serbian captors told women that they were trying to impregnate them. In doing so, they would create "Chetnik babies" who would kill Muslims when they grew up. Furthermore, "they repeatedly said their President had ordered them to do this."[59] One woman, detained at the rape camp in the northern Bosnian town of Doboj, reported that women who became pregnant had to remain in the camp for seven or eight months.[60] Gynecologists examined the women, and those women found pregnant were segregated from the rest and received meals and other "special privileges."[61] Only after it was too late for these women to get an abortion were they released and usually taken to Serbia.[62] The frequently reported intent of Serbian soldiers to impregnate Muslim and Catholic Croats, the presence of

---

54. Bassiouni and McCormick, *Sexual Violence*, 17.

55. UN Security Council, *Final Report*, §247.

56. See ibid., §248.

57. In male camps, this public form of sexual assault took place as well. In one documented instance, a prisoner was forced to bite off the genitals of another (Bassiouni and McCormick, *Sexual Violence*, 17–18).

58. Allen, *Rape Warfare*, 65.

59. UN Security Council, *Final Report*, §248.

60. Alexandra Stiglmayer, "The Rapes in Bosnia-Herzegovina," in *Mass Rape*, ed. A. Stiglmayer, 82, 119 (hereinafter "Rapes").

61. Niarchos, "Women, War, and Rape," 657.

62. Stiglmayer, "Rapes," 118–19.

gynecologists to examine the women, and the intentional holding of pregnant women until it was too late legally or safely to procure an abortion all
point to a systematic, planned policy to utilize rape and forced impregnation
as a form of ethnic cleansing.

A fifth pattern of sexual violence occurred in "bordello" camps.[63] Rather
than a form of punishment, women were held in these camps to provide sex
for men returning from the front lines. While many of the women in the
other camps were eventually exchanged for other civilian prisoners, these
women were generally killed.[64]

Through an analysis of these five patterns of rape as well as other data, the
commission detected a number of characteristics indicating an overall Serbian systematic policy: similar characteristics in the practice of sexual assault
and rape in noncontiguous areas; concomitant acts of other international
humanitarian law violations; simultaneous military activity; simultaneous
activity to displace civilian populations; common characteristics in commis-
sioning rape aimed at maximizing shame and humiliation of the victim, her
family, and her community; and the timing of the rapes, with the majority of
documented cases occurring from April to November 1992.[65] Particularly
significant is the large number of rapes, "approximately 600 of the 1,100
documented cases," that occurred in detention camps:[66] "These rapes in detention do not appear to be random, and they indicate at least a policy of
encouraging rape supported by the deliberate failure of camp commanders
and local authorities to exercise command and control over the personnel
under their authority."[67]

The Genocidal Purpose of Sexual Assault

Beverly Allen rightly points out that although the five patterns of rape delin-
eated by the commission exemplify various practices of sexual assault, they
do not clearly indicate the genocidal nature and purpose of those assaults.[68]
Consequently, she labels as "genocidal rape" the Serbian military policy of

---

63. UN Security Council, *Final Report*, §249.
64. See ibid.
65. See ibid., §252.
66. Bassiouni and McCormick, *Sexual Violence*, 10. This figure differs from that of the
Final Report, which states that "out of 514 allegations which are included in the database, 327
occurred in places of detention" (§252, n. 71). The discrepancy between these numbers is most
likely due to the fact that the database in Geneva was not adequate to handle the immense
amount of information accumulated by the Commission of Experts (about 65,000 pages of
documents and three hundred hours of videotape). The information could only be thoroughly
processed subsequently when an adequate database was established at DePaul University under
the direction of M. Cherif Bassiouni, the commission's rapporteur on the gathering and analysis
of facts.
67. UN Security Council, *Final Report*, § 252.
68. Allen, *Rape Warfare*, 155–56 n. 7.

rape for the purpose of genocide and ethnic cleansing, distinguishing three forms of this policy. First, prior to the arrival of the Serbian military (Yugoslav army or Bosnian Serb forces), Serb militias, civilians, or Chetniks would enter a village and terrorize the inhabitants, especially through the use of public rape and sexual assault.[69] Frequently the women recognized their assailants as neighbors, law enforcement personnel, or other members of the community. Recognition seemed an important part of Serbian policy. The persecuted would be less likely to return to their towns and villages if their assailants were local inhabitants rather than men from distant territories. Consequently, invading Serbian military personnel would frequently employ local Serbs through force, threats, or psychological pressure to participate in the atrocities.[70] Word of these atrocities would quickly spread throughout the town or village instilling fear in the inhabitants. Subsequently, official Serbian military forces would arrive offering safe passage for the townspeople out of the village if they would agree never to return.[71] In this way, the goal of ethnically cleansing a particular town, village, or region was attained.

The second form of genocidal rape occurred in Serb concentration camps where Bosnian-Herzegovinian and Croatian women (and sometimes men) were randomly chosen to be raped.[72] The victim was often murdered after the sexual assault.[73]

The third form of genocidal rape occurred in "rape/death camps." Bosnian-Herzegovinian women were arrested and imprisoned in these camps and systematically raped for an extended period of time by Serb, Bosnian Serb, and Croatian Serb soldiers, Bosnian Serb militias, and Chetniks.[74] Either the women were raped as a form of torture preceding death or with the purpose of forced impregnation. As noted earlier, if a woman became pregnant, she would be held in the concentration camp until it was too late to procure an abortion safely.[75] In cases where the victims were murdered following repeated rapes and sexual assaults, the genocidal intent is obvious. Not so obvious, however, is genocide in the form of forced impregnation. Is not the propagation of a species the antithesis of genocide? How would the forced impregnation of Muslim and Croat women serve the objective of creating a greater Serbia?

---

69. Ibid., vii, 62–63.
70. See Stiglmayer, "Rapes," 160–61.
71. See Allen, *Rape Warfare*, vii, 62.
72. Bassiouni and McCormick, *Sexual Violence*, 18.
73. See Allen, *Rape Warfare*, 63.
74. See ibid.
75. See Bassiouni and McCormick, *Sexual Violence*, 18.

Number of Forced Pregnancies due to Rape

Even though the exact number of Bosnian women raped by Serbs and the pregnancies resulting from those acts of violence will probably never be known, in January 1993 the United Nations sent a team of five people to investigate reports of the widespread occurrence of rape and, in particular, the systematic use of rape, especially in Bosnia-Herzegovina, for the goal of ethnic cleansing.[76] Though limited by temporal, personnel, and financial constraints, the team's findings were revealing. The team of experts spent twelve days (12–23 January 1993) interviewing physicians and reviewing medical records from six major medical centers in Zagreb, Sarajevo, Zenica, and Belgrade. Through their investigations, they identified 119 pregnancies resulting from rape during 1992.[77] Of these pregnant women, eighty-eight received abortions.[78] In Zenica, sixteen women between the ages of seventeen and twenty-two were more than twenty weeks pregnant and, therefore, could not receive abortions.[79]

Medical studies estimate that a single act of intercourse results in pregnancy between 1 and 4 percent of the time.[80] Due to the trauma of rape, the lower percentage more accurately reflects these occurrences. Consequently, this suggests that the 119 pregnancies were a result of approximately 11,900 cases of rape. In analyzing these figures, there are several variables that must be taken into consideration. First, the majority of women were raped more than once, and in the case of rape/death camps where some women reported being held for several months, women were raped hundreds of times. Such frequency of repeated rapes on an individual would lower the overall total of women raped.

Second, the team of experts only investigated six medical facilities throughout the former Yugoslavia. Women could have aborted pregnancies resulting from rape in countless other existing hospitals and clinics. In addition, many women did not have access to medical facilities and either tried to induce abortion themselves, gave birth to the baby and abandoned

---

76. See ibid., 7–8.

77. UN Economic and Social Council, *Report on the Situation of Human Rights in the Territory of the Former Yugoslavia Submitted by Mr. Tadeusz Mazowiecki, Special Rapporteur of the Commission on Human Rights, pursuant to Commission Resolution 1992/S-1/1 of 14 August 1992* (Document E/CN.4/1993/50; 10 February 1993), 64–65 (hereinafter *Report on the Situation*).

78. Ibid., §§10–14.

79. Stiglmayer asserts that out of the 119 pregnancies 104 women decided to abort the pregnancy. In her table (135), she lists nineteen abortions out of nineteen pregnancies in Zenica. The report, however, states that of the nineteen women, sixteen "were more than 20 weeks pregnant as a result of rape and could not receive abortions." See Stiglmayer, "Rapes," 134–35.

80. Shana Swiss and Joan E. Giller, "Rape as a Crime of War: A Medical Perspective," *JAMA* 270 (1993): 612–13; see also UN Economic and Social Council, *Report on the Situation*, §3.

it, or acted as if the child belonged to their husbands to avoid the possibility of being ostracized and rejected. Thus, the number of impregnated women is most likely much higher than the 119 discovered by the investigative team.

Third, even in the hospitals that the team of experts did visit and investigate, the policy of some personnel is not to inquire of women requesting abortions whether or not they had been raped. Indeed, it seems highly probable that women would not admit to being raped even if asked. Some women did not disclose having been raped until after their request for an abortion was denied.[81] In some hospitals in Zagreb, doctors actively shielded rape survivors from public exposure.[82]

Fourth, the investigation took place in the early months of 1992 when the conflict in Bosnia-Herzegovina was only a year old. Some people maintain that such rape camps still existed as late as the spring of 1996. Thus, there are four additional years where women may have become pregnant due to rape.

Fifth, in 1992 the clinic in Sarajevo that the team of experts visited reported that the number of abortions performed doubled in September, October, and November (four hundred to five hundred per month) compared to prewar rates (approximately two hundred per month).[83] During this time, the number of patient visits decreased by half.[84] This indicates a phenomenal increase in unwanted pregnancies. One could speculate that rape accounted for this increase. The report warns that such an analysis might not be accurate: "While this increase could reflect a rise in pregnancies due to rape, it could also reflect a more general response to economic and social instability created by war."[85] Finally, coercion and intimidation from the fear of ostracism by a woman's family, society, or community, fear of reprisals by their attackers either on themselves or their families and communities, and a sense of futility among the women for any possibility of justice prevented many women from reporting these crimes.

All of these factors combined make it impossible to arrive at any accurate statistics on the number of rapes, the number of rape survivors, and the number of pregnancies that resulted from these rapes. Estimates vary anywhere from 20,000 rape survivors reported by the UN special rapporteur[86] to as

---

81. UN Economic and Social Council, *Report on the Situation*, §8.

82. World Council of Churches, "Rape of Women in War: Report of the Ecumenical Women's Team Visit—Zagreb (December 1992)" (printed by the World Council of Churches on behalf of the Ecumenical Women's Team, December 1992), 9.

83. UN Economic and Social Council, *Report on the Situation*, §16.

84. See ibid.

85. UN Economic and Social Council, *Report on the Situation*, 67, §27.

86. See UN Economic and Social Council, *Contemporary Forms of Slavery* (Document E/CN.4/Sub.2/1995/38; 13 July 1995), §4.

many as 50,000–70,000 reported by the Bosnian government.[87] The Bosnian government estimated that some 35,000 women, primarily Muslim but also Croat, became pregnant from rape.[88] Given medical estimates of the percentage of pregnancies from rape, this would indicate some 3,500,000 incidents! This shocking statistic reveals another shortcoming in obtaining accurate information on the number of rapes and pregnancies resulting from rape: namely, the use of statistics for propaganda to incite the masses. Though the statistics vary, sometimes radically depending on the source, what is undeniable is that the practice of rape, and in particular rape with the intent to impregnate the victim, was both widespread and systematic among the Serbian forces, paramilitary groups,[89] and civilians.

Reproduction as Genocide?

The third form of genocidal rape identified by Beverly Allen,[90] rape and forced impregnation, is one of the most heinous crimes targeting the female body. Allen is correct in questioning the Serbian logic that motivates this practice: How can it be that rape, enforced pregnancy, and enforced childbirth equal genocide?[91]

According to Allen, this equation becomes conceivable only if one denies both science and culture.[92] Biologically, the fetus shares an equal amount of genetic material between the non-Serb mother and the Serbian father. Culturally, unless that child is raised by the father within a Serbian community, he or she will assimilate the cultural, ethnic, religious, and national identity of the mother. Allen summarizes: "Serb 'ethnic cleansing' by means of rape, enforced pregnancy, and childbirth is based on the uninformed, hallucinatory fantasy of ultranationalists whose most salient characteristic, after their violence, is their ignorance."[93] We concur with Allen that this mentality, what we label the genetic and cultural patriarchal myth, is indeed ignorant. However, the acceptance of this myth is not limited to Serbs but is supported by Muslim and Catholic men and women as well. The idea that the male determines a child's ethnic identity is cross-cultural and com-

---

87. World Council of Churches, "Rape of Women in War," 9.

88. See Allen, *Rape Warfare*, 9.

89. These groups included traditional groups such as Chetniks, known for their atrocities during World War II, as well as more recent groups such as Arkan's Tigers and the White Eagles. As Mujeeb R. Kahn, "From Hegel to Genocide in Bosnia, Some Moral and Philosophical Concerns," *Institute of Muslim Minority Affairs* 15 (January and July 1994): 6, points out, it "is important to note...that these professional killers were armed and directed in their 'cleansing operations' directly by the Belgrade government."

90. See Allen, *Rape Warfare*, 63; see above "The Genocidal Purpose of Sexual Assault," pp. 74–75.

91. Allen, *Rape Warfare*, 95.

92. See ibid., 96–97.

93. Ibid., 97.

mon, though misinformed. No matter how much one argues against such a perspective, a person's (mis)perceptions often dictate both how he or she perceives reality and his concrete practices, regardless of the facts.

Just as this genetic myth is based on a patriarchal system, so too is the ignorance that it cultivates. In the Balkans, a patriarchal society, the family name passes on through the male, regardless of religion or ethnicity. Even though biologically the child shares an equal amount of genetic material from the male and female, this fact does not overcome the sense that a child born from rape by a Serb will always be considered Serbian. Culturally, where it is recognized that the baby's father is Serbian, if the child is brought up in the Muslim or Catholic culture, he or she will oftentimes not be assimilated entirely within that culture given the circumstances of conception.[94] The very practice of rape and impregnation as a form of genocide depends not only upon the perpetrators buying into the genetic and cultural myth but the victims, their families, and their communities accepting the myth as well. As demonstrated by the response of Catholic and Muslim women who refer to their fetuses as "filth" and "that thing," the Serbs are not the only group who accept this myth.[95]

A report by the World Council of Churches (WCC) maintained that "the use of rape as a weapon of war is perceived as having its roots in patriarchal systems. Destruction and violation of women can be one way of attacking male opponents who regard the women as 'theirs' and whose male identity is therefore bound up with protection of 'their' women."[96] From the perpetrator's perspective, or the policy that he follows, the resultant child is considered Serbian, receiving his or her ethnic identity only from the Serbian father. In fact, many of the raped women interviewed reported that their assailants frequently claimed that they intended to impregnate them so that they would have a Serbian or "Chetnik baby."[97] When asked about reports of the deliberate impregnation of women to create "Serbian babies," a typical response representative of a patriarchal society was that if the biological father was Serb, the child "would always be considered in some way Serb."[98] In this way, Serbian seed becomes implanted and spread through non-Serbian women, even though the resulting baby is only half-Serb genetically speaking.

From the victim's perspective, because of the humiliation and terror experienced and the fact that the perpetrators were often neighbors or people from their community, many victims do not wish to return to their

---

94. See Stacy Sullivan, "Born under a Bad Sign," *Newsweek*, 23 September 1996, 50.
95. Ibid. See also Stiglmayer, "Rapes," 137.
96. World Council of Churches, "Rape of Women in War," 22.
97. See Stiglmayer, "Rapes," 92, 96, 104, 109, 118–119, 130, 132, 135.
98. World Council of Churches, "Rape of Women in War," 20.

homeland. Also, many women sustained physical injuries to such an extent through the process of sexual assault, torture, and rape that they are now unable to conceive. This fulfills one of the UN criteria that defines an act of genocide as one "intended to prevent births within the group."[99] In cases where women did become pregnant, the children may serve as constant reminders of their experiences and prolong the intended trauma of this practice.

Genocide is further accomplished through rejection of the victim by her husband because of the disgrace that the rape brings to him and his family. Often blamed for the rape, the woman faces ostracism from her family and community. Furthermore, those women impregnated as a result of rape are often viewed as tainted and unworthy for reproduction. All these components function to remove non-Serbs from Serbian territories and to break down the very social fabric of non-Serbian cultures. Not only does the practice of rape and rape for impregnation ethnically cleanse Serbian territories, but it functions to kill, in whole or in part, the non-Serb culture and reproductive capabilities once people have fled Serbian territories. The impact of this practice is far-reaching, and its success is based on the unilateral acceptance of a patriarchal system.

The Secondary Victimization of Rape Victims: Religious, Cultural, and Ethical Responses

The systematic rape of Muslim and Catholic Croat women with the explicit purpose of impregnation to create "Chetnik babies," to effect ethnic cleansing, and to attain a greater Serbia is an atrocious usurpation of the female body as a weapon of war. Perhaps the only atrocity that could compare to this is the treatment, perception, and exploitation of these women if and when their experiences become public knowledge. This section examines the religious and cultural responses to these women, the media's treatment of them, and the failure thus far of the international community to bring the perpetrators of genocidal rape to justice. All of these elements have contributed to the secondary victimization of these women, thus prolonging their physical, emotional, and psychological healing processes.

Religious Responses

Islamic Responses

A traditional Muslim aphorism states, "As our women are, so also is our community."[100] Islamic religious culture strongly emphasizes the protection

---

99. UN General Assembly, *Genocide Convention*, art. II(d).
100. Azra Zahihic Kaurin, "The Muslim Woman," in *Mass Rape*, ed. A. Stiglmayer, 171.

of a woman's dignity and honor. Bosnian Muslims frequently recount the story of Emina, a young Muslim woman who attempted to defend her village against loyalist Serbian Chetniks during World War II. Unable to hold off the advancing Serbs, when she fell into their hands, her one request was, "Only leave me my honor; I will forgive you my death."[101] To be raped, humiliated, and defiled was a fate worse than death for this Muslim woman, so high is the virtue of "honor" held within Islam. The point of the story is that a woman's purity in Islam and the Muslim patriarchal culture is not only held sacred but is seen as an essential element to insure the stability of the society and culture. This is true even though this concept of female honor has come under increasing and justifiable scrutiny.[102] Also relevant is that there is a vast chasm, not always recognized in Islamic sexual ethical mores, between a woman who is violated through rape and a woman who freely engages in a premarital or extramarital sexual relationship. The violation of a woman's honor, as is the case for raped Muslim women in Bosnia, produces various, often contradictory, religious and cultural responses.

First of all, the Koran does not extensively address the issue of rape among Muslims, let alone between Muslims and non-Muslims. This may be a result of its rather explicit view of the social roles of women in Islamic culture and the requirement that men accompany women in public.[103] This being the case, rape is considered to be a relatively infrequent occurrence. When a rape does occur, society generally concludes that since the woman was unaccompanied by a male guardian (husband, father, brother), she was "on the make" and perhaps looking for a sexual encounter; in such a case, sexual intercourse, even if violent, could be warranted given the woman's violation of religious customs.[104] In the event that a woman accuses a man of rape, the case goes before the religious court. If found guilty, the man faces a penalty of death by stoning or a lengthy jail term. In order to be found guilty, however, four respectable Muslims must have witnessed the event.[105] In the unlikely event of producing such witnesses, the woman must further prove that she has lived an exemplary or chaste life.[106] Even though the Muslim jurists who interpret the Koran address the issue of rape and sanction

---

101. Ibid., 173.

102. Niarchos, "Women, War, and Rape," 672–76; see also Anne Tierney Goldstein, *Recognizing Forced Impregnation as a War Crime under International Law* (New York: The Center for Reproductive Law and Policy, 1993), 20–22 (hereinafter *Forced Impregnation*).

103. In some conservative areas of Pakistan, the traditional *chador* and *chardiwari*—"the veil and four walls"—is still practiced. According to this custom, a woman should only go out of the house three times in her life: when she is born, when she leaves for her husband's home after marriage, and when she dies and is taken to be buried. Jan Goodwin, *Price of Honor: Muslim Women Lift the Veil of Silence* (Boston: Little, Brown, 1994), 56.

104. See ibid.

105. See ibid., 151.

106. "Women Jailed for Being Raped," *Marie Claire* 3 (October 1996): 74–76.

severe penalties for perpetrators of this crime, the prosecution of rapists in Muslim society occurs rather infrequently. More likely, the women will be accused of *zina*—sex outside marriage including adultery, fornication, and rape—by her assailant and will herself be sent to jail.[107] (This has happened in many rape cases in Pakistan.) This travesty of justice is not unlike the difference between the religious ideals of the Bosnian Muslim community and the actual practices of that community when Muslim women are raped by non-Muslims.

In interviews with Bosnian Muslim religious leaders, the WCC reported that leaders have taken measures to insure that victims of rape will be treated compassionately on several accounts.[108] Within the religious community itself, according to Aruna Gnanadason, a member of the WCC commission, religious leaders consider raped women heroines and receive them unconditionally into the communities.[109] Her claim, however, conflicts with reports asserting that raped women are frequently stigmatized and ostracized within these communities. The international community frequently voices its concern that if her experience becomes public knowledge, a raped woman will be considered an outcast in certain cultures; her husband will abandon her, or in the case of an unmarried woman, she will be unable to marry if she so desires because of the stigma associated with the event. Muslim leaders, however, assured the WCC commission that "young men of the community have been pledged to marry women victims."[110] In the case of impregnation, religious leaders have sympathized with the situation of these women and have condoned abortions up until the 120–day legal limit.[111] For those women held past the limit, or those who chose not to abort, there were offers of adoption by international Muslim communities.[112] The official WCC report substantiated Gnanadason's claim from a religious perspective. It added, however, that practically and culturally speaking, such openness and receptivity are not always evident.[113]

---

107. See Goodwin, *Price of Honor*, 51.

108. World Council of Churches, "Rape of Women in War," 9, 20.

109. Aruna Gnanadason, interview by WCC, Geneva, Switzerland, 16 July 1996.

110. World Council of Churches, "Rape of Women in War," 9.

111. Ibid. According to the *Hanafi* jurists' interpretation of the *hadith* (sayings, practices, judgments, and attitudes of Muhammad), ensoulment takes place 120 days after conception. They allow for abortion during this time "only for juridically valid reasons." "Abortion," *The Oxford Encyclopedia of the Modern Islamic World*, ed. John L. Esposito (New York: Oxford University Press, 1995), 4:18. Mirjana Rasevic, "Abortion as a Method of Birth Control," *Yugoslav Survey* 31 (1990): 103, asserts that abortion is regularly used and accepted as a predominant form of birth control in the former Yugoslavia without any social stigma attached to it. See Ivan Felice et al., "Bosnia-Herzegovina: Cultural Profile," *International Journal of Refugee Law* 6 (1994): 435.

112. World Council of Churches, "Rape of Women in War," 20.

113. Ibid., 20, 23.

Catholic Response

The Croatian Catholic response to victims of rape suffers from similar tensions between religious ideology and cultural practice. In an address by Pope John Paul II to Archbishop Vinko Pulijic of Sarajevo, the pope called for the entire community to "be close to these women who have been so tragically offended and to their families, in order to help them transform the act of violence into an act of love and acceptance."[114] The terms "rape" and "abortion" are noticeably absent from this document. For "rape," the pope substituted phrases such as "mothers, wives and young women who have been subjected to violence because of an outburst of racial hatred and brutal lust." Instead of "abortion," he said, "[S]ince the unborn child is in no way responsible for the disgraceful acts accomplished, he or she is innocent and therefore cannot be treated as the aggressor."[115] The omission of these terms seems somewhat curious. One could speculate that because of the political and religious tensions between the various groups in the former Yugoslavia, the pope consciously attempted to remain diplomatic in his address and avoided terms that would highlight the atrocities committed (rape) and the potential outcome of those atrocities (abortion). Instead, he focused on the need for reconciliation. The call for support and solidarity from the community and the assertion of the sanctity of the family and its role in bringing about healing prove noteworthy. This challenge of solidarity, so key to overcoming the factions within families and the social and cultural genocide that rape causes, can also serve to remove the power and genocidal motivation from this practice. If the culture, society, and family do not react according to the Serb's projections, but instead stand by these women and support them in solidarity, an impetus for the practice is removed. The Serbian policy of rape for the purpose of ethnic cleansing is dependent not only upon the complicity of Serbs as perpetrators but also on the Muslims and Catholics as the victims and the anticipated cultural responses toward those victims. If the victims are met with love and acceptance instead of fear and hatred, a link in the chain of genocide is removed.

The major difference between Catholicism and Islam is the possibility of obtaining an abortion in the case of rape. While Muslim religious leaders allow abortion up to the 120–day legal limit in the case of rape, the Catholic Church officially condemns abortion even in the case of rape, and according to some Croatian women's groups, many Catholic hospitals will not perform this operation. This claim, however, has been disputed by Croatian doctors who maintain that they will perform abortions in cases of rape

---

114. Pope John Paul II, "Change Violence into Acceptance," *The Pope Speaks* 38 (1993): 220.

115. Ibid., 219–20.

unless serious medical reasons militate against it.[116] As mentioned above, of the 119 pregnancies from rape documented by the UN special commission, eighty-eight were terminated by abortions. Thus, while in theory the religious position may dictate against abortion, it is commonly practiced, even in Catholic Croatia.

Cultural and Social Practice

Frequently a stark contrast develops between religious ideologies and the actual responses of Muslims and Catholics to rape survivors. Within Muslim, Catholic, and Serbian cultures, victims of rape tend to experience alienation in varying degrees. First of all, many women refuse to discuss the rape because of the shame and humiliation associated with it, as well as the stigmatization from family, friends, and the community. These attitudes do not facilitate an openness to sharing experiences and often hamper the ability to heal emotionally, physically, and psychologically. Also, women sometimes feel responsible in some way for the rape, and this misconception can be reinforced by attitudes and comments from peers.[117] Especially in cultures where women raped in peacetime are frequently blamed for the attack, whether because of the clothes they were wearing or being out alone in public, in a wartime situation women may internalize these speculations.[118] Often, even other women who have been raped do not encourage peers to talk about the incident for fear that they will themselves be implicated as rape victims and stigmatized and ostracized by their families, husbands, or communities. Fear of reprisals toward detained family members or other women being detained poses another very real threat to these women if they speak about the event.[119] Finally, society has developed suspicions as to whether or not women fabricate these events, especially in the Bosnian conflict where propaganda has played a major role on all sides. All of these factors tend to dissuade women from talking about their experiences with friends and family as well as seeking psychological counseling.

Research shows, however, that if raped women are supported emotionally by family and friends or peers in refugee camps, the psychological disorders of these women do not persist as long as for those who keep the rape a

---

116. Stiglmayer, "Rapes," 135–36.

117. Ivan Felice et al., "Women Refugees from Bosnia-Herzegovina: Developing a Culturally Sensitive Counseling Framework," *International Journal of Refugee Law* 6 (1994): 213.

118. The special rapporteur to the United Nations points out that "women's experience of rape can be intensified by cultural and religious views which often blame the victim." UN Economic and Social Council, *Rape and Abuse of Women in the Former Yugoslavia: Report of the Secretary-General* (Document E/CN4/1994/5; 30 June 1993), §60 (hereinafter *Rape and Abuse*).

119. UN Economic and Social Council, *Situation of Human Rights in the Territory of the Former Yugoslavia* (E/CN.4/1993/50; 10 February 1993) 66, §24.

secret or speak only to a therapist.[120] Rape is just one of the many layers of trauma that these women have experienced. They are still attempting to cope with witnessing the torture and execution of fathers, husbands, or sons, the rape of their own daughters or mothers, being detained in a camp, or losing their homes and personal belongings. To heal from these traumas takes love, support, compassion, and acceptance from one's family, friends, and community. Unfortunately, this support does not always exist.

A second consideration that can aggravate the trauma and suffering of the victim is the husband's response to the event. In interviews conducted with rape survivors, one of the recurring concerns is that if their husbands found out about the rape, their husbands would not take them back or might violently abuse, or in some cases even kill, them.[121] What causes such responses from the one to whom the victim should be able to turn for love, comfort, support, and understanding? Although the psychological reasons are complex and beyond full comprehension by this author, some justifications are rooted in the masculine myth perpetrated by a patriarchal ideal that men are responsible for "their" women. This myth, which is not limited to a particular religion, culture, or sociological stratus, demonstrates a model of masculine-feminine relations in which men possess, rather than relate with, women. According to this myth, when a "man's woman" is violated through rape, it is often very difficult for him to accept the humiliation of such an event. He has failed to live up to his masculine duty and the obligation to defend "his woman," regardless of the circumstances. Frequently, though illogically, this belief translates into alienation or violence directed toward the only one whom he can punish, the woman. Empathy and compassion for the woman sometimes become displaced by masculine self-pity, humiliation, and suffering as a result of her rape.

The cultural and social practices of alienation and expulsion all too frequently oppose the religious ideology calling for compassion, love, and acceptance of rape victims. The phenomenon of secondary victimization caused by this occurrence merely prolongs the recuperation process of victims and implicitly supports the very goal of rape and forced impregnation for the sake of genocide. Not only does this violation destroy the women physically, psychologically, and emotionally, but because of the masculine images that prevail in a patriarchal society, it destroys the very fabric of that

---

120. Vera Folnegovic-Smalc, "Psychiatric Aspects of the Rapes in the War against the Republics of Croatia and Bosnia Herzegovina" in *Mass Rape*, ed. A. Stiglmayer, 175.

121. See ibid., 179 n. 2; Laurel Fletcher et al., *No Justice, No Peace: Accountability for Rape and Gender-Based Violence in the Former Yugoslavia* (Washington, D.C.: International Human Rights Law Group, 1993), 27; Stiglmayer, "Rapes," 137; Ruth Seifert, "War and Rape: A Preliminary Analysis," in *Mass Rape: The War against Women in Bosnia-Herzegovina*, ed. Alexandra Stiglmayer, trans. Marion Faber (Lincoln: University of Nebraska Press, 1994), 59; and Lance Morrow, "Unspeakable," *Time*, 22 February 1993, 28.

society. Although patriarchal attitudes typify the Muslim culture, frequently singling out its inability to accept raped women back into its familial and social structure, Catholic Croats and Orthodox Serbs are no less plagued by this phenomenon.[122]

Media, Propaganda, and Exploitation

The media has played a significant role in the Bosnian war. Milosevic used the media for a blatant propaganda campaign to instill fear and hatred and to incite Serbian nationalism, manifested as genocide toward non-Serbs. Not so blatant is the sometimes harmful effect of the media, even by the most well-intentioned humanitarian groups, on the very people whom they hope to help.[123] The WCC report on raped women in Bosnia, for example, contained as an appendix a letter issued by the Zagreb Women's Lobby entitled "Letter of Intentions to Women's and Peace Organizations All Over the World."[124] While praising the support of international women's groups and peace organizations, the Zagreb Women's Lobby voiced concern regarding the involvement of some of these groups with the actual victims. First, concern exists that the process of helping raped women is being taken over by governmental institutions, and that the occurrence of rape thus will be used in political propaganda to spread hatred and call for revenge against the enemy, thereby encouraging further violence against women.[125] The second concern addresses those groups who have encouraged women to share their experiences publicly with promises of help and support yet who do not provide that support to the victims in the long term. The letter criticizes "sensationalistic journalist" approach, which has frightened and upset raped women, prolonging their recuperation.[126] The letter continued, "The development of serious women's support projects needs understanding of the problem, patience and time. Otherwise, the good intentions could turn out to be useless or even harmful, bringing some relief only to the conscience of the support-givers."[127] Tadeusz Mazowiecki of the United Nations and his team of investigators also voiced such concern, reporting that some of the women "felt exploited by the media and the many missions 'studying' rape in the former Yugoslavia.... There have been reports of women attempting suicide after being interviewed by the media and well-meaning delegations."[128]

---

122. Fletcher et al., *No Justice, No Peace*, 23 n. 8; and Allen, *Rape Warfare*, 92.
123. See Stiglmayer, "Rapes," 162–63.
124. World Council of Churches, "Rape of Women in War," app. VI.
125. See ibid.
126. Ibid.
127. Ibid.
128. UN General Assembly, *Rape and Abuse*, 5, § 13.

An employee of the UN high commissioner for refugees (UNHCR) reported that when news of widespread, systematic rape of Muslim and Croat women and children by Serbs reached the world, women's groups flocked to Zagreb to obtain information and interviews from women who had suffered these atrocities.[129] Often, the presence of these groups left the women feeling exploited and used, without providing extensive care to the victims themselves and without empowering them to regain a sense of human dignity. Physical rape is an atrocity in itself, but the psychological and emotional consequences can be prolonged and exacerbated through insensitivity toward the victims.[130] The point here is not to cast blame on the media and well intentioned humanitarian or women's groups. It is merely to sensitize them to the delicate nature of the situation and the need for prolonged support and care in the psychological and emotional recuperation of the traumatized women. This recuperation requires limiting the occurrences of secondary victimization.

While the media and propaganda have had a negative impact on women rape survivors in some respects, they also have had a positive impact by alerting the international community to the atrocities committed and, in effect, mobilizing aid efforts from the international community on behalf of the victims to try to stop the violence and bring the perpetrators to justice.[131]

No Justice?: International Humanitarian Law and the War Crimes Tribunal

Not only is rape one of the most underreported crimes worldwide, but it is also one of the least punished in the aftermath of a war. Occurrences of rape are frequently considered an inevitable by-product of war with the non sequitur "Boys will be boys." As a result, rape as a gender-specific war crime often has been ignored or considered under the auspices of human rights violations. In the former Yugoslavia, where the woman's body was not only targeted through rape but also through forced impregnation as a form of genocide, it is important to recognize this offense as a gender-specific crime directed against women for at least two reasons. First, this practice demonstrates a novel and demented form of warfare directly targeting noncombatants on the basis of their gender and reproductive capabilities. International legislation needs to recognize this as a unique and novel weapon of war and a distinct violation of human rights that incorporates rape and genocide into a single practice.

---

129. Unpublished interview at UNHCR headquarters, Geneva, Switzerland, 15 August 1996.
130. See Allen, *Rape Warfare*, 92–94.
131. See, e.g., Gutman, *A Witness to Genocide.*

Second, establishing laws that will specifically punish this crime may bring a sense of justice to those who have been violated. Part of the recuperation process of these women, especially to restore their faith in the moral and political order, is that the perpetrators be held accountable.[132] To send a clear message that the systematic usurpation of the female body to further one's military objective is morally reprehensible and will not be tolerated, the international community must recognize the unique nature and severity of this crime and prosecute the perpetrators accordingly. There has been an internationally supported move to indict, try, and punish those responsible for these atrocities. The UN Security Council's establishment of a research team in 1991 and an international war crimes tribunal in February 1993 to investigate these reports and bring the perpetrators to justice, respectively, are steps to correct this void in international law and justice.

Rape, Forced Impregnation, and International Humanitarian Law

Several international laws exist under which those responsible for rape in the Bosnian war can be held accountable. The Fourth Geneva Convention of 1949,[133] although it had an implicit precedent from previous codes and declarations, provided the first clearly articulated prohibition of rape as a crime against women in article 27. While calling for the humane treatment and protection of all people against any act of violence, it specifically states that "[w]omen shall be especially protected against any attack on their honour, in particular against rape, enforced prostitution, or any form of indecent assault."[134] In article 147, the convention refers to the violations described within article 27 as war crimes, though it does not specifically mention rape.[135] In addition, protocol II of the Geneva Convention contains specific legal sanctions protecting victims of internal armed conflicts while protocol I protects victims of international armed conflicts from rape.

Given the genocidal motivation of the rapes, the perpetrators are also subject to prosecution under the Genocide Convention of 1948, in particular, article II: "Killing members of a [national, ethnical, racial or religious] group; [c]ausing serious bodily or mental harm to members of the group; [d]eliberately inflicting on the group conditions of life calculated to bring about its physical destruction in whole or in part; [i]mposing measures intended to prevent births within the group; [and] [f]orcibly transferring

---

132. Fletcher et al., *No Justice, No Peace*, 14.

133. *Geneva Convention Relative to the Protection of Civilian Persons in Time of War*, art. 27, opened for signature 12 August 1949.

134. Niarchos, "Women, War, and Rape," 673.

135. *Geneva Convention*, arts. 147, 388. For a description and commentary on the historical development of international humanitarian law, see Niarchos, "Women, War, and Rape," 672–79; and Goldstein, *Forced Impregnation*.

children of the group to another group"[136] are all considered forms of genocide and are punishable under international law. Psychological trauma and physical torture of rape, which sometimes has included foreign objects such as gun barrels, constitute aspects of genocide as well.

Further, genocidal consequences of the rapes arise through the reduction of birth rates in non-Serbian societies. For example, the cultural response to women who have been raped could result in the prevention of births: unmarried women will not be married within the community, or those who are married may be rejected by their husbands. In either case, reproduction is impaired within a specific community. In cases where women have suffered physical damage and are thus incapable of reproducing, the genocidal objective is clearly accomplished. Where forced impregnation was the goal, children have been considered by both Serbs and non-Serbs to carry the father's genealogy, thus allowing the Serbs to transfer what they perceive as "their children" to the Muslim or Catholic group. Cultural genocide therefore results because the presence of these children and the knowledge of the circumstances under which they were conceived causes strife and resentment within the community and serves as a constant reminder of Serbian oppression and violence. Reports that pregnant Muslim and Catholic women were released from detention camps and sent to Serbia to give birth to "Serbian children" further helps to propagate the Serbian population, as the "Serbian child" is not considered tarnished by the mother's genes in Serbia as it is with the father's genes in Catholic or Muslim Croatia. Although international law has clear guidelines for prosecuting those guilty of rape, the intention to rape for the purpose of impregnation, though implicit under genocide, is not explicitly stated as a separate crime under international law. This is a gap that requires an amendment given the atrocities in Bosnia: rape, forced impregnation, and genocide.[137]

Finally, rape also constitutes a crime against humanity that entails the intention to systematically persecute a particular group. Even though there are numerous stipulations under international humanitarian law to prosecute those responsible for rape and even rape for the purpose of impregnation,[138] the question is whether or not such prosecutions will come to fruition.

---

136. UN General Assembly, *The 1948 Convention on the Prevention and Punishment of the Crime of Genocide* (12 January 1951), art. II.

137. Goldstein, *Forced Impregnation*, 13 n. 32, notes that a task force of the American Bar Association has recently recommended that article 5 (g) of the International Tribunal's statute on rape should read: "rape *including enforced prostitution and enforced pregnancy, and other forms of sexual assault*" (addition in italics). See "Report on the International Tribunal to Adjudicate War Crimes Committed in the Former Yugoslavia," *American Bar Association Special Task Force of the Section on International Law and Practice,* 15 (1993).

138. For an extensive discussion of categorizing forced impregnation under numerous violations of international law, see Goldstein, *Forced Impregnation*, 14–28.

Rape and the International Criminal Tribunal

To insure that perpetrators are brought to trial and prosecuted, the UN Security Council passed Resolution 808 in February 1993, establishing the International Criminal Tribunal for the former Yugoslavia. The tribunal's mandate is to prosecute those people responsible for serious humanitarian law violations committed in the former Yugoslavia since January 1991. Articles 2 through 5 stipulate prosecution for sexual assault, including rape.[139] However, the tribunal has no specific statute condemning forced impregnation despite the fact that the UN Commission of Experts documented five patterns of rape, one of which explicitly addresses this practice, and several of the women victims interviewed recounted the perpetrators' intent to impregnate them.[140] Notwithstanding any clear prohibition of forced impregnation in international law, the UN Commission of Experts responsible for analyzing the data and considering human rights violations of the Geneva Conventions and other humanitarian laws in the former Yugoslavia concluded that

> there is no doubt about the prohibition of rape and sexual assault in the Geneva Conventions and other applicable sources of the international humanitarian law. Furthermore, the commission finds that the relevant provisions of the statute of the International Tribunal adequately and correctly state the applicable law to this crime.[141]

Thus, the commission did not see a need to amend the law to include forced impregnation as a particular violation distinct from rape.

In an address to the New England School of Law on 14 January 1998, David Scheffer, ambassador at large for war crimes issues, gave an update on the proceedings of the War Crimes Tribunal. As of mid-January 1998, seventy-nine individuals had been publicly indicted by the tribunal: fifty-seven ethnic Serbs, nineteen ethnic Croats, and three ethnic Bosniaks. Three indictees had died, meaning that there are currently seventy-six known indictees now living. Fifty-four remain at large, and nineteen are in custody at The Hague. The indictments against three ethnic Croats were subsequently withdrawn, and they were released from custody. Of those indictees at large, fifty-two are ethnic Serbs, and two are ethnic Croats. Furthermore, only three ethnic Serbs, thirteen ethnic Croats, and three ethnic Bosniaks remain in custody.[142]

---

139. UN General Assembly, *Rape and Abuse*, 9, §26.

140. UN Security Council, *Final Report*, 59, §248.

141. Ibid., annex, sec. II J, § 109.

142. David J. Scheffer, "Challenges Confronting International Justice" (unpublished paper, 14 January 1998). From these numbers, it is clear that ethnic Serbs, while having the greatest number of indictments, have been the least cooperative with the International War Crimes

From the number of indictments, it is impossible to ascertain the indictees accused of rape for the purpose of forced impregnation, as this is not a specific violation under international humanitarian law. Consequently, the numbers of those who committed this crime will probably never be known. Nonetheless, given the prevalence of reported rapes and the United Nations' own task force that interviewed victims, collected data and testimonies from eyewitnesses and medical professionals, and identified nearly eight hundred victims and six hundred alleged perpetrators by name, one could question the seriousness of the international effort to bring the perpetrators to justice. No wonder many women have an attitude of "What's the use?" and refuse to come forward to testify. The fear of exposing themselves and reliving the nightmare as well as the risk of reprisals, given the slim possibility of an indictment, let alone the prosecution of the perpetrator, is cause for despair. Not only does this hinder the recuperation process of rape victims, but it also sends a message to the world that women are second-class citizens and sexual crimes against them are not taken seriously by the international justice system. Although the War Crimes Tribunal conducted in The Hague thus far has not given much cause for hope that justice will be served, it is certainly a step forward in recognizing the severity of the crime.[143]

Conclusion

The war in the former Yugoslavia has provided documented evidence of rape and forced impregnation used as a weapon of war for achieving ethnic cleansing and has raised international awareness concerning the usurpation of the female body and her reproductive capacities to fulfill political and military objectives. This evidence proves that not only were women caught up in a circle of violence waged and executed by men in power but also that they were specifically targeted as a means of attaining a military end. This frightening occurrence in war tactics and military strategy has caused the international community grave concern, but much remains to be accom-

---

Tribunal. Scheffer notes that what has bedeviled the tribunal from its creation is "state co-operation." "The worst offenders are Republika Srpska and Serbia-Montenegro. Neither has apprehended or orchestrated the voluntary surrender of a single indictee." Thus, while the International War Crimes Tribunal has improved on its number of indictments, as the number of known perpetrators of rape indicates, it still has a long way to go before there is any semblance of justice for the women who suffered atrocities during the conflict in the former Yugoslavia. This task is especially difficult given the lack of cooperation among the states harboring these suspected criminals. For information on those indicted and the specific indictments against them, visit the website www.un.org/icty/i-b-ens.htm#2.

143. In a landmark ruling on 10 December 1998, the War Crimes Tribunal found a Croatian commander, Anto Furundzia, guilty of standing by while a subordinate raped a female prisoner. This decision was the ultimate step in making rape a war crime and was upheld on appeal on 21 July 2000. See the *New York Times*, 21 July 2000.

plished to put an end to present violations, to punish the perpetrators, and to prevent these acts from occurring in future conflicts. Man's inhumanity to man and woman knows no bounds. To remain passive in light of such injustice is a moral abomination and betrays those who have suffered, and will suffer, from this treatment. Protection against rape and rape for the purpose of impregnation must be insured under international humanitarian law as well as guarantees providing for swift punishment of the perpetrators.

In addition, to reduce the disparity between religious ideology and cultural practice, communities should be sensitized to receive rape victims and their children in love, compassion, and empathy to foster healing not only among the women but within the community as a whole. The success of genocide in the form of rape and forced impregnation is dependent upon the patriarchal myth that supports its very practice. As is evident from the responses toward many of the women who have suffered this tragedy, this myth is still very much alive.[144]

---

144. I would like to thank my wife, Katy Salzman, for her friendship, support, and assistance in attaining invaluable documentation for this article from UNHCR (UN High Commissioner for Refugees). I also wish to thank Maarit Kohonen at the UN Center for Human Rights for her generous contribution of extensive resource materials.

6

Rwanda

Women Speak

HUMAN RIGHTS WATCH

JANE

Jane had witnessed the rape, mutilation, and killing of women who were speared through their vaginas:

I was at my house with my aunt and her five children when a group of Interahamwe came shouting and making noise. We tried to escape. Everywhere, people were being killed. I was caught by a group of Interahamwe on 1 April 1994, along with about twenty other women, and we were held by them in Gatare sector. Some of them decided to rape us before killing us. Others of them refused to rape us. The ones that wanted to rape us began to rape the women one by one. About ten of them would gang-rape a woman, and when they had finished, they would kill her by pushing a sharpened stick the size of a broomstick into her vagina until she was bleeding and almost dead. I saw them do this to several women. All the time, they were saying things like, "We want to have a taste of Tutsi women." One of them told us that they were going to chop the Tutsi women into pieces over days—one leg today, another arm tomorrow—until we died slowly. I managed to escape from them while they were raping and hid in the bushes until 2 May when the RPF [Rwanda Patriotic Front] saved us.

CLAUDINE

Claudine is another Hutu woman who was married to a Tutsi man. When the war began, she and her husband were living in Kanzenze commune,

These accounts are taken from Binaifer Nowrojee, *Shattered Lives: Sexual Violence during the Rwandan Genocide and Its Aftermath* (New York: Human Rights Watch, 1996), and are used with permission of the publisher.

Kigali prefecture, with their five children. At the time, she was thirty years old and seven months pregnant. She said:

My husband was in Kigali the day the war broke out and they started the killings. I stayed in my house because I was too pregnant to run. They came and killed my children. After they took my children, I went into labor and later my baby was born dead. The next day, I went out to find the bodies of my children. I saw an Interahamwe there taking the clothes of the dead people lying on the ground. He grabbed me and cut me with a knife on the arms and legs. I begged him to kill me. He raped me and then left me thinking I was dead. After a few days, I crawled to a sugarcane plantation and stayed there in hiding. One day, I saw a group of people. I went to them. I did not care who they were or if they killed me. They were the RPF. They took me to Gitarama. There were many others like me who were raped during the genocide.

ROSE

Other Hutu women were targeted because they tried to protect Tutsis. Rose, a twenty-eight-year-old woman, was raped after being accused of hiding Tutsis. Today, she has a child from the rape. She said:

I am a Hutu woman. During the genocide, three of my Tutsi friends came to hide in my house. I was living with my family because I was not married. In the middle of April, the Interahamwe came to our house and asked for all the Tutsis. We denied that there were any Tutsis. The first time they left without doing anything. They came back a second time and said that they knew that I was hiding Tutsis. They searched the house but could not find anyone, so they accused me of letting them get away. They threatened to kill me for hiding Tutsis. One of the Interahamwe, Nzabonimana David—about fifty years old; he was killed by the RPA later—asked me for money. I told him that I didn't have any. He told me that I was going to die because I had hidden people and now was not prepared to pay. He put a long knife at my throat and told me that he was going to kill me the way he wanted to. He took me out to the coffee bushes and pushed me on the ground and raped me. After he raped me, he told the other Interahamwe that I was useless and could not give them any money. He also told the others not to rape me because I might have AIDS and could contaminate them. I think he told them that to defend me from being raped by the others. After the Interahamwe left, I tried to go home. I was not badly wounded, but I was hurt and could not walk properly. I still wonder, even today, if I have been given AIDS. I have never seen a doctor because I have no money.

ALPHONSINE

Alphonsine was nineteen years old and living with her grandparents in Taba commune when the Interahamwe attacked them on 12 April 1994. She escaped through a window at the back but was caught by one Interahamwe. She said:

He told me that he knew that even though I was Hutu that my grandparents were Tutsi (my mother is Tutsi) and that he would kill them if I did not submit to him. He took me to the sorghum field and raped me on the ground there. Before he left, he asked me to tell him where we kept all our money. After they left, I escaped to my parents' house. I never saw a doctor after the rape, but a few months later, I realized I was pregnant. I was angry about the pregnancy and even thought about getting an abortion, but I had no money and no way to do it. I gave birth to twins in January 1995. At the time, I accepted them. I could not think about killing them. They survived for eleven months, but died. When I took them to the hospital, they couldn't find anything wrong. . . . My family knew that I had children of an Interahamwe. They all accepted it, but sometimes my mother would complain about the children and say that they were not children of this family. Sometimes when they cried, my mother would tell me to stop the noise or to give these children back to their father. I still think a lot about the rape. I wonder if I have AIDS.

Rwanda's Living Casualties

LAURA FLANDERS

For fifty-two years, the term "crimes against humanity" has applied to wartime offenses so heinous and so widespread that they threaten humanity itself. The International Military Tribunal came up with the definition at Nuremberg in the 1940s. That doesn't mean that anyone has managed to

---

"Rwanda's Living Casualties" was first published in *Ms.* (March/April 1998) and is reprinted with permission of the publisher.

make such crimes stop. In this decade alone, crimes against humanity have happened at least twice: in the former Yugoslavia beginning in 1991 and again in Rwanda in 1994.

Between April and July of 1994, Rwandan murderers killed between 500,000 and 1 million men, women, and children in the culmination of an all-out war that followed years of pogroms, expulsions, casualties, and flight. Allies and members of the ruling Hutu government targeted members of the Tutsi minority for genocide, and they massacred moderate Hutus for loving, hiding, living with, or working with Tutsis—or for no reason at all. According to human rights observers and Rwandan medical workers, rape was the rule, not the exception: an integral part of the genocide. The number of pregnancies said to be caused by force suggest that so-called genocidaires raped 250,000 to 500,000 women and girls in less than one hundred days. Up to the present, in Rwanda as in the former Yugoslavia, most of those genocidaires stand a pretty good change of getting away with murder. As for getting away with mass rape—their chances are better still.

When I visited Rwanda in May 1997 with Vivian Stromberg, the executive director of MADRE, a U.S.-based international women's human rights organization, we sat in the homes of Rwandan women and heard their stories. The reality could not have been clearer: "crimes against humanity" don't begin and end tidily, as the TV news stories do. The roots of the Rwandan genocide—and the rape—lie deep in Rwanda's history. The effects will be felt forever.

The Banyarwandans, as they were known before colonialism, ran a relatively successful state. "Hutu" and "Tutsi" were not so much ethnic groups as social strata—defined by their relation to property and power—and the lines between the groups could and did get crossed. When Belgian colonialists found a productive state with a single language in the middle of Africa, they explained the state's (to them) surprising success by applying prevailing nineteenth-century race theory. They classified the groups as racially distinct and attributed Tutsi "superiority" to mythical European roots. Colonists backed the Tutsi aristocracy's often brutal suppression of the Hutu. Then in the 1930s, the Belgians issued ID cards and registered every Rwandan according to her or his group. Researchers Alex de Waal and Rakiva Omaar report that "people with ten or more cows were Tutsi (in perpetuity); those with fewer were Hutu." Slender or not, the distinction was deadly. With independence came pogroms against the ruling Tutsi minority (who'd been abandoned by then by their colonial patrons), and from 1959, when revolt against colonial rule began, to the present, through many waves of violence, those cow-counting ID cards carried sentences of death.

And rape. According to European racialized mythology, Rwandan Tutsi women were said to be more beautiful ("European-looking") than their

Hutu counterparts. Rising against the Tutsi, Hutus repeatedly warned their men to beware of Tutsi seductress spies, and in the lead-up to the 1994 genocide, Hutu propaganda stoked Hutu men to take revenge. Proslaughter propagandists dubbed Tutsis "cockroaches," and the women "serpents" and worse. Stereotypes portrayed Tutsi women as arrogant and deceptive—and sexually special. Fetishized parts of the Tutsis' supposedly "European" physiology were singled out for mutilation: noses, necks, fingers—as well as genitals. Survivors murmur that their rapists wanted to "see what Tutsis look like inside."

The genocide of 1994 began for a number of reasons. For one, Tutsi exiles (the Rwandan Patriotic Front, or RPF) had been waging a civil war since 1990. During exactly the same period, the International Monetary Fund's relentless Western donors demanded austere economic "adjustments" in exchange for foreign loans. This led to a currency devaluation that hobbled the economy. In the government, enemies of democracy were fighting with both Hutu and Tutsi advocates of reform, and on 6 April 1994, the president's plane was shot down, leaving the country without a leader. The scene for the slaughter was set, and it began.

Hutu extremists blamed President Juvenil Habyarimana's death on the RPF and broadcast their claims on the radio. In fact, propagandists blamed the rebels and all Tutsis for everything: the war, the financial collapse, the fear. And the so-called international community, as Madeleine Albright, then U.S. ambassador to the UN, admits now, looked on and did nothing. "The international community should have identified the atrocities in 1994 sooner for what they were: genocide," acknowledged Albright in December 1997. But the time for action in Rwanda is far from over. "Rape and genocide both are crimes in perpetuity," says Vivian Stromberg, "against survivors, their families, and the communities who endure the repercussions indefinitely."

Today, 70 percent of Rwanda's population is female, and of the adults and adolescents, observers agree that the vast majority have lived through rape. Common among women anywhere who have been raped is the feeling of being dehumanized. In Rwanda, dehumanization was a goal of the genocide, committed against a group whom society had already eschewed. Rwanda's traditional law forbids women from inheriting property or engaging in business without their husbands' consent. Women are barely educated and mostly illiterate. Their worth has been weighed in children: pregenocide, the average woman had 6.2—one of the highest averages in the world. Now, as before the war, Rwandan women have next to no power, poor health, poor education, and little in the way of realizable human rights. "We are not protected against anything. . . . We are the living dead," one widow told a member of Human Rights Watch.

For the genocide to be defeated, Rwandan women must be brought back to life. That's what women's organizations across Rwanda are trying to do and what MADRE is trying to help make happen. Building on its experience in Central America, Haiti, and the former Yugoslavia, MADRE is now working in Rwanda with local organizations to provide for women's immediate needs—like health care and employment—and to support their longer-term efforts to get justice and economic development for themselves and the communities they support.

The Clinic of Hope in Kigali is one such organization. Cofounded by Peace Bikunda, a nurse, it offers medical treatment and counseling to women who survived 1994. Some of the hundreds of women Bikunda counsels were gang-raped next to their dead husbands. She herself "lost" her husband and two of her four children. What she gained were two scars above her sternum where a spear entered and left her chest. On this day, eighty-four rape survivors meet in the Clinic of Hope. Their physical wounds are formidable. Some you can see: in a neck, where a machete tried to separate a woman's spinal cord from her skull; on an ankle, where kidnappers tried to hobble their captive for good. Others you have to imagine: ripped-out uteri, perforated placentas, dislodged intestines, savaged labia, and bleeding that will not stop. "When they were raping these women," says Bikunda, "what drove it was deep hate."

It's possible to heal some of the effects of hate with law: by finding the perpetrators, acknowledging the crimes, exacting punishment. In Rwanda, there are two legal machines in motion: a domestic process and an international criminal tribunal for Rwanda that has the ability to apprehend criminals who fled abroad. On the domestic front, Gerald Gahima, deputy minister in Rwanda's Justice Department, says that about 100,000 men and women are currently imprisoned. Most are not charged, not fully investigated, but accused predominately of mass murder. And resources are impossibly short. Judges are poorly housed, investigators have inadequate protection, and witnesses are in danger. The UN Human Rights Field Office in Kigali reports that at least two hundred survivors of the genocide were assassinated in the first four months of 1997 in attacks that many Rwandans characterize as attempts to prevent them from testifying in any court of law.

But trials and prosecutions only go so far. The genocidaires destroyed not only lives, but also livelihoods. Survivors had their houses, as well as their households, demolished in the effort to eradicate them from the land.

Organizations have been mobilized to help. An example is Pro-Femmes, an umbrella organization of thirty-five women's groups that supports development projects serving Rwandan women and works to transform traditional patriarchal law. Executive Secretary Immaculée Habiyambere says that the women she works with are traumatized by poverty, as well as by bloodshed. Women are the sole heads of 50 percent of all households postgenocide. Rwandan women face harsh legal discrimination when it comes to succession rights, which often prevents them from inheriting their husbands' property. Now widowed in massive numbers, many women are opting for abusive forced marriages, simply to avoid being alone and vulnerable and in the streets.

As for health, AIDS was rampant before the war, and an AIDS awareness center in Kigali claims that the percentage of HIV-positive Rwandans remains at around 25 percent. Women working with rape survivors say that many avoid getting medical treatment for fear they'll be diagnosed with AIDS. (There is no treatment for HIV in Rwanda except for aspirin and, occasionally, useless antibiotics.) Women bleeding from illegal, botched abortions piled into hospitals after the war, but the new government has still refused to legalize the procedure.

The next generation also bears scars. Observers estimate that almost every child over four has witnessed killings. Even children as young as seven years old have been named by investigators who believe they played a role in genocide. Children conceived in the midst of the chaos face agonizing questions about their parentage. Their mothers are ambivalent. In the space of an hour's interview, the same woman who told me that Rwandans cherished every life after the genocide, admitted she'd required months of help before she could introduce anyone to the child she'd borne after being raped during the war. No one knows how many children labeled *enfants de mauvais souvenir*—refugees of their mothers' "bad memories"—have been abandoned.

"If we don't take care of the vulnerable, can we call that peace?" Habiyambere asks. "Girls and boys left alone in the streets will become either victims or dangerous; whores or bandits. Is that peace?"

As this is written, the forces of evil that spurred the 1994 genocide are still at work. In December, Hutu guerrillas attacked a Tutsi refugee camp in northwestern Rwanda, killing at least 272 people. The *New York Times* reported that the killers left "nothing but burning tents and leaflets preaching genocide." Achieving national reconciliation in the wake of genocide is a historic challenge facing Rwanda. Women need to be empowered to meet that challenge if the society is to survive.

Note: Rwanda Tribunal

The International Criminal Tribunal for Rwanda, located in Arusha, Tanzania, was established in 1994, following the massacre of more than 500,000 Tutsis by allies and members of the then Hutu government. So far, three defendants have been brought before the tribunal—and those only in early 1997—although tens of thousands of suspects have been in custody.

Prosecutors consistently failed to specifically pursue crimes of sexual violence against women until last June, when Chief Prosecutor Louise Arbour revised an indictment against Jean-Paul Akayesu, the court's first defendant, to include charges of sexual violence. Her action was prompted by the submission of an amicus brief coordinated by the Montreal-based International Centre for Human Rights and Democratic Development, which urged that all indictments include rape and other sexual abuses. The court has also had its funding increased and new staff—including a new deputy prosecutor—appointed. But with more women likely to be coming forward to testify, some activists are worried about witness protection. "The safe houses for the prosecution witnesses and safe houses for the defense witnesses are across the street from each other. That's not safety," says Rhonda Copelon of the New York City-based International Women's Human Rights Law Clinic.

7

What Are You Doing to Stop Violence against Women and Girls in Africa?

PAULINE MUCHINA

Introduction

To understand violence against women in Kenya, one needs to imagine the worldview in which they live. I begin this article with a picture of the world-view of an African woman, followed by an analysis of the forms of violence she endures, focusing on domestic and political violence against Kenyan women. I shall also examine the role of the state, the church, local and international organizations, and the society as a whole and explore how African women are responding to the crisis. Eighty percent of the Kenyan population claims to be Christian, therefore making it necessary for us to analyze the role of the church on the issue of violence against women in Kenya. To defend the human rights of African women—the right to a safe environment—one must dig into the fabric of the African societies, social, religious, cultural, and political ideologies that govern these communities.[1] With Africa being a diverse continent, an attempt to address the issue in the whole continent proves futile. On the basis of this reality, this article will focus on Kenya, my home country.

The Worldview of an African Woman

The African woman lives in a complex world filled with the joys and pains of life. The contradictions that exist in an African woman's world provide both the power to survive and the challenges by which she is confronted. Having entered this world as a free spirit, the contradictions between life and death; joy and sadness; love and hatred; freedom and oppression; poverty and richness; Christianity, Islam, and African religion; and beings or nonbeings become the ragged path in which she must walk. Patriarchy and

1. Mercy Amba Oduyoye, *Daughters of Anowa: African Women and Patriarchy* (New York: Maryknoll, 1995), 79–131.

poverty are not her only cross to carry. An African woman lives in a world of violence: colonialism, imperialism, conflict and war, domestic violence, globalization, and HIV/AIDS pandemic.[2]

The African woman exists in community. The concept of community presents itself as a harbinger, even amidst the current trend to urbanization. As the African woman struggles to survive, her livelihood is intimately tied to her community. The survival of her community is contingent upon her providing shelter, food, care for the children and the elderly, and spiritual guidance. Today, however, the community may depend on her for its survival, but she has little hope in the new patriarchal structures established to keep her in "her place." Faced with the many challenges rampant in Africa, the African woman is forced to give everything she has, her strength, her spirit, her wisdom (though not often sought), her body and mind, often at her own expense, making great sacrifices in her life.[3]

Many of us are inspired and challenged by the African woman's ability to find means of survival in situations that seem impossible. The African woman is always creating, making life possible for her community. Her creativity and resilience are portrayed in different expressions: music, dance, and folklore, as exhibited by the humming of a song or saying as she moves her hands, feet, and whole body; food preparation; farming; and sawing.[4] The joy that permeates the surroundings of the African woman as she works is a source of unending strength, empowering her to face every challenge with full determination and courage. Her faith in God and the spirits of the ancestors also empower her and her community to fight for life and hope for a better tomorrow. Needless to say, however, the African woman is not a superwoman. The constant bombardment from all directions finally does take a toll. Some African women die very young due to hard work and improper medical care. Many African women live subject to domestic violence, suffering all the physical and psychological pain involved. Others venture into prostitution in order to sustain themselves and their families financially, while many African women lose their sense of self-worth. Currently, thousands of African women are roaming the continent as displaced persons, others are refugees in their neighboring countries, and still others

---

2. For more information, see Aguibou Y. Yansane, ed., *Decolonization and Dependency* (Westport, Conn.: Greenwood Press, 1980), 13f.

3. See Linda Gordon, *Heroes of Their Own Lives: The Politics and History of Family Violence* (New York: Viking, 1988); and Mechthild Reh and Gudren Ludwar-Ene, eds., *Gender and Identity in Africa* (Münster: Lit, 1995), 50. See also Gwendolyn Mikell, ed., *African Feminism: The Politics of Survival in Sub-Saharan Africa* (Philadelphia: University of Pennsylvania Press, 1997), 2–3; and Bella S. Abzug, et al., *Women: Looking beyond 2000* (New York: United Nations, 1995), 87–92.

4. See Oduyoye, *Daughters of Anowa*, 99–101.

are at the receiving end of the blatant military atrocities under civil wars and dictatorship.[5]

The political and economic structures in Africa seem to kill rather than give life. Internal and external forces turn the African woman into a refugee in her own land. The global economic structures tie her down in debt, crippled with draconian economic policies that make life impossible for her and her community.[6] Although her country gained independence from the Western colonial masters in the late fifties or early sixties, corruption, imperialism, and neocolonialism govern her world.[7] The environmental degradation takes a toll on her. The rains do not come, and when they do, the floods kill her children and sweep away her home, animals, and crops.[8] The toxic waste imported from rich Western countries make her sick and her children disfigured. HIV/AIDS threatens every section of her community. She continues to bury her young ones and to care for the sick, while her community remains in denial.[9] In addition, she is a woman and therefore....

> She awakes one day only to realize that her biological and physical features, with which God has so beautifully accorded her, automatically make her less human in the eyes of many men. Although she exists, her existence is at the mercy of the society. She knows that she is a full human being, yet her identity is only acknowledged through the men she relates to (father, husband, or sons). She tries to find out who she is; she is struggling, for she is confused and cannot see clearly. All that the society tells her about herself is contrary to her inner being. Deep inside her, she knows that her freedom, identity, and humanity are God-given. She knows that she has the right to exist and exercise freedom of choice like other human beings. Oh yes, she knows she is created by God in God's image. She knows in her heart that she deserves respect and justice like anyone else. She very well knows that she

---

5. See Elizabeth G. Ferris, *Uprooted! Refugees and Forced Migrants* (New York: Friendship Press, 1998), 19–33.

6. See Karuti Kanyinga and Susie Ibutu, *Report of the Proceeding of the Workshop on Structural Adjustment Programmes (SAPS) in Kenya, Implications on the Lives of Women* (Nairobi, Kenya: NCCK, 1994). See also Mary Getui and Grace Wamue, eds., *Violence against Women* (Nairobi, Kenya: Acton Publishers, 1996), 3; Elizabeth Amoah, ed., *Where God Reigns* (Accra, Ghana: Sam-Woode Ltd., 1997), 177; and Gordon, *Heroes of Their Own Lives*, 251.

7. Kenya achieved its independence in 1963.

8. The El Niño rains have caused devastating problems in Africa. In Kenya, the rains completely destroyed the roads. Other parts of Africa, including northern Kenya, have been experiencing drought and famine in the last two decades. See the *Nairobi Daily Nation*, 25 February 1999.

9. Out of the 23 million people in the world who are infected with HIV/AIDS, 14 million reside in Africa. For more information, see UNDP, *UN Development Programme 1997 Report* (Geneva: United Nations, 1997), 9–12.

did not bring a curse to the world, and neither is she cursed because of her womanhood. She knows that her sexuality is good and has no inherent evil in it. She is meant to enjoy it without anyone curtailing it. She knows that she was not created to be a scapegoat for the evils in the society, and neither was she born to be enslaved, ridiculed, abused, and insulted from one generation to the other. As she trods the beaten path, she is fully aware that her pain was not meant to be. She asserts that she was not born stupid, weak, and evil; she has strengths and abilities, both God-given and learned. Oh yes, she understands that she and God are working toward the salvation of the world, herself included. She knows that she deserves love, justice, and peace; she is meant to have life and have it more abundantly.[10]

Violence against African Women

Violence against women in Africa takes various shapes. It ranges from unpaid hard labor and exploitation, battering, sexual abuse and harassment, sexist humor and sarcasm, to being treated as second-class citizens or nonhuman.[11] Violence against women is a silent war that spreads to the whole society. The campaign to combat violence against African women is ultimately a struggle for the human rights of African women.[12] Each day, the human rights of African women are violated. They continue to lose their right to a violence-free environment, the right to emotional and psychological well-being, the right to economic development, to education and health services, and the right to be recognized as full human beings with full citizenship in their respective countries.[13]

Thousands of African women are languishing in domestic violence—psychological, emotional, physical abuse—and under abject poverty. In civil wars, thousands of African women have been killed, maimed, or crippled. Others have become refugees, subjected to the violence and dehumanization prevalent in refugee camps.[14] The suffering is exacerbated by the fact that

---

10. This is my own reflection based on personal experiences and other African women's experiences.

11. See United Nations, *Women: Looking beyond 2000*, 24.

12. See Micheline Beaudry, *Battered Women* (Montreal, Que., and Buffalo, N.Y.: Black Rose Books, 1985), 72; and Reh and Ludwar-Ene, *Gender and Identity in Africa*, 183. See also Aruna Gnanadason, *No Longer a Secret: The Church and Violence against Women* (Geneva: WCC, 1993), 37–39.

13. For a better understanding of what it means for African women to be second-class citizens, see Buchi Emecheta, *Second Class Citizen* (New York: George Braziller, 1975).

14. Refugee Somali women were raped by Kenyan soldiers in a refugee camp in 1995. For more information on the plight of Somali refugees, see Gina Baijs, *Women: Crossing Boundaries and Changing Identities* (Oxford and Providence: Berg, 1993); and Codak Ka Yimi Soomaaliya, *Voices from Somalia* (London: London Minority Rights Group, 1991).

African women continue to be excluded from decision-making processes. They have been denied the right to determine the political and economic systems in which they operate. Left to them are the consequences of decisions and plans made and carried out mainly by men.[15] Observing this reality Maria Nzomo, a Kenyan woman political scientist, notes

> Like women in many other parts of the world, Kenyan women have had difficulty penetrating the patriarchal decision-making structures and processes of the state and party.... Although post-1963 independent government brought new possibilities for political involvement, Kenyan women were not granted the same political access as men were. Democratic participation at the level of gender and class has yet to be attained.[16]

Violence against Women in Politically Instigated Ethnic Clashes in Kenya / Armed Conflict in Africa

The politically instigated ethnic clashes are another form of insidious violence against Kenya women. Kenyan women caught in this male showdown (those with political hegemony subjugating their opposition) have suffered unprecedented violence—physical, economic, and psychological. Thousands of people in Kenya have been killed, are disabled, or have been displaced in Kenya following the politically instigated clashes. Kenyan Kikuyu women have taken the full brunt of these clashes.[17] Their husbands and sons have been killed, they have been raped, and many are homeless today, struggling to survive with their children. Since Kenya is not officially in a civil war, violence against these people may never come to the International Criminal Court or the International War Tribunal. Their offenders walk free, just as the domestic-violence offenders in Kenya do. The Beijing Platform for Action shows that women throughout the world are exposed to violence in times of conflict:

> While the entire communities suffer the consequences of armed conflict and terrorism, women and girls are particularly affected because of their status in society and their sex. Parties to conflict often rape women with impunity, sometimes using systematic rape as a tactic of war and terrorism. The impact of violence against women and violation of the human rights of women in such situations is experienced by

---

15. See Mikell, *African Feminism*, 232–57.
16. Ibid., 232–33. See also Getui and Wamue, *Violence against Women*, 78.
17. Women from other ethnic groups have suffered under the political ethnic clashes.

women of all ages, who suffer displacement, loss of home and property, loss or involuntary disappearance of close relatives, poverty and family separation and disintegration, and who are victims of acts of murder, terrorism, torture, involuntary disappearance, sexual slavery, rape, sexual abuse and forced pregnancy in situations of armed conflict, especially as a result of policies of ethnic cleansing and other new emerging forms of violence. This is compounded by the life-long social, economic and psychological traumatic consequences of armed conflict and foreign occupation and alien domination.[18]

In January 1998, while visiting my sister in Nakuru area, in the Rift Valley Province of Kenya, I heard people screaming followed by loud gunshots. I left the telephone booth where I was making a phone call and ran toward my sister's house. People were running from all directions. In the confusion, I took a wrong turn. Then I heard my brother-in-law, who was with me at the time, calling, "Duck down and run this way." I followed until we reached a friend's house. When we got back to my sister's house, my cousin from the outskirts of the city had arrived with her children. She told us that they tried to take refuge in the nearby church, but it was too crowded and there were fears that the "warriors" might break into the church.[19] My cousin was heavily pregnant. That night, she went into labor, after running the whole day trying to save her children. The next day, the Langalanga road in Nakuru was filled with women and children and their belongings, going toward the city. Some were in tears as they narrated their experiences of terror, how their loved ones were murdered in cold blood, how some had been raped, and how their houses burned, destroying all their belongings. As I watched these women walk down the road, stand to converse with bystanders, and urge their children to quicken their steps, I remembered my aunt who lost her husband in Burnt Forest in 1992. Their house in Burnt Forest was burnt down, and my uncle and five of their neighbors were slashed into pieces by the so-called Kalenjin warriors. I stood in silence and realized that I was shaking. I searched for somewhere to sit down and wondered what had become of my country.[20] There in front of me were women casualties of a political war that they had nothing to do with. And in my memory were

---

18. See United Nations, *Platform for Action and the Beijing Declaration: Fourth World Conference on Women* (New York: United Nations, 1996), 84.

19. The observation among the victims of the violence is that the attackers are well-trained people. Many people fear that they might be trained by the Kenyan government. The association with the government comes as a result of the government's reluctance to deal with these warriors effectively and the fact that senior politicians in the country are known to incite people in their constituencies to attack people of other ethnic groups. See also the *Nairobi Daily Nation*, 26 January 1998.

20. The Burnt Forest violence killed hundreds of Kikuyus who had settled in this area and left many homeless.

two women in my family, one whose husband was prematurely snatched from her by violence and the other fighting for her life and that of her premature baby, praying that her husband escaped unharmed. An Amnesty International report on Kenya indicates that

> Scores of people were killed by government groups during 1993, particularly in areas near Burnt Forest, Molo and Nakuru towns in Rift Valley Province and near Mount Elgon in Western Province, many of them apparently victims of extrajudicial executions. In particular cases as in Londiani in June and Molo in July, the violence was carried out by organized groups known as "Kalenjin warriors" armed with bows and arrows and composed of as many as 300 members of the Kalenjin ethnic group to which President Moi belongs. Police failed to protect the victims, who were perceived as supporting opposition parties, or belonged to other ethnic groups, particularly the Kikuyu, although Kalenjins also suffered violent reprisals in some areas.[21]

The economic violence meted against these women is unprecedented. Most of the Kikuyu women earn their living through farming and small businesses. Since the beginning of the clashes, they have nowhere to farm, and they have no source of income. After taking temporary shelter from relatives and good Samaritans, these women turn to the street markets in big cities. They buy agricultural produce and sell them in the streets. They can no longer afford to send their children to school or clothe them. As they mingle with city women, it becomes difficult to tell who they are. The darkness of the experiences they left behind clouds their conversations as they reminisce about the old good days. These women will tell you that their Kalenjin neighbors did not chase them out of their land; unknown "warriors" are responsible for the atrocities. The emotional and psychological impact on these women cannot be measured. Some swear never to go back to the place where they witnessed the murders of their loved ones. Others wait for peace to return so that they can return to their homes. Their once peaceful homes, and a source of their livelihood, will never be the same again. As political tensions intensify in Kenya, and the economic conditions continue to deteriorate, many Kenyans wonder whether they will ever live in peace again and whether they will ever overcome poverty.[22]

Meanwhile, the Kenyan government continues to fortify its military power. Even though Kenya is not at war with any of its neighboring coun-

---

21. See Amnesty International, *Amnesty International Report 1994* (New York: Amnesty International USA, 1994), 183. Political tensions, fear, and suspicion remain in the Rift Valley Province.

22. The coastal area and the Rift Valley Province are the two areas that have been severely affected by the violence.

tries, the Kenyan government in 1998 spent a fortune to buy antiriot vehicles used by the antiriot police in the apartheid regime in South Africa. These antiriot vehicles are the remains of the apartheid regime's tools of war. Why would the Kenyan government invest in them? This question is even more pertinent when asked in light of the economic crisis and food shortages in Kenya and the deteriorating infrastructure in the country—lack of sufficient health services, the collapse of the transportation system, a high unemployment rate, and insufficient education facilities. In this light, the Kenyan government sets itself as a perpetrator of violence against women in Kenya. The government's violence against women falls in different categories—the possible use of the antiriot gear to suppress Kenyans fighting for their political freedom, the taking of money from starving children to buy military equipment, the investment in military and political fortification at the expense of thousands of Kenyan children with no access to education, and direct violence against women during economic and political instability in the country.[23]

Like that of their male counterparts, African women's participation in democracy and protection of their human rights are threatened by politically instigated ethnic armed conflict. As some scholars rightly articulate, not all forms of ethnic rivalry in Africa are primordial. They have emerged from political and economic groupings resulting from colonialism or postcolonialism.[24] Ethnic conflicts in Africa arise from the struggle to have access to the resources and power of the state, which are concentrated often in one particular area or among a group of people.[25]

It has been argued that decentralizing power and resources and distributing the same throughout the state may help end ethnic tensions that exist in most parts of Africa. However, the danger still lies in how this redistribution is carried out. Take, for example, Kenya—the Kenyan African National Union (KANU) government proposed "Majimboism" to curtail multipartyism, but the process resulted in efforts to remove all other ethnic groups from the Rift Valley, leaving only those groups deemed "native" before colonialism. This led to the politically instigated so-called ethnic clashes that left thousands of people dead and thousands more landless and homeless. Under Majimboism, people from other ethnic groups in Kenya who

23. The Kenyan government spends 60 percent of its GNP on military and 2 percent on women-related social issues. See also the "Women of the World's Peace Petition to the Governments of the World" (New York: WCC Office at the United Nations, 1997).

24. Harvey Glickmann, ed., *Ethnic Conflict and Democratization in Africa* (Atlanta: African Studies Association Press, 1995), 10. See also Christopher Lee, *Land and Class in Kenya* (Toronto, Ont., and Buffalo, N.Y.: University of Toronto Press, 1984), 27–34; and H. J. Nyamu, *Aspects of Kenya's Development: A Participant's View* (Nairobi, Kenya: East Africa Publishing House, 1980), 2–10.

25. Glickmann, *Ethnic Conflict*, 161.

reside in the Rift Valley would be discriminated against in education, the licensing of businesses, voting rights, issuance of new national identification cards, employment opportunities, and land distribution.[26]

Given the present ethnic integration in Kenya, organizing along ethnic lines politically or economically is unrealistic. Different ethnic groups coexist in the Rift Valley and most of the cities and towns throughout Kenya. In addition, current political ethnic organizations would encourage the marginalization of groups of people who are the minority in particular places of Kenya.[27] In the pursuit for democracy, Kenyan women must aim at transcending ethnicity. This does not mean ignoring people's cultural differences or ethnic origins but instead working together for beneficial change.

Realizing that ethnic organization is not to their advantage, African women at the Fourth World Conference on Women in Beijing in 1995 called for solidarity across ethnic boundaries.[28] The need for solidarity across ethnic boundaries was also reiterated at the Pan-African Circle of Concerned Women Theologians' Conference in Nairobi in August of 1996. At this conference, it was emphasized that democracy and peace in Africa can only be achieved through building communities based on love and justice. These African women pointed out that it is the African men who start the wars, but it is the women and children who become the victims of these wars.[29] African women are aware that poverty in Africa does not discriminate along ethnic lines. The elite and political leaders can well afford to fight over who is superior to whom, but the African women's concerns are over peace, food, shelter, and health facilities. Indeed, it is worth noting that the leaders of ethnic political organizations live in the suburbs of the cities. These are places where ethnic boundaries have no meaning. Wealth and political involvement are the determinants. The same applies to the poor living in

---

26. See Human Rights Watch/Africa Watch, *Divide and Rule: State Sponsored Ethnic Violence in Kenya* (New York and London: Human Rights Watch, 1993), 12; and *Human Rights Watch World Report 1997* (New York: Human Rights Watch, 1997) 31. In the summer of 1996, I went home and tried to get a new national ID. Although my parents migrated from central Kenya to the Rift Valley in the 1940s and I was born and raised in the Rift Valley, I was told to go back to central Kenya for the new ID.

27. Such as the Luos and Kikuyus in the Rift Valley or the Kalenjins in Nairobi and central Kenya.

28. I participated in this dialogue in Beijing. The dialogue was between African women politicians and women representing NGOs from Africa.

29. An official report of this conference is in the process of preparation and will be published in *Amka*, the official journal of the organization. Most of the papers presented at the conference are being edited and will be published in two books, scheduled to be released next year by Acton Publishers, Nairobi, Kenya. The information here is based on personal notes from the speeches, discussion groups, and individual conversations with women at the conference. See also Mercy Amba Oduyoye, ed., *Transforming Power: Women in the Household of God—Proceedings of the Pan-African Conference of the Circle of Concerned African Women Theologians* (Accra, Ghana: Sam-Woode Ltd., 1997).

slums, where people of all ethnic groups live in abject poverty. It is also important to bear in mind that during the 1992 politically instigated "ethnic clashes," neighbors of different ethnic groups tried to help each other. The question, then, arises—who was doing the killing and the burning and destroying of people's property during the clashes? Various organizations such as the Human Rights Watch, Amnesty International, and the National Council of Churches of Kenya claim that the Kenyan government was behind this violence.[30]

The ongoing Akiwumi Commission on this ethnic violence has revealed that not only were government officials reluctant to protect the victims but that in some cases they were actually present when victims were attacked.[31] The commission has also heard that some prominent KANU leaders made inciting remarks that provoked violence against the Kikuyus. Speaking to this reality, Githu Muigai of Nairobi University observes that "authoritative observation of the ethnic clashes laid the blame squarely at the door of the government. All the objective reports implicated senior party and government officials. . . . The government's response was lukewarm, giving credence to allegations of state complicity in the clashes."[32]

In these circumstances, one has to wonder what kind of democracy operates in Kenya. Kenyan women's understanding of democracy, like that of other African women, is not limited to elections or political rhetoric. They perceive democracy as a vehicle of liberation from violence, conditions of poverty, violation of human rights, and male domination. The exercise of democracy in Kenya, therefore, cannot exclude the human rights of women.[33] However, democracy will not effect change and reform if Kenyan women are excluded from direct participation in reformulating this possibility. They are in the best position from experience and knowledge to create a thriving country. Kenyan women's participation in the current reconstruction of the Kenyan Constitution is crucial to ensure that violence against women is eliminated and perpetrators of it brought to justice. The constitution should ensure the protection of all Kenyan citizens against all forms of violence, including the domestic violence that plagues Kenyan society.

---

30. See Human Rights Watch/Africa Watch, *Divide and Rule*, 40–44; Amnesty International, *Amnesty International Report 1994*, 182–84; and National Council of Churches of Kenya, *Deception, Dispersal, and Abandonment* (Nairobi, Kenya: NCCK, 1993); and *The Cursed Arrow: Contemporary Report on the Politicized Land Clashes in Rift Valley, Nyanza, and Western Province* (Nairobi, Kenya: NCCK, 1992).

31. The Akiwumi Commission was set by the Kenyan government to investigate the violence. Most Kenyans think this is just a hoax, and they are waiting to see what the commission will do to the guilty parties.

32. Glickmann, *Ethnic Conflict*, 178–79.

33. Stephen P. Riley, *Democratic Transition in Africa: An End to One Party State?* (London: Research Institute for the Study of Conflict and Terrorism, 1991), 5.

Domestic Violence against Women in Kenya

In most traditional African communities, physical violence against women was regarded as taboo. A man who abused a woman was condemned by the whole community. Depending on the kind of abuse, the community's elders prescribed the punishment. In some African communities, rape, especially of young girls, was punishable by excommunication from the community, condemnation never to marry, or curse never to have children of one's own. Wife battering was also addressed by the whole community. Women shamed the wife batterer in public, and the community warned and fined the offender. Failure to cease the abuse resulted in the perpetrator's being chastised by the whole community. Even his fellow men would not keep company, go hunting, or farm with him.[34]

Today, however, the situation is different. Most African women, including Kenyan women, are left to fight against violence on their own. The structures in place within communities to deal with this issue have broken down. Communal condemnation of violence against women has been replaced with a deadly silence. The community does not talk about it. The churches do not talk about it, and the law does not seem to protect women. The law enforcement officers (policemen) have no consciousness about violence against women.[35] Many of them have been known to rape women who go to them for help. If a woman chooses to make public any form of violence against her, she, the victim, is regarded as the troublemaker. In case of rape, she might be blamed for tempting the rapist. If the charge is wife battering, the woman is said to have a big mouth, which is why her husband had to discipline her. Domestic violence has become prevalent in Africa. Eight out of ten women will have suffered some form of violence from their spouses.[36] As the economic conditions in Africa continue to deteriorate, violence against women drastically rises. Women in Africa, therefore, have to bear not only the full brunt of economic violence, but they also suffer the anger of frustrated and depressed men. As most men turn to drugs and alcohol to ease their economic despair, women are suffering from unprecedented violence from men.[37] This kind of violence is experienced by other women in other parts of the world. As the World Council of Churches' *Report of the Consultation on the Programme to Overcome Violence* states:

---

34. This information is derived primarily from oral tradition. Among the Kikuyus of Kenya, rape was considered a heinous crime punishable by castration or animal sacrifice. Oral tradition also tells of how women were protected from male violence by the community.

35. Police in Kenya do not respond immediately to calls concerning domestic violence. If they do respond, they are most likely to side with the man, dismissing wife battering as a family feud to be settled within the family.

36. See United Nations, *Platform for Action.*

37. See the *Nairobi Daily Nation*, 26 January 1999, front page.

Violence originates in part from systems and structures that rob people of the opportunity for humane living conditions which help sustain their lives. One such system is globalization, the transnationalization of capital and production based on a single, world-wide logic of exchange. Globalization increasingly centralizes control and power, removing decisions about fundamental matters of economic, social and political life from the local and national level to the global level. This system also imposes on individuals and societies world-wide norms of economic growth, consumerism, privatization, individualism, and the presumption of winners and losers. These norms, accompanied by such remote control, accentuate and accelerate human fragmentation, isolation, and exclusion for the profit of the few, contributing significantly to violence among individuals, groups, and nations.[38]

Growing up in a little town (Tambach) in Kenya, I witnessed or heard about wife battering almost every week. Sometimes our dinner or sleep was interrupted by shrieking sounds of a woman or her children calling for help. I remember my parents running to their aid, trying to talk to the male offender. Sometimes, the beating would break up only to resume in the middle of the night, after the man returned from his drinking break. The images of scared, cold, and crying children, huddled in a corner or running toward the rescuers, flood my mind. My mother would pick up the children and bring them back to our house, while my father and other neighbors would break up the fight or take the battered woman to our local health center. In most cases, the children would be hungry and frightened. Some would talk about their father's threats to kill their mother, saying, "I thought he was going to kill her." Other children would just be too scared to utter a word. The next day, early in the morning, the battered woman would come looking for her children. The bandage on her face or other parts of her body was the physical manifestation of the violation of her body by someone who claims to love her. In the absence of a bandage, the shadow on the woman's face told the story of her deep-seated agony. In the meantime, she would try so hard to forget yesterday by talking about other things or events.

The police in our little town did nothing to help these women. Sometimes they would respond to the screams, and other times they did not respond. When they did, they would always tell the woman to take refuge with her neighbors for the night. They never arrested the offender or advised the women to file charges against their abusers. Among the many ethnic groups in this town, wife battering had become an accepted phenomenon, usually

---

38. See World Council of Churches, *Report of the Consultation on the Programme to Overcome Violence: Rio de Janeiro, 13–18 April 1996* (Geneva: World Council of Churches, 1996), 9.

used to discipline women.[39] The state did nothing to stop it, the society condoned it, and the church enhanced it by teaching women to be submissive to their husbands.[40]

In recent years, domestic violence against women has been brought close to home through the experiences of two of my sisters. One of my older sisters lived in an abusive marriage for twenty-nine years. The marriage began with little incidence of verbal abuse, but it intensified as the years went by. At the time of her divorce three years ago, my sister had suffered a broken leg and emotional depression and had lost everything she had worked for all her life. She also lost housing and moved in with my parents for a couple of months. Of her six children, two of her youngest sons, who are now twenty-one and nineteen years old, were the most affected. In addition to dropping out of school, as soon as my sister left, my nephews have gone through depression and imprisonment and cannot find any kind of employment.[41] This is the story of many Kenyan women and children running away from abusive men.

In 1996, one of my younger sisters left her husband of eight years after he abused her. Fortunately, my sister escaped without contracting HIV/AIDS, a constant threat to their marriage, given his lifestyle. However, the psychological and emotional damage done to her and her children will take years to heal. She left with her two sons, seven and eight years old. My eight-year-old nephew, in narrating to us how his father would sleep with a knife under his pillow after he attacked my sister, said,"Baba alisema ataua mama na kisu kama yule mtu wa gaseti" [My dad said that he will kill my mother with a knife like the man in the newspapers did last week]. My sister reported this incident to the police, but they took no action. My whole family supported my sister to leave him immediately. Efforts to secure child support through the Federation of International Women Lawyers (FIDA) have failed.

I share these experiences to show how widespread domestic violence is in Kenya. My sisters were married in two different parts of Kenya, and I grew up in the Rift Valley Province. Also working in the diocese of Eldoret, I witnessed and ministered to women and girls who had suffered domestic violence in six districts in the Rift Valley Province (Elgeyo Markwet, Nandi, Turkana, Transzoia, Uasingishu, and West Pokot). The Kenyan newspapers have countless reports on women, battered, killed, disabled, or raped by known and unknown men. Indeed, the news in Kenya has become a litany of violence against women (rape, female genital mutilation, battering, and

---

39. Even though Tambach is a small town, people from different ethnic groups, such as Kalenjin, Turkana, Luo, Luhya, Taita, Kikuyu, Kisii, and Masaai, reside there.

40. Katarina Tomaserki, *Women and Human Rights* (London and Atlantic Highlands, N.J.: Zed Books, 1993), 84–90; and Amoah, *Where God Reigns*, 135–92.

41. See Getui and Wamue, *Violence against Women*, 13.

other offenses).[42] Many Kenyan women also suffer tremendous psychological violence from their spouses or men in the society who use derogatory
language toward women.

Domestic violence against women in Kenya has escalated in the last three
decades. Some analysts ascribe the increase to the economic deterioration
and political instability in the country. This is the same in other parts of
Africa.[43] As more and more men become unemployed, lose their ability to
control their families through economic means, and are confronted with political insecurity and uncertainty, they turn to alcohol and drugs. Some of
these men air their frustrations through abusing their wives and women in
their community. Although women in Kenya can now file charges against
abusive husbands or male offenders, the local police are not trained to deal
with these issues. The rampant corruption in Kenya also makes it possible
for the offenders to buy their freedom from the police. Sometimes, the policeman responding to the call may himself be a wife batterer and may
easily dismiss the incident as a domestic feud.[44] This leaves many Kenyan
women with hardly any legal recourse when they are subjected to violence.
Furthermore, the local and international efforts to combat this evil have
been minimal, and the need for concerted efforts to end violence against
women persists.

Local and International Response to Violence against Women— the Church, Kenyan Women, the Kenyan Government, and the International Community

Response to Domestic Violence

To end violence against women in Kenya will require a combined effort
from all groups that recognize violence against women as a violation of
their human rights. This involves the society at large that stands at a loss if
over half of its population lives under fear and at risk of physical and psychological attacks every minute. The government has a great role to play in
the protection of its citizens through the law and in creating a safe environment both in the urban areas and in the country.[45] The Kenyan government

---

42. Getui and Wamue, *Violence against Women*, 78. See also the *Nairobi Daily Nation*,
25 December 1998.

43. See Getui and Wamue, *Violence against Women*, 13. This is also happening in other
parts of Africa; see Ciru Gatecha and Jesimen Chipika, eds., *Zimbabwe Women's Voices*
(Harare: Zimbabwe Women's Resource Center and Network, 1995), 129–35.

44. See United Nations, *Platform for Action*, 72, Rubric 121; and Jalma Hanmer, *Women,
Policing, and Male Violence: International Perspectives* (London and New York: Routledge,
1989), 200–207. In January 1999, Kenyan women were in an uproar calling the police to arrest
a policeman who had killed his wife. The police did not arrest him for two weeks.

45. See United Nations, *Platform for Action*, 76–93.

needs to educate its law enforcement officers, public administrators, and politicians on violence against women. As it is now in Kenya, many Kenyan women are violated with the knowledge of government officials who choose to do nothing about it either out of misogyny or ignorance. Given the fact that all forms of violence against women are related, the Kenyan government also has the responsibility to end the politically instigated ethnic violence, curtail the use of drugs and excessive alcohol, cut its military spending, and solve the economic crisis that has become the breeding station of violence against women in Kenya.

Since the Kenyan government was one of the first countries to ratify the Convention on the Declaration on the Elimination of Violence against Women (CEDAW), it would only be just if they were to implement the demands of this convention and the Beijing Declaration. For example, the convention calls governments to condemn violence against women without hiding behind any customs, tradition, or religious norms; facilitate the achievement of justice for victims through the law and the bringing of perpetrators to justice; deal with problems of gender in their public policies; ensure that the education system does not sanction violence against women; and provide counseling for the victims. Kenyan women must hold the Kenyan government accountable for the implementation of CEDAW. Talk is cheap; actions speak louder than words.

Religious institutions in Kenya also have a crucial role in stopping violence against women. It has been documented that most men who feel they are superior to women base their argument on some form of religious teachings. Some of the religious scriptures contain myths about creation, gender difference, and the role of women and men that seem to sanction or perpetuate violence against women. Take, for example, Christianity, the dominant religion in Kenya. The prevalent Christian teaching in Kenya is that man was created first and the woman was created out of the man's rib. Therefore, the man is the head of the house, and the woman is supposed to be submissive to her husband. These elements give many Kenyan Christian men the attitude that they are to be in control and women are to submit to them at all costs. When these men meet resistance to their dominance, the results are always violent—physical or psychological. They use scripture to justify themselves. Kenyan Christian women who refuse this male hegemony are regarded as non-Christians.

In addition, for the most part, the churches in Kenya have remained silent about violence against women. Many churches continue to preach to and to teach Kenyan women to be submissive to men.[46] Through the exclu-

---

46. Oduyoye, *Daughters of Anowa*, 172–88; Musimbi R. A. Kanyoro and Nyambura J. Njoroge, *Groaning in Faith: Women in the Household of God* (Nairobi, Kenya: Acton Publishers, 1996), 16–23; and Getui and Wamue, *Violence against Women*, 68–78.

sion of Kenyan women from the ministry and positions of leadership in the churches, the Kenyan churches condone and perpetuate violence against women. Many pastors/ministers are known to advise women to stay in abusive marriages: "Dada, vumilia na Yesu" [Sister, patience with Jesus] or "Dada mulete kwa Yesu" [Sister, bring him to Jesus]. The churches in Kenya must preach and teach that violence against women is a sin. They must set an example by changing their teachings and traditions that discriminate against women and make them susceptible to violence. Eighty percent of the Kenyan population claims to be Christian.[47] The majority of Kenyans are churchgoers. In what more perfect place can consciousness-raising take place? The churches can have women's programs in their dioceses, parishes, and local churches. However, they cannot fight against domestic violence if they do not start preaching about the equality of men and women, against the sin of discrimination against women on the basis of their gender, and the dignity and full humanity of women who are created in the image of God. A Christian husband who thinks that his wife should be submissive to him should not be backed by the church. A woman who chooses to divorce an abusive husband should be supported by the church, and if possible, the church should provide her with legal representation.

The churches in Kenya need to revisit the teachings of Jesus, relearn how Jesus related to women, and see who are the care holders of the gospel. The injustice meted out against women in the Kenyan society should not be duplicated in the churches. This is a cry for justice and for a violence-free environment. Will the Kenyan churches respond to this cry?[48] (The same question applies to other religions present in Kenya.) As Kenyan women continue to receive misguided information from the churches, they need to consider suing the churches for wrongful advise. If a woman is hurt by her spouse and the church advises her to stay in that abusive marriage, the pastor or the church should be held accountable. In time, women will be able to sue the churches for perpetuating violence against them through their teachings.

Silence on violence has been broken. Kenyan women refuse to hide any form of violence.[49] They are shouting at the top of their voices, bringing all forms of violence to the attention of the whole society. Like their sisters in other parts of the world, Kenyan women assert that violence threatens not only the lives of women but that of the whole society. They are also making linkages between all forms of violence. They are educating the communities to know that the private violence is also public. Acts of violence done in the

---

47. Elizabeth Isechei, *A History of Christianity in Africa* (Grand Rapids: Eerdmans, 1995), 1–11.

48. See Getui and Wamue, *Violence against Women*, 68–78. This a cry for women all over the world. See also Gnanadason, *No Longer a Secret*.

49. See Getui and Wamue, *Violence against Women*, 5–12.

privacy of the home or in the dark corners of the cities are crimes against the individual and the whole society as well. Claiming our vanishing heritage, African women call for the whole community to be involved in the issues of violence against women.

In December 1998, while attending the World Council of Churches' Conference in Harare, I bought several T-shirts with the words "What are you doing to stop violence against women and girls?" "Violence against women is everybody's responsibility," and "No means no." I brought the T-shirts back to Kenya for my sisters and myself. I also brought back large posters on violence against women produced for the week on the global campaign on violence against women. I wore the T-shirt in the city (Nairobi) several times and put the posters at my sister's clinic in the outskirts of Nairobi. The reactions we got from many people were very telling. One man told me that even though he believes that violence against women is wrong, he did not think we should put the posters in a public place. He said, "This is private. You do not need to advertise it." Another man asked me what he should do to stop violence if he is not the one committing the crime.

The insensitivity on issues of violence against women confronts the Kenyan society from all directions. Consider the following incident. In January 1998 while riding in the *matatu* (public transportation), I saw a picture of a woman on the front mirror of the minibus with the words "A woman is like a matatu, you ride her today and tomorrow she is gone and you take another one." When I alighted from the *matatu*, I asked the conductor why he had such derogatory words on his vehicle. At first he was surprised, and he started laughing. But I insisted, "Seriously, why do you have those words on your car? Are your mother and sister and wife, if you have one, like *matatus*?" After a moment of deep thought he answered, "No, I love them. I promise to remove that picture today." These incidents indicate how far behind we are in educating one another about violence against women. I believe that it is everyone's responsibility to stop violence against women and girls. The Kenyan society needs to focus more on raising people's consciousness about violence against women so that if a woman is beaten by her husband and the people around her do not respond to her cries, they are as guilty as the abusive husband. If the government does not crack down on obscene messages about women in *matatus* and other places, they are failing in their responsibility to protect the women of Kenya.

As women's organizations such as FIDA provide the legal means by which African women demand justice, the churches should be at the forefront teaching against violence of all forms against women.[50] African women are also finding ways to end violence and to care for women who are recovering

---

50. See D. B. Abbey-Mensah, in *Where God Reigns*, ed. E. Amoah, 180–81.

from various forms of violence. Mothers in Action is a women's organization in Kenya that formed in 1994 after nineteen girls were killed, seventy-seven raped, and hundreds traumatized by their schoolmates at St. Kizito boarding high school. Women in Kenya were horrified by the way the legal processes in Kenya failed to deal with these boys who committed the murders and injured other girls for the rest of their lives. Most of them got away with a slap on the hand: some were expelled from school, while others stayed on. The girls however were so traumatized that they are undergoing long-term therapy. Their lives were shattered, and their dreams for a better life threatened in a manner from which some may never recover.[51]

More and more women's organizations and individuals in Kenya are raising their voices, condemning any form of violence against women. Some organizations focus on educating women on their human rights, discussing what strategies are available to them in case of abuse. Some of these organizations are providing legal representation and are calling for tighter laws and legal procedures to protect the human rights of women.[52] The Kenyan Constitution states that all people in Kenya are equal and are to be treated justly, regardless of their race or ethnic background. While the Kenyan Constitution condemns discrimination of persons based on race, tribe, residence, place of origin, political opinion, or religious affiliation, it categorically states that "any law that discriminates against any person is permitted with respect to issues of personal law such as adoption, marriage, divorce, burial, and succession or the application of customary laws."[53] Under this provision, discrimination in marriage is not against the law, and all kinds of physical and psychological abuses present within the family go unchallenged.[54]

In the case of divorce, Kenyan women stand the risk of losing not only everything they have worked for and have registered in the man's name but child support too.[55] Kenyan women are also exposed to discriminatory laws when it comes to issues of rape within marriage, polygamy, adultery,

---

51. See Joyce K. Umbima, "Kenya: Mothers in Action," in *Women, Violence, and Non-Violent Change* (Geneva: WCC), 96–102. See also Margot Kasemann, *Overcoming Violence: The Challenge for the Churches in All Places* (Geneva: WCC, 1998), 46; and Mikell, *African Feminism*, 243.

52. Organizations such as the Women's Political Caucus, the Coalition on Violence against Women, and the National Council of Churches of Kenya Gender Desk.

53. See Maria Nzomo, ed., *Empowering Kenya Women* (Nairobi, Kenya: National Committee on the Status of Women, 1993), 15–18; *The Pocket Constitution of Kenya* (Nairobi, Kenya: A Public Law Institute Publication, 1988), 27; and Getui and Wamue, *Violence against Women*, 51–53.

54. See Mikell, *African Feminism*, 241–42; and Getui and Wamue, *Violence against Women*, 51.

55. Margaret Snyder and Mary Tadesse, *African Women and Development: A History* (Johannesburg: Witwatersrand University Press, 1995), 22–23.

inheritance, and widowhood. Wamboi Otieno's case is a classic example of gender discrimination based on customary law. Wamboi lost the right to bury her husband on their farm, which they bought together, to Mr. Otieno's kinsmen (brothers), who had had little to do with him when he was alive. The Luo custom requires that a widow be married by the deceased husband's brother or next of kin, giving him the right to inherit everything, including children.[56] Fortunately, Wamboi lost only her husband's body. She managed to keep her children and some property, except the property that contains her husband's place of burial.[57] Writing about the human rights of women in Kenya, Maria Nzomo challenges Kenyan women saying, "Women must, for example, demand that the government repeal or amend certain laws that discriminate against them, and they must communicate the political, social, and economic costs that it will incur if such demands are not met."[58]

Kenyan women have joined the Kenyan masses to call for constitutional reforms. To ensure that women's human rights are protected in the Kenyan Constitution, women must demand full participation in reformulating it. The public, and especially women, need to be educated on all that is at stake so that they have the ability to protest any omissions or inclusions that do not consider their well-being.[59] Some efforts are already in place. In the 1992 elections, Kenyan women advocated for democracy. They realized that unless they have proper representation in Parliament and decision-making bodies throughout the country, women's rights and those of children will always be violated.[60] Beside putting forth women candidates for parliamentary and local government positions, the League of Kenyan Women Voters passed a resolution to educate women on their rights and the role of the civil government. So far, women's organizations such as the Center for Democracy, women's church groups, and other NGOs have organized seminars, workshops, and conferences to educate women. One of these organizations, FIDA, provides women with legal education pertaining to their rights and legal intervention and representation in courts for women who are abused by their husbands or other men.[61]

This is the beginning of what a democratic Kenya will be like in the eyes of women—the welfare of women and children will be safeguarded by the constitution, and those who violate these rights will be brought to justice.

---

56. Reh and Ludwar-Ene, *Gender and Identity in Africa*, 173–74. See also Mikell, *African Feminism*, 245.

57. See Reh and Ludwar-Ene, *Gender and Identity in Africa*, 173–74; and Getui and Wamue, *Violence against Women*, 51.

58. See Mikell, *African Feminism*, 246.

59. See United Nations, *Platform for Action*, Rubric 173.

60. See Obioma Nnaemeka, ed., *Sisterhood, Feminisms, and Power: From Africa to the Diaspora* (Trenton, N.J.: Africa World Press, 1998), 84, 133, and 144.

61. Nzomo, *Empowering Kenya Women*, 11–12.

However, it is going to be a long journey. The present government has only reactionary solutions to the problems of women and children.[62]

Although the Kenyan government was one of the first governments to ratify the Commission on the Elimination of Discrimination against Women (CEDAW), it has a long way to go in implementing it. At the moment, the government is not involved in programs to educate the Kenyan society to change its harmful attitudes and practices toward women. Work of this nature is being undertaken by nongovernmental organizations and individuals. The school curricula remain hostile and discriminatory toward girls. Children are not learning anything in school that teaches them how to relate to one another. This has to change. Boys in school have to take the responsibility for their actions, and girls must learn to have zero tolerance toward violence. Only then shall we build a generation of people who treat each other justly and with respect. The Kiswahili saying is "Mtoto umuleyavyo ndivyo akuavyo" [Raise a child the way they grow].

Response to Violence against Women in Political/Armed Conflict

The Kenya churches have played a significant role in condemning politically instigated ethnic violence. The churches continue to preach peace and reconciliation. They have called upon the Kenyan government to end these clashes. Victims of the clashes have often found refuge in churches. Some churches have provided food and medical services to victims running away from the Rift Valley. And the churches have called for the ongoing inquiry on the killings of innocent people. Kenyans await to see whether anyone will be indicted. There is a strong feeling that the inquiry is a hoax since some of the prominent government leaders continue to incite their people to chase Kikuyus from their areas. Sadly, some clergypersons have been cited as inciters of the clashes. The National Council of Churches of Kenya has taken a strong stand calling the government to end this violence.[63]

During the UN Commission on the Status of Women's Conference in March 1998, African women issued a statement on violence against women in armed conflict. In their statement, African women stated that while the perpetuators of violence in Africa are fully responsible for the violence and murders of thousands of people in Africa, those who supply arms to them are equally responsible as enablers. The African women's statement went further saying that some nations, especially in the West, sell arms to poor African nations, who then use these weapons to subjugate their citizens. The ongoing campaign against land mines derives its force from women

---

62. Aruna Gnanadason et al., *Women, Violence, and Non-Violent Change* (Geneva: WCC, 1996), 96–103; and Getui and Wamue, *Violence against Women*, 68–78.

63. See National Council of Churches of Kenya, *Deception, Dispersal, and Abandonment*.

who are tired of seeing children in Africa and other parts of the world killed or maimed by land mines manufactured in the West.

Who benefits from armed conflict? Obviously the people who sell arms and keep their hands clean from the actual bloodshed are the benefactors. Their economy thrives at the expense of human life in other parts of the world. It is not surprising then that most of these countries resist any treaty or policy that would place any limits on the arms trade.[64] Reflecting on this issue, the World Council of Churches' *Report of the Consultation on the Programme to Overcome Violence* states

> Many of the old industrial economies in both the West and East harbor deeply entrenched weapons and war related production complexes, most of which are largely disconnected from widely-shared, realistic assessments about requirements for these nations' security. Many newly industrialized economies employ weapons production and arms trade primarily as a strategy for economic growth rather than meeting defense needs. Manufacturing and trade in armaments and weaponry for profit contributes to war within and between nations. Military stockpiles and arms races drain societies of resources necessary to meet human needs. Military research and development divert precious skills and technology from addressing pressing social problems. Militarism pervades many societies, resulting in human degradation, isolation and exclusion. Pervasive armaments, together with the concept that military might leads to national security, fosters violence within and between countries.[65]

There has been an outcry from women all over the world to end the age of militarism. As indicated previously, excessive military expenditure hinders governments from taking care of their citizens adequately and creates an environment in which the human rights of women are violated. Kenyan women must join the women of the world calling for their government and other governments of the world to invest in social services rather than in militarism. The "Women of the World's Peace Petition to the Governments of the World" must be echoed by all women and all peace-loving people in the world. The petition reads

> We are horrified at the level of violence witnessed during this century and that women and children are the primary victims of war and poverty. On behalf of society at large, we, the undersigned women of

---

64. See Meredeth Turshen and Clotilde Twagiramariya, eds., *What Women Do in Wartime: Gender and Conflict in Africa* (London and New York: Zed Books, 1998), 150–62.

65. World Council of Churches, *Report of the Consultation on the Programme to Overcome Violence*, 9–10.

the world, demand that annually, for the next five years, at least five percent of the national military expenditures be redirected to health, education and employment programmes. By doing so, one half billion dollars a day would be released world wide for programmes to improve living standards.

We also demand that war, like slavery, colonialism and apartheid, be delegitimized as an acceptable form of social behavior, and that governments and civil society together develop new institutions that do not resort to violence for the settlement of disputes.

Together we commit ourselves, as half of the world's population, to use our power to ensure that these demands, which will promote international peace and security, are met through legislation and action. We resolve that we will inaugurate a new century that rejects warfare and promotes well-being, justice and human rights.[66]

Recent events in conflict-torn places such as Africa's Great Lakes region, the Balkans, the Gulf region, and other parts of the world demonstrate that a military solution to any conflict is only temporary. The opponents withdraw only to regroup and strike again. It also does not seem to address the root causes of the conflict. As long as the source of conflict remains unresolved, any military solution is a Band-Aid, and conflict is bound to explode again soon or later. Therefore, the powers that be must listen to the women of the world's petition. They must find ways of resolving conflict without violence. Governments must cease to invest in militarism and begin to invest in the children of their countries—education, health care, and food. If they do not invest in them in healthy ways, or if they do so as others have done by turning them into soldiers before they even see their teenage years, the circle of violence will continue.

Conclusion

The campaign to end violence against women and girls is ultimately a struggle against all forms of violence.[67] All forms of violence are connected; therefore, our struggles need to be connected. Fundamentally, we must challenge the political and ideological structures that legalize any form of violence. The killing of women and children in Iraq through cruise missiles is as evil as the killing of women and children in Rwanda by machetes.

---

66. This peace petition was initiated by the World Council of Churches' liaison office at the United Nations in New York and was sponsored by dozens of women's organizations throughout the world in 1997.

67. See Pamela Cooper-White, *The Cry of Tamar: Violence against Women and the Churches' Response* (Minneapolis: Fortress Press, 1995), 20–44.

Equally evil is the daily murder of thousands of children living under abject poverty throughout the world.

We must join our collective power to struggle against these evils in our societies. Violence against women is not a natural phenomenon. It can be eradicated through combined efforts from all those who care about humanity. We can no longer remain silent because silence in the face of violence sanctions it or gives approval to the perpetrators. Any religious institution, government, and cultural tradition that teaches or emphasizes the subjugation of women is an accomplice to the murder and the physical and psychological violence of thousands of domestic-violence victims, who suffer in the hands of men who believe that they have a right to discipline their wives.

In Africa, women must find ways to stand together in their resistance to violence. For example, we must find ways to be in solidarity with our sisters in Southern Sudan who are languishing in a civil war and slavery, while the whole world is silent about it.[68] We must find ways in which to support those women living in refugee camps and displacement camps throughout the continent because their homes have become the battlefields of men. We must learn to reach out to those living in domestic violence throughout the continent, stand up against draconian local and international economic policies that subject our communities to a slow death, reject educational systems and religious and cultural traditions that perpetuate violence, and strive to eradicate violence against women and girls in the twenty-first century.

---

68. Human Rights Watch, *Civilian Devastation: Abuses by All Parties in the War in Southern Sudan* (New York: Human Rights Watch, 1994).

8

Guatemala

"We Thought It Was Only the Men They Would Kill"

MARION CIBORSKI

Paulina Iboy Osorio...Dominga Sanchez Chen...Dorotea Osorio Chen ...Marcela Iboy Osorio...Juliana Osorio Osorio...Juana Iboy Osorio...Guillerma Osorio Chen...Narsaria Tum Sanchez...Luisa Osorio Sanchez...Vicenta Iboy Chen...Narcisa Chen Chen...Francisca Sanchez Chen.... These are the names, 177 in all, inscribed on the face of a giant, concrete monument in the municipal cemetery outside the remote mountain town of Rabinal in central Guatemala. The monument honors the 70 women and 107 children from the Achí Maya village of Río Negro who were raped and brutally killed on 13 March 1982, in one of four massacres that virtually exterminated the village. The women and children named on the monument were murdered by a government-sponsored civil defense patrol and several officials from the Guatemalan army in one of most vicious atrocities of Guatemala's thirty-six-year-old civil war. That day, two adult women escaped, and eighteen children were taken to a neighboring town as slaves. By denouncing the massacre and building the monument eleven years later, surviving members of the community of Río Negro risked their lives in order to tell the world what happened.

In 1982, the village of Río Negro was home to five hundred Maya Achí people, whose homes dotted the winding river valley that creates the northern border of the department of Baja Verapaz. They were subsistence farmers, growing corn, beans, and some vegetables and fruit, which they sold in markets in nearby villages. At the time of the massacres, the community was resisting an eviction order issued by the state-owned electric company. Río Negro was one of five villages located in the flood path of a 100-meter hydroelectric dam to be built five miles downriver. The dam was part of the Chixoy Hydroelectric Project, which was designed to solve the extreme electricity shortage faced by Guatemala since the 1970s. The violent destruction of Río Negro occurred after the failure of several years of resettlement negotiations between the community and the electric company.

124

Between 1995 and 1997, I worked in Guatemala for Witness for Peace, documenting the suffering caused by U.S. policy.[1] During that time, I was privileged to meet the survivors of Río Negro, hear their testimony, and witness their courageous efforts to overcome the terror of the war and speak out about the crimes committed against them. I also watched firsthand as the women, children, and families tried to cope with this legacy of violence that almost exceeds comprehension. The long war destroyed the social framework of Guatemala, and its survivors continue to live with the trauma inflicted on them by the state-sponsored reign of terror. Women, children, and families throughout Guatemala today bear the scars of the war's violence and suffer social, psychological, and physical consequences. The case of Río Negro is one example of this legacy.

The War

The horrifying brutality committed against the women and children of Río Negro on 13 March 1982 was standard practice by the Guatemalan army throughout the counterinsurgency war against the rebel Guatemalan National Revolutionary Unity. The Guatemalan government's military campaign of the 1970s and early 1980s decimated the nation's primarily indigenous population. Although other factors affected the disastrous fate of Río Negro, including the construction of the Chixoy Hydroelectric Project, it is important to understand the massacre of the village in the context of the war.

Civil war in Guatemala broke out after the 1954 overthrow of President Jacobo Arbenz, who along with his predecessor Juan José Arévalo had initiated a program of democratic reforms, including an attempt to address the unequal distribution of land in the country. The 1954 coup against Arbenz, orchestrated by the Central Intelligence Agency of the United States, began thirty years of consecutive repressive military regimes that unleashed unremitting state-sponsored violence against the civilian population.

The first organized opposition guerrilla forces appeared in 1961, formed by disillusioned military officers who protested the tyranny of their government, calling it a puppet of American imperialism.[2] The guerrillas found support in the Guatemala countryside, where the Mayan peasant majority, disenfranchised by the elite landowning class, had lived in extreme poverty

---

1. Witness for Peace is a grassroots, faith-based, and politically independent organization that seeks to change U.S. economic and political policies that cause suffering and oppression in Latin America and the Caribbean and to promote just alternatives. To that end, Witness for Peace sponsors advocacy campaigns and nonviolent actions and leads delegations of U.S. citizens to witness and accompany people in seeking justice in Latin America and the Caribbean.

2. Stephen Schlesinger and Stephen Kinzer, *Bitter Fruit: The Untold Story of the American Coup in Guatemala* (Garden City, N.Y.: Anchor Press/Doubleday, 1983), 240.

for generations. In response, the government militarized the country, and for the next two decades, the Guatemalan armed forces systematically combed the countryside killing rebel forces and antigovernment activists.

By 1966, a full-blown counterinsurgency war was raging across Guatemala. Right-wing death squads had spread into all sectors of Guatemalan society. They terrorized civilians and carried out thousands of political assassinations, killing anyone who organized against political or economic injustice. According to Amnesty International, from the mid-1960s to the end of the 1970s, more than thirty thousand people were kidnapped, tortured, and killed by the Guatemalan armed forces.[3]

In 1978, wealthy landowner General Lucas Garcia became Guatemala's president through a fraudulent election, and the extent of the state-sponsored violence engulfing the Guatemalan countryside increased. In a largely successful attempt to suppress all opposition, the army killed anyone in a position to organize around a cause—including lawyers, teachers, labor and human rights activists, religious workers, students, and women leaders. Disappearances, torture, and murders were tactics used not only to eliminate the "enemies" of the Guatemalan state but also to terrorize the population, subduing and ensuring silence from the survivors.[4]

In 1981, Lucas Garcia's government organized men from rural villages across Guatemala into Civil Defense Patrols (PACs), which functioned as a network of community-based militias under the control of the army. Participation in one's local PAC was mandatory, and refusal often resulted in torture and death for both the patroller and his family. The PACs were forced to patrol their villages and the surrounding areas, searching for guerrillas or any suspicious activity. They were made to inform the army about goings-on in their villages, detain and interrogate strangers, and serve as cover for the army during skirmishes with the guerrillas.

At the height of the war there were an estimated 900,000 men in PACs. They have been accused of being responsible for many of the worst human rights abuses of the war. Indoctrinated with anticommunist zealotry, patrollers were persuaded by their military leaders that anyone who challenged the army in any manner was a subversive and must be denounced and eliminated. In this way, the PACs were an effective part of the counterinsurgency strategy. Their existence helped maintain the army's reign of terror over the population, increased suspicion between villages and among neighbors, and caused people to denounce others as guerrillas.[5]

---

3. Amnesty International, *Guatemala: A Government Program of Political Murder* (London: Amnesty International, 1981), 3, 5.

4. Schlesinger and Kinzer, *Bitter Fruit*, 251.

5. Gary MacEoin, "Guatemalan Villagers in Fight for Survival," *National Catholic Reporter*, 20 January 1995.

In 1982, the four principal guerrilla organizations opposing the Guatemalan government formed a joint command called the Guatemalan National Revolutionary Unity (URNG). That year, after an election marked by fraud and political confusion, General Efraín Ríos Montt took control of the presidency. The savage killing in the countryside intensified as the army continued the "scorched earth" campaign against the rural population begun under President Lucas Garcia. With the goal of depopulating the conflict zones, the army slaughtered inhabitants and burned their villages to the ground. By the time Guatemala made a transition to civilian rule in 1985, the counterinsurgency campaign had destroyed 440 entire villages, and more than 250,000 refugees had fled to Mexico. The war killed over 150,000 people, internally displaced more than 1 million, and left hundreds of thousands of widows and orphans.

The year of the Río Negro massacres was one of the bloodiest years of the war. The Guatemalan army committed several of the war's most notorious human rights atrocities in 1982. On 14 March, 324 men, women, and children were killed in Cuarto Pueblo, Ixcán, Quiché. On 16–18 July, 350 were killed in San Francisco, Nentón, Huehuetenango. On 18 July, 200 were killed in Plan de Sanchez, Rabinal, Baja Verapaz. On 4–6 December, more than 200 were killed in Dos Erres, La Libertad, el Petén. These mass killings completely devastated large areas of Mayan Guatemala.

The department of Baja Verapaz in central Guatemala, home to the Achí Mayas, was one of the regions of Guatemala most affected by the war. In the mid-1980s, it became what a local priest has called a giant clandestine cemetery, with more than five thousand people buried in twenty to twenty-five mass graves in the area.

The Massacre of Río Negro

The Maya Achí are one of twenty-one ethnic groups indigenous to Guatemala. Long before the Spanish conquest of Central America, the Achí people inhabited central Guatemala, in what is now the department of Baja Verapaz. Achí villages are scattered along an isolated valley surrounded by steep, rugged mountains, and most are only accessible on foot. Like most indigenous Guatemalans, the Maya Achí survive on subsistence farming, growing the traditional corn, beans, and some vegetables and occasionally raising livestock.

Unlike other Mayan villages that suffered the devastation of the war, the community of Río Negro was affected by the additional circumstance of the construction of the Chixoy Hydroelectric Project. In 1976, the National Institute of Electrification (INDE), Guatemala's state-owned electric company, had informed the people of Río Negro that the 100-meter Chixoy dam would be built downriver from their village and that the subsequent flood would submerge the entire valley, which had been their home for generations. Although reluctant to leave their ancestral lands, the villagers formed a committee to negotiate a resettlement package with the electric company. An initial agreement mandated a new village with cement-block houses, free water and electricity, five acres of land for each family, and cash compensation for crops and orchards that would be lost to the flooding.

However, in early 1980, the relationship between INDE and the villagers soured when the community rejected the cramped, urban setting of Pacux—their newly built resettlement village—located just outside the town of Rabinal, some eight hours south of Río Negro on foot. With resettlement negotiations completely stalled, INDE resorted to a series of deceitful and violent scare tactics to persuade the community to leave their lands. First, the electric company forced the community to surrender their land titles, later claiming to have never received them and leaving the people with no record of how much property they were losing to the flooding. Then in March 1980, some community members were accused of stealing food from the warehouse at the dam construction site. When the military police arrived in Río Negro to arrest the alleged thieves, there was a violent standoff that killed seven community members and one of the soldiers. INDE blamed the community for the incident, and according to one former resident of Río Negro, the electric company then began to denounce the villagers as guerrillas. Four months later, members of Río Negro's negotiating committee disappeared while en route to meet with the INDE officials. They were carrying the community's only written record of the resettlement agreement.[6]

The first of four massacres occurred on 13 February 1982 when seventy-three men and women from Río Negro were tortured and killed in the neighboring town of Xococ by the local civil patrol. One woman escaped while the patrollers were raping several adolescent girls, and she ran all night to Río Negro. Hearing what had happened, the men fled to the mountains to hide, never thinking that the PAC would kill women and children left behind.

One month later, on 13 March 1982, ten army soldiers and twenty-five civil patrollers from Xococ arrived in Río Negro at dawn. Angry that the men of the village were missing, they demanded that the women tell them where "the guerrillas" were hiding. They began to raid the houses, pulling the women and children out, eating their food, looting and breaking their possessions. The women protested that they did not know any guerrillas and that there were no guerrillas in Río Negro. The armed men then marched

---

6. Julie Stewart et al., *A People Dammed: The Impact of the World Bank Hydroelectric Project in Guatemala* (Washington, D.C.: Witness for Peace, 1996), 16.

the women up the mountainside, hitting them with sticks. Part way up the mountain, they stopped and forced the women to dance, insulting them and calling them guerrilla whores. One fourteen-year-old girl was dragged into the weeds and raped.

At the top of the mountain, in a rocky hollow full of dry grasses and scrubby trees, the women and children were divided into several groups. "Pablo,"[7] a ten-year-old boy in 1982, was one of the eighteen children who survived the massacre but were taken as slaves by members of the Xococ PAC. He recalled:

> *The patrollers began to cut sticks from branches. They had rope which they had taken from our houses in Río Negro. While they were doing this, the soldiers began to take the young girls off from the group and rape them in the bushes. Later the patrollers began to rape as well. . . . We saw the women and girls brought back one by one, beaten, crying and with their clothes torn. . . . the soldiers took the girls between the ages of fourteen and sixteen, and the patrollers took the rest of the women and girls.*[8]

The patrollers then brutally killed the women and children. Some were strangled with sticks and ropes, some beaten with clubs and guns, kicked and punched. Some children were killed as the soldiers and patrollers swung them by their ankles and smashed their heads and bodies against trees and rocks. Pablo remembered:

> *The patrollers would grab the women one by one and drag them to the edge of the ravine. There they would slaughter them and throw them over the edge. The sandals of the patrollers were covered and full of blood.*[9]

A few dozen residents of Río Negro, both men and women, survived the massacre because they were hiding or not home on 13 March. These people spent the next two years living and hiding in the mountains, without permanent shelter or food other than roots, seeds, and raw fish. They could not build fires for fear of revealing their hiding places to the army; helicopters often passed overhead bombing and shooting machine guns over the mountainside. During this exile, the weak, the sick, the elderly, and many children died due to these difficult living conditions. Others were killed in the two subsequent massacres. On 14 May 1982, eighty-four refugees from Río Negro were killed by the Xococ PAC in the village of Los Encuentros, located

---

7. The names of all individuals who gave testimony of the violence are pseudonyms.
8. Based on unpublished interviews of survivors by Grahame Russell, 1995.
9. Ibid.

five miles from Río Negro. And on 13 September 1982, thirty-five orphans from Río Negro were killed when the Xococ PAC massacred the population of nearby Agua Fria, machine-gunning and burning ninety-two people to death. In total, 369 residents of Río Negro were killed between March and September 1982.

With the completion of the dam at the end of 1982, the waters of the Chixoy reservoir gradually rose and flooded the Río Negro valley. Over the next few years, surviving residents regrouped in the resettlement village of Pacux.

The Survivors

For the survivors of Río Negro, the terror of the massacres and the anguish caused by the extended war have left deep emotional scars. A majority of the former members of the Xococ PAC have continued to live unpunished in Baja Verapaz since the killings. Many Río Negro survivors cross paths with their loved ones' killers on their way to the market or while working in the fields.[10] Over a decade of suppressing their pain, sorrow, and anger has made recovery from the trauma nearly impossible. Without punishment of those responsible and without some public acknowledgment of the carnage that robbed them of their families, it has been difficult for many survivors to make sense of the past and to build productive lives and functioning communities.

In 1994, ten Río Negro families left Pacux and returned to the banks of the Chixoy reservoir to live on the steep hillside above their former homes, now submerged. The reservoir winds between the brown, treeless hills that rise straight out of the water. It is a stark and desolate place, at once eerie, beautiful, and peaceful. The families of the "new" Río Negro live in primitive conditions and extreme poverty, in huts made of poles, without electricity or plumbing and with barely enough food. But each family has chosen to live there in order to be near their ancestral lands and the memory of those who died in 1982. On 20 February 1997, a Witness for Peace delegation of twenty-two U.S. citizens visited the "new" Río Negro. That day, sitting on the dusty ground in the shade of the wood-plank schoolhouse, the delegation listened as survivor after survivor spoke of their experience of the Río Negro massacres. For many of the women, this was the first time they had recounted their testimonies to outsiders.[11]

---

10. Grahame Russell, "Assassins Walk Free with Impunity," unpublished manuscript, December 1994.

11. Unless otherwise cited, all testimony in this section is taken from interviews by this author with survivors during January and February 1997.

"Maria" was sixteen in 1982. She lives in the new Río Negro with her husband and their five young children. Her husband's first wife and his children were killed in the 13 March massacre. That day, Maria and her mother had traveled before dawn to sell some vegetables and buy supplies at the weekly market in another town:

When we returned to Río Negro, there was no one there. Our house was empty, and everything inside was destroyed. We could not see anyone, not at my sister's house, nor my aunt's house. I remember that I began to cry, "Where is everyone? What happened to them?" We were very afraid. Later, after some of the men had found the bodies, we climbed up to see them. There was so much blood, blood everywhere. My two sisters, my aunt, and her children were all dead—you could not even recognize all the dead; their faces and bodies had been cut and smashed. We did not bury them; we were too afraid to stay there for very long. I live always with sadness in my heart and the memory of what happened to our people.

"Lilia" and her husband have six children now, the oldest born before the dam was built. She is normally a talkative, jolly woman, but the memories of the violence suffered by her village and of loved ones she lost in the massacre are still too painful for her to recount. She can only shake her head as the tears roll down her face, apologizing for her inability to speak.

Only two adults survived the massacre. One was "Aurelia," who was marched up the mountainside along with her mother, grandmother, aunt, and daughter. When the raping and killing began at the top, Aurelia told her mother that she would rather be shot than wait her turn to die beaten and strangled to death, and she dove down the steep side of the ravine next to the massacre site.[12] Although perhaps lucky that the soldiers' bullets missed her, more than a decade later she still lives with the pain and horror of witnessing the horrible deaths of her family and neighbors.

"Ana Maria" lives in the highest dwelling above the reservoir with her husband and two sons. One son was born before the massacres, but his father and siblings were killed in the violence. Her new husband lost seventeen relatives in the 13 March massacre, including his wife, several daughters, sisters, and daughters-in-law. Ana Maria lost her mother, sister, three nieces and nephews, and two small children. She herself escaped the death march halfway to the summit by hiding behind a boulder on the steep banks of the path:

The soldiers got to my house when I was making tortillas for my children's breakfast at 5 A.M. They came into my house and took the

---

12. Stewart et al., *A People Dammed.*

food I was cooking and smashed everything. They pulled us out of the house and made us walk up the mountain. No one could stop to rest; they hit us with sticks like we were cattle. My children and my mother were ahead of me, but I could not get to them. I knew we were all going to die. I prayed to God to spare my family and threw myself down the hill and hid behind a big rock. I did not move for a long time, I was so afraid. Sometimes it is hard to go on remembering how they all died; it's hard to remember all that we lost. There will always be a sadness here, like a shadow hanging over us.

The violence perpetrated against Río Negro had grave effects on the survivors beyond the sorrow of their still vivid memories. During the time I spent visiting the communities of Pacux and Río Negro in the mid-1990s, the women in particular often described suffering from physical and psychological ailments as a consequence of living through years of violence. In many of the women, the resulting emotional trauma has manifested itself as various illnesses—headaches, dizziness, ulcers, lack of energy, and, in particular, severe depression. These physical conditions are worsened by the unending hard work necessary to provide food for their families. These physical symptoms have been documented throughout Guatemala in the war's aftermath.

"Magdalena" is a widow who lives with her children, her sister, and her sister's husband in Pacux. Her large eyes always appear heavy with fatigue and melancholy. She speaks in a low voice, talking with the quiet desperation of a woman now resigned to what she sees as a joyless fate:

There is no other choice but to keep going somehow, waiting as my time for living passes.... Everything that we of Río Negro suffered brought us to this situation. Sometimes I feel as if there is no way out [of the poverty]. The struggle is very tiring.

"Carmen" is another widow who lives in Pacux. She lives in the standard issue two-room house with her four daughters, one grandchild, and a younger sister who is married and has a daughter. Carmen works all day in Rabinal washing clothes and cleaning for a middle-class family. She also cultivates a small plot of land to grow corn to supplement what she must buy in town in order to make enough tortillas to feed her large family. Exhaustion and undernourishment show in her thin face from this daily routine of hard work. She reports that she is often sick, suffering from frequent headaches and chest pain:

It's difficult to find enough money to buy food. Women like me, who have no husbands, we have to do the work of both the man and the woman to support our families. After a week of washing, working the land to plant and cultivate corn is too much—I am always tired. But buying corn in town is very expensive; the prices are always rising. So we all have to work hard to keep going forward.

The villages in the valley around Rabinal are full of women who watched as their husbands, children and other relatives died at the hands of the Guatemalan army and local civil defense patrols. "Sylvia" is a community activist from Nimacabaj, a small town near Rabinal. Like those living in Río Negro, the residents of Nimacabaj suffered terrible violence during the war. Now Sylvia heads a coalition of widows' groups in the region, helping women organize around human rights issues or small agricultural and livestock projects sponsored by national community development organizations. In addition to working long hours with little or no financial compensation, Sylvia gives her testimony in public, recounting how her husband was killed in front of her and thrown in a well near her house. Sylvia suffers from chronic pain—a tightening in her chest and stabbing pains in her head. Sometimes the pain is so overwhelming that she thinks she might die. It is accompanied by a great despair, which she describes as a cloud hanging over her head. Bouts of this illness, for which doctors have not been able to help her, attack her at random.

The gross effects of the violence extend beyond individual physical sickness and deep emotional turmoil. Numerous social problems in Pacux have their roots in the posttraumatic effects of the violence. Poverty further disintegrates families already broken by the death of a father and husband; the need for additional income forces widows to send younger children to work. Young women often move to Guatemala City to work as domestic servants, and entire families spend three months a year as seasonal workers on the south coast coffee and sugar plantations. Society often labels widows as whores because of their desperation for a partner who would alleviate their poverty and the weight of their double workload. Remarriage is not possible for widows with children, as most men reject the expense of supporting another man's children.[13]

A particularly frustrating effect of the violence that I experienced while working in Baja Verapaz is that the broken sense of community hampers postwar development and reconstruction attempted by both national and international organizations. The war destroyed the social fabric of communities all across Guatemala; the targeted assassinations carried out by the army robbed the population of a generation of community leaders, priests, teachers, and intellectuals. Many villagers still feel fear and suspicion of outsiders as a result of the indoctrination by the army during the war. The

---

13. Interview by Witness for Peace with Rolando Alecio of Equipo de Estudios Comunitarios y Acción Psicosocial, Rabinal, Guatemala, February 1997.

outcome is a fear and resistance to organizing in general, accompanied by an intense jealousy of those people with the courage to organize. Thus, when a group of people participate in a community development initiative, like a cooperative poultry or vegetable-growing project, fear and jealousy lead to internal divisions, deepening the fragmentation and instability of the community and inevitably undermining the project. For the Achí Maya, with their strong tradition of cooperative organizing, these effects are particularly tragic.

The poverty endured by the survivors of Río Negro magnifies the devastation afflicted on them by the war, especially for the widows. The electric company provided each surviving family with only half the land promised by the resettlement agreements. Households headed by women who are able to work the land have had limited success, citing the dry and rocky soil, sadly comparing it to the fertile land of the former Río Negro valley. Opportunities to earn money to supplement subsistence agriculture are rare. Pacux is located in an economically depressed area, where permanent employment is virtually impossible to find, particularly for women. Many work eight to ten hours shelling pumpkin seeds to earn twenty cents a day. In the end, women of Río Negro and Pacux struggle to survive the same way women do all over Guatemala—any way they can—while trying each day to put the horror of the past behind them.

Understanding the Violence

The scope and insidious characteristics of the violence in Guatemala's history beg a deeper understanding of the war. Such an analysis helps to explain the severity of the war's effects on the people of Río Negro and on communities all across Guatemala, despite the passage of time.

The war in Guatemala has been likened to an ethnic cleansing, with the objective of eliminating the Mayan indigenous people as a social and political entity. Indeed, the racist roots of the modern Guatemalan state can be traced from the Spanish conquest to the present, through a history of land seizures, physical enslavement, and cultural oppression against the Mayan people.[14] During the counterinsurgency war against the URNG, Guatemala's consecutive military governments—in the service of the nation's landowning class and supported by the U.S. government—lashed out at the indigenous population in order to maintain and protect the political and economic status quo of the previous five hundred years. The 1954 U.S.-staged coup that marked the beginning of the state-sponsored violence was engineered

---

14. *Nunca Más*, "Opresíon y Discriminacíon Cultural" 2, no. 9 (November 1994).

in order to end the ten-year social experiment of land reform and political democratization of the Arévalo and Arbenz presidencies. Fear that the peasant majority might unify behind the armed guerrilla movement, and thereby threaten the power of the ruling aristocracy, fueled more than thirty subsequent years of violent backlash against the civilian population.

The Guatemalan army's counterinsurgency strategy included using the PACs to create a culture of violence in the rural indigenous communities of the Guatemalan highlands. Complete political indoctrination, psychological domination, and the terror of mortal punishment for disobedience induced the patrols to commit atrocities in their own communities, against neighbors and even friends. And despite the tremendous hardship that the indigenous people suffered at the hands of the military, those who became PAC leaders often relished their positions as lackeys of the institution that was so feared by the civilian population.[15]

The dynamics of this power structure—with the PAC commanders as the representatives of the dominant military to a cowering population—gave the PAC commanders unprecedented influence in their own communities. They dominated all aspects of community life and operated with the same impunity enjoyed by the army. The head of a PAC possessed the ultimate threat against his rivals: the power to denounce or force others to denounce an individual or community as guerrillas, bringing certain death to the accused. Motivated by fear, accusers denounced others in hopes of a guarantee of their own safety. In this way, the army was able to take advantage of and heighten existing tensions or rivalries between villages, using rumors and revenge to pit one community against another.[16]

In the Río Negro case, there existed a history of rivalry between Río Negro and Xococ, which was aggravated by rumors and accusations surrounding the construction of the Chixoy dam. The Xococ PAC formed after the village had already suffered years of torture, murder, and disappearances from the counterinsurgency campaign. Instigated by the military, the PAC turned violently against their neighbors in Río Negro, denouncing them as guerrillas and thereby providing the army with justification for its murderous attack on the village.[17]

Whether or not there was a guerrilla presence in Río Negro cannot be definitively known. There were, however, connections between members of the community and the Committee for Peasant Unity (CUC), a militant indigenous organization formed in the late 1970s in response to the waves

15. MacEoin, "Guatemalan Villagers in Fight for Survival."
16. The Campaign for Peace and Life in Guatemala, "Guatemala's Civil Defense Patrols: Social Control through Terror" (Washington, D.C.: Campaign for Peace and Life in Guatemala, 1994).
17. Stewart et al., *A People Dammed*.

of disappearances carried out by the military during that decade.[18] The Guatemalan government considered CUC organizers to be subversives and therefore enemies of the state. During the late 1970s and early 1980s, CUC led a campaign to raise the wages paid to the migrant workers of the Pacific Coast plantations. Many Río Negro families traveled to the coast each year to work harvesting coffee, sugarcane, or cotton. When the difficulties arose in the resettlement negotiations, Río Negro residents turned to CUC organizers for help. In Guatemala at that time, association with an organization such as CUC was more than enough reason for the military government to label a community as insurgent and to justify its elimination.

The construction of the Chixoy dam is another factor essential to understanding the violence against Río Negro. Evidence exists that the army targeted Río Negro, not because of guerrilla activity in the area, but because of the community's resistance to relocation.[19] This resistance threatened the successful and timely completion of the hydroelectric plant. But more than the goal for cheap and abundant electricity motivated the government to turn violently against the people of Río Negro. The project itself was a part of the army's strategy in the region; its location in the center of the country facilitated a strong military presence to cut off support and communication between the northern and southern areas of guerrilla activity.[20] And the project was an incredible source of wealth for government officials who siphoned off hundreds of millions of dollars from the international funds being sent to Guatemala for the dam's construction.[21]

Overcoming the Terror of the Past

> We must learn to speak [about the past] and lose our fear. We must do it now; if we don't we will condemn our future. Talking about the past we help to guarantee that it will not repeat itself.
>   —Representative of the Archbishop's Office
>   on Human Rights, August 1995

After a decade of sporadic negotiations, thirty-six years of civil war in Guatemala officially ended on 29 December 1996. The URNG and the Gua-

---

18. Interview with Rolando Alecio, Equipo de Estudios Comunitarios y Acción Psicosocial, Rabinal, Guatemala, July 1996.

19. Stewart et al., *A People Dammed.*

20. Interview with Alecio, 1996.

21. Ironically, the Chixoy project was a technical failure. The cost of its construction exceeded initial estimates by more than 500 percent. The plant has never operated at more than 70 percent of its production capacity and has been plagued by mechanical problems needing costly repairs. Despite the investment of more than a billion dollars in the project, the majority of Guatemalans have no electricity. Julie Stewart et al. *A People Dammed,* 25–27.

temalan government signed peace agreements that address a wide range of topics, including human rights, the role of the military in peacetime, disarming the URNG, and social and economic reforms. Although these agreements on paper constitute the first steps toward demilitarizing one of the most repressive regimes in the hemisphere, the road to true peace in Guatemala will be long and arduous. Ending the war does not instantly erase the people's deep distrust of government institutions nor reform a corrupt and ineffective judicial system nor establish a lasting rule of law. The peace accords themselves do not reconcile the deep societal divisions left behind by the violence or heal the pain of a still fearful population, the majority of whom still live in extreme poverty.

In considering the prospects for peace in Guatemala, many people have recognized the need for reconciliation on a national level between the sectors of society affected by the war. Experience with the people of Río Negro confirms that indeed reconciliation is one of the crucial first steps toward healing the emotional, social, and physical wounds suffered by so many. Reconciliation must consist of the full public acknowledgment of the human rights abuses committed by both sides and bring about the freedom to talk openly, without fear of reprisal, about what happened. It includes the opportunity to mourn the dead and to seek punishment for those responsible for their deaths.

When these conditions exist, reconciliation will be possible—a reconciliation that can truly ease the confusion and agony caused by the sudden and senseless loss of loved ones. Then the Guatemalans victimized by the war will be able to transform their fear and suspicion into a confidence that the past will not repeat itself. Then people will have the strength, initiative, and motivation to organize and cooperate productively addressing the social ills that continue to plague them.

The women, children, and families of Río Negro are among the growing number of Guatemalans who have courageously taken the first steps by publicly speaking out against the violence they endured. In 1993, survivors of the 13 March 1982 massacre officially denounced the killing to the authorities and demanded the exhumation of the mass grave. A team of forensic anthropologists completed the exhumation in November 1993, and in April 1994 the remains of the 177 women and children were reburied in the Rabinal municipal cemetery. When the small graveside monument was destroyed, presumably by those fearful of the truth, the community pledged to build a new one that would stand as an unforgettable memory to what happened in Río Negro. In March 1995, the community dedicated a giant, concrete monument topped by a cross, built with the help of the Campaign for Peace and Life in Guatemala, a U.S.-based coalition of solidarity organizations. The monument names all 177 women and children killed on 13 March 1982, states the dates and places of the other three massacres against the Río Negro population, and states for the world to see that members of the Xococ PAC committed these atrocities.

Many other individuals and organizations are working to contribute to the healing of Guatemala's postwar trauma. Human rights organizations are documenting survivors' testimonies and helping communities through the legal process denouncing abuses and coordinating exhumations of clandestine graves. In 1998, the Archbishop's Office on Human Rights released a report about the violence, compiled from hundreds of testimonies gathered from survivors throughout the countryside and intended to serve as a public disclosure of the human rights abuse committed during the war. In Rabinal, the Community Studies and Psychosocial Action Team has promoted a holistic approach to treating the trauma. The group has documented effects of the violence and formed psychotherapy groups for survivors, working in tandem with the local health center to treat the physical illnesses and supporting other human rights groups taking testimony or coordinating exhumations.[22]

On the hills of Rabinal and all across Guatemala, many small, fearful communities yearn to honor slain loved ones with the customs and ceremonies traditional to their culture, openly and with dignity. Meanwhile, burdened with social and psychological scars inconceivable to most North Americans, the surviving families struggle daily to free themselves—and their children—from the legacy of violence, terror, and trauma.

---

22. Interview with Alecio, 1997.

9

Nicaragua

"In My Country of Water and Fire..."

DONNA VUKELICH

This essay examines Nicaragua's long history of violence and war in an analysis informed by how those phenomena have been experienced by Nicaraguan women—always affected by the country's upheavals but rarely taken into account unless the discussion centers specifically around "women's issues." Violence has wracked the country since the times of the Spanish conquest, leading to internecine wars between the country's elite (with the poor serving as the foot soldiers) during the nineteenth century that left thousands dead and caused substantial physical damage to the nation's principal cities. This legacy of violence was further reinforced by heavy-handed U.S. military intervention during the early part of the twentieth century, intervention that led to the imposition of a repressive dictatorship that has left an indelible mark on Nicaragua's political character as well as its psyche. Economic paternalism—semifeudalism, according to some experts—combined with a somewhat burlesque populism permeated all levels of society and social relations with violence, or the threat of violence. Perhaps not surprisingly, then, the Somoza dictatorship ultimately ceded only to an armed revolution, and then only after bitter warfare that further battered the country. On the heels of the revolution, and advancing almost simultaneously to it, was the perhaps inevitable counterrevolution, which so pummeled Nicaragua that today war-related psychological trauma is virtually endemic. While the military violence has subsided, the country today is hardly "at peace," and the lessons of the past have not been heeded by the country's increasingly powerful and unresponsive political class.

Poet Gioconda Belli asks of her country, "What are you, Nicaragua, but a small triangle of land, lost in the middle of the world?"[1] Small though it

---

1. Author's translation of an excerpt from Gioconda Belli's poem "Qué Sos Nicaragua?" in ...*A Puro Golpe de Amor: Seis Poetas Contemporáneas de Nicaragua* (Mexico City: Casa

may be, the country has a convulsive history, one that reveals a patchwork of violence upon violence, to such a degree that it evokes the wreckage Walter Benjamin's angel of history gazes upon.[2] The specter of war has cast its shadow over so many years of Nicaraguan history that violence in wartime is an absolutely fundamental issue for anyone attempting to understand the reality of the country, yet it is also one that cannot be completely understood without a more complex understanding of the nation's tragic history and the reality that unabashed, open violence continues today, under the broad, if tattered, umbrella of "democracy" and "peacetime." Nicaragua's recent history is almost overwhelmingly polarized. And if one were to imagine the country's history as a mirror and then imagine that mirror shattered into multiple, sometimes tiny, fragments, each fragment could be found to contain a bit—though never all—of the truth. This article cannot presume to make the mirror whole, yet it does offer one crucial part of the overall story.

Looking more closely at the war years in Nicaragua and their impact on women is imperative. Much work has been done of late about violence—including domestic violence—in Nicaragua, and thousands of pages were published during the 1980s that discussed and documented the war. Since the 1990 elections and change in government, a number of so-called post-mortems have been published as well, many of them extremely useful to furthering an understanding of that complex decade.[3] However, few, if any, studies have looked specifically at the particular suffering of women during the war and how that shapes their collective identity as Nicaragua attempts to move forward into the twenty-first century.

Since the Spanish conquest of Central America, Nicaragua has lived with the burden of ongoing, often daily, violence. It is a brutal legacy resonating throughout Nicaragua's history and one that remains relevant today. While the conquest was clearly one of Spanish, white domination over indigenous peoples, it was also an eminently patriarchal phenomenon, and the fruits of that sexual and social violence are seared into Nicaragua's subconscious.[4]

Like other conquered nations, Nicaragua can be understood in one sense as the violated woman. History since the arrival of the Spanish *conquistadores*—almost invariably men—has been shot through with the realities of rape and domination, and Nicaragua's *mestizo* (literally, the mixture of

---

de las Imágenes, 1989). Likewise, the subtitle of this chapter is a paraphrase of a line from Gioconda Belli's poem "Canción de cuna para un país suelto en llanto."

2. "This is how one pictures the angel of history. His face is turned toward the past. Where we perceive a chain of events, he sees one single catastrophe which keeps piling wreckage and hurls it in front of his feet" (Walter Benjamin, "Theses on the Philosophy of History," IX).

3. See, e.g., the work of Alejandro Bendaña, Center for International Studies in Managua; selected issues of *envío*, the monthly magazine of the Central American University in Managua.

4. See Verena Stolcke, "Conquered Women," in *Report on the Americas* (New York: NACLA), 24, no. 5.

Spanish and Indian blood) identity rests on that troubled past. Shortly after the arrival of the Spanish in the early 1500s, hundreds of thousands of Indians were sent to the Andean region as slaves to work, and often die, in the mines. Thomas Walker notes that much of the Indian population was thus decimated.[5] Many of the indigenous people who remained later tried to blend into the larger fabric of Nicaragua's new *mestizo* identity, hoping thus to avoid discrimination. At the same time, the elite tried to negate indigenous identity in a number of communities in an attempt to deny the communities their corresponding property rights.[6]

During the colonial years and continuing well into the postindependence period, Nicaragua saw the emergence of the *patrón*—or patriarch, oftentimes the owner of enormous extensions of land that poorer people worked—as an extremely strong figure in political, social, and economic terms. E. Bradford Burns's excellent historical overview of Nicaragua discusses cultural traditions that became entrenched early on and remain relevant even today. According to Burns, the country's political structure was infused with family symbols, and political power was understood very much as the "domination of father over family."[7] Thus did president-as-father become the model for Nicaraguan politics. Nicaragua's "family," then, revolves around an overwhelmingly powerful father who anoints favored male relatives with power, protecting and controlling female relatives and exercising enormous amounts of influence over the various servants attached to his family through complex ties of patronage and fictive kinship So, while Nicaraguan law explicitly stated otherwise, political power became inextricably linked to one's ability to accrue, maintain, and expand personal power.[8]

As Burns describes the patriarchs, they were invariably representatives of the elite classes. Thus independence from Spain cannot really be thought of in liberating terms for the majority of the population. Many of the poorest of Nicaragua's peasants were pressed into service in the private armies of the warring Conservatives and Liberals, whose ongoing struggles during the aptly named "period of anarchy" in the early nineteenth century had nothing to do with the well-being of the poor and virtually everything to do with their own economic and political ambitions.

---

5. Thomas W. Walker, *Nicaragua: The Land of Sandino*, 3d ed. (Boulder: Westview Press, 1991), 10–11.

6. Gould discusses the differences in property legislation as it pertained to the indigenous and *mestizo* communities and examines the way in which a "myth" of Nicaragua as a *mestizo* nation was born.

7. E. Bradford Burns, *Patriarch and Folk: The Emergence of Nicaragua 1798–1858* (Cambridge: Harvard University Press, 1991), 71.

8. Burns notes that although the different Constitutions officially set a more institutional course for the country, political power continued to be wielded "on a personal basis in a patriarchal style," with "the blur between family and national matters remain[ing] characteristic of Nicaragua." See *Patriarch and Folk*, 72.

Nicaragua in the postindependence period was marked by an anarchy that left a legacy of highly personalized politics—stable political institutions were almost nonexistent and the solidity of a given regime depended more on the strength or charisma of the caudillo of the day. Bitter internal conflicts finally erupted in a devastating civil war in the 1850s, which turned into one of the more bizarre episodes of Nicaraguan history when U.S. citizen William Walker came to Nicaragua, initially at the behest of the Liberal Party. Walker ended up declaring himself president, proclaiming English the national language, and making public his intent to conquer all of Central America. That eventually led the elite to a Liberal-Conservative alliance, and with assistance from other Central American nations, Walker was thrown out of the country.[9] Aside from the physical destruction left in Walker's path, the affair revealed a disturbing tendency among the Nicaraguan elite to sell out their national interests for immediate or short-term financial gain.

A period of relative stability following Walker's invasion was ruptured by the conflict touched off with the United States during the presidential administration of José Santos Zelaya. Zelaya, a stalwart Liberal, took over the country in 1893 and soon made it clear that he intended to move forward with the construction of an interoceanic canal. For decades, Nicaragua had been discussed as the most feasible site for a canal connecting the two oceans, but Zelaya ran afoul of the United States when he made it clear that the canal would be controlled by Nicaraguans, with financing coming from a variety of sources. That led to ongoing tensions, and Zelaya was forced out by the United States in 1909, paving the way for years of on-and-off U.S. Marine presence in the country. An ongoing U.S. presence, particularly when it involved military force, was in many ways upping the ante of patriarchal power in the country—the homegrown patriarchs were now handpicked by the United States, functioning as extensions, to a certain degree, of northern power inside their own country.

A Family Dynasty

With no single military force in place, the long-feuding Liberals and Conservatives battled each other in small groups of armed men, united by their allegiance to one single man, or caudillo. In 1927, U.S. intervention in the country secured a so-called peace accord—calling for Marine supervision of the 1928 elections and the formation of a new military force, the National

9. See Alejandro Bolaños's exhaustive biography of Walker for a deeper understanding of the man and the implications of the so-called Walker affair for Nicaraguans. Alejandro Bolaños, *William Walker, the Gray-eyed Man of Destiny* (Lake St. Louis, Mo.: A. Bolaños-Geyer, 1988–91).

Guard,[10] which was conceived from the very beginning as a sort of U.S. proxy force in Nicaragua. Thus the model installed by the United States in Nicaragua is that of an often errant, but ultimately spoiled, child whose worst misbehavior warrants little more than slaps on the hand and who is clearly always under the domination of the strong father to the north.[11]

Just one of the warring generals refused to sign the 1927 accord, citing what he called the danger of full-scale U.S. influence in his small country. General Augusto César Sandino headed to the mountainous region of Las Segovias, near the border with Honduras, and began a five-year war against the U.S. Marines. Sandino is generally regarded as first and foremost a nationalist, but he also had an interesting spiritual component to his thought.[12] Charges of violence against civilians by the Marines sent to Nicaragua in the late 1920s and early 1930s were frequent, and more recent research discusses the sometimes extreme violence used by both sides. Sandino eventually defeated the Marines but was assassinated shortly thereafter by National Guardsmen in a mission planned by the guard's new director, General Anastasio Somoza García.

The Somoza dynasty rested on two key foundations—his National Liberal Party and the National Guard. The National Guard functioned as the shock troops of the dictatorship. While officers lived well and had many privileges, the rank-and-file soldiers were often treated poorly.[13] María Teresa Blandón, a well-known feminist in Nicaragua today, calls the Somoza dictatorship "a combination of military repression with populism."[14] The National Guard, she says, was an expression of "absolute, arbitrary power." Richard Millett's thorough study of the National Guard, *Guardians of the Dynasty*, notes that by the mid-1970s, "Nicaragua was clearly a nation occupied by its own army."[15] That army was an ever more deliberate manifestation of U.S. power in the region, as evidenced by the fact that thousands of guard officers were trained at the infamous School of the Americas (then located in the Panama Canal zone).

---

10. For a thorough examination of the origins of the National Guard and a discussion of the May 1927 Espino Negro pact, see Richard Millett, *Guardians of the Dynasty: A History of the U.S. Created Guardia Nacional de Nicaragua and the Somoza Family* (Maryknoll, N.Y.: Orbis, 1977).

11. The notorious quote by Cordell Hull, secretary of state to FDR, succinctly sums up the U.S. attitude: "Somoza is a son of a bitch, but he's *our* son of a bitch."

12. Guillermo Pérez Leiva (lecture on Sandino, Managua, February 1999). Pérez Leiva, speaking as a critical Sandinista, said, "We must recover that spiritual element" if the party is to regain its once massive base of support. Many in the Nicaraguan women's movement also today speak forcefully of the need for a spiritual component in any political project that is to be both successful and long-lived.

13. See Doris Tijerino, as told to Margaret Randall, *Inside the Nicaraguan Revolution* (Vancouver, B.C.: New Star Books, 1978), 57.

14. María Teresa Blandón (lecture series, Managua, February 1999).

15. Millett, *Guardians of the Dynasty*, 251.

As Somoza's years in power dragged on, the figure of the caudillo became dangerously entrenched, with the dictatorship itself increasingly cast as a quintessentially macho, or patriarchal, phenomenon with the father figure at the top unassailable, for all practical purposes. Even in the wake of the devastating 1972 earthquake that leveled much of Managua and left severe psychic scars still to heal, Somoza remained virtually untouchable. Still, the earthquake did mark a significant turning point for Nicaragua and Somoza in that many Nicaraguans refer to it as the single event that eventually forced Somoza out of power. Somoza's "insatiable greed"[16] and nearly criminal ineptitude during the postearthquake reconstruction period alienated growing numbers of Nicaraguans. As he and his cronies accumulated huge amounts of wealth and property, many Nicaraguans struggled to cope with enormous losses and long-term trauma, the consequences of which contributed on some level to Somoza's downfall.[17]

Though the Sandinista movement was founded in 1961, it had little impact on Nicaraguan society as a whole until the mid to late 1970s. Because of the extremely repressive nature of the Somoza dictatorship—civic opposition was met with violence, and electoral channels were simply not viable[18]—the Sandinista movement emerged as a paramilitary, clandestine movement, heavily influenced by the recent example of the Cuban revolution. María Teresa Blandón, who joined the Sandinistas as a teenager and is now active in the independent women's movement, talks about the context in which the Sandinistas emerged and developed as an organization. To live in Nicaragua at that time, she says, was to live in a culture of intolerance and authoritarianism. The cultural patterns thus passed on took their toll in ways far beyond the most obvious and immediate impact of the repression. As Blandón notes, it was perhaps inevitable that "to a degree, we reproduced that culture" within the Sandinista Front for National Liberation (FSLN).[19]

As events, both internal and international, changed the political context in Nicaragua, opposition to Somoza mounted, including, but not limited to, armed actions by the Sandinista Front. Sandinista guerrilla identity quickly took on a certain mystique, one that has been a long time in wearing thin. That identity was eminently male, enshrined in several well-known texts by

---

16. The characterization comes from Richard Crawley, *Nicaragua in Perspective* (New York: St. Martin's Press, 1979).

17. So many people had lost everything during the earthquake that, as one Nicaraguan said, "We also lost our fear." He and many others later became the backbone of the insurrection in Managua.

18. One example is the opposition demonstration of 22 January 1967. Thousands of protestors, convoked by the Conservative Party, marched in downtown Managua. The National Guard opened fire on the unarmed demonstrators, and some three hundred were killed (see Crawley, *Nicaragua in Perspective*, 135). Elections were invariably won by Somoza.

19. Maria Teresa Blandón (lecture series, Managua, February 1999).

guerrilla commanders turned poets.[20] Literary critic Ileana Rodríguez notes that "in masculine guerrilla literature woman comes into the text largely as an erotic, sentimental, or familiar subject."[21] Ultimately, says Rodríguez, "woman is dismissed as 'romantic.'"[22] While certainly not the only image of women in currency once the Sandinistas came to power, it remained a potent one in revolutionary discourse during the 1980s.

Despite this somewhat demobilizing image, women were very active in the opposition to Somoza during the late 1970s—a good many of them primarily, if not exclusively, as mothers. There is a deep-seated cult of motherhood in Nicaragua, linked to the particular brand of Catholicism that took hold in Nicaragua, which includes an unusually intense devotion to the Virgin Mary. In fact, the Feast of the Immaculate Conception (celebrated in Nicaragua on 7 December as *La Purísima*) is the single most important holiday in Nicaraguan Catholicism, still the religion of the overwhelming majority of Nicaraguans.

Motherhood in Nicaragua

To have been born a woman means:
putting your body at the service of others
giving your time to others
thinking only about others....
To have been born a woman means:
that your body does not belong to you
that your time does not belong to you
that your thoughts do not belong to you.[23]

To be a mother in Nicaragua is to be self-denying, to suffer often, and generally to put one's needs absolute last on any family list of priorities.[24] First and foremost is not one's job, one's husband or *compañero*, or one's own self—it is one's children. This will last long after children are grown, even if

---

20. One of the most famous is *La montaña es algo más que una inmensa estepa verde* by Omar Cabezas (translated into English as *Fire from the Mountain*). Other works include those written by Tomás Borge and Carlos Guadamuz. Daniel Ortega (who later became president of Nicaragua) spent some seven years in prison, penning at one point a poem called "I Never Saw Managua in Miniskirts."

21. Ileana Rodriguez, *House/Garden/Nation: Space, Gender and Ethnicity in Post-Colonial Latin American Literatures by Women* (Durham, N.C.: Duke University Press, 1994), 172.

22. Ibid.

23. Excerpts of Daisy Zamora's poem "Ser Mujer" [To Be a Woman], author's translation.

24. This is underscored by the following anecdote: A U.S. student accompanying a health brigade on their visit to a hurricane refugee settlement not far from Managua in early 1999 commented that one woman had brought her sick child for care and made no mention of her own problems—even though she had a huge and obviously infected wound in her leg. Only after the health professionals present insisted did she allow herself to be checked.

they have moved away from home, and is particularly true with adult males, who in the end are infantilized by the harsh strictures of machismo. Adult female children are friends, often mothers themselves, but they are seldom babied or cared for in the same way that adult male children frequently are.[25]

One anthropological study of contemporary Nicaragua observes how little boys are often provoked and teased until they "display an appropriate rage," while little girls are already being taught to suppress their anger, understand their often restrictive physical boundaries, and the like—in other words, internalizing that they must put themselves last.[26] This is carried on into adulthood, with marriage still understood by many women as something that is supposed to last, whatever the problems may be: "When a woman marries a man, she's agreeing to put up with whatever he decides to do."[27] Still in use in Nicaraguan Spanish is the reference to unmarried women as *niña*, or little girl, with the implication that you remain a girl until a man "makes" you a woman. This is a profound negation of the existence of women as individuals in and of themselves and could be said to represent a truly insidious form of psychological violence.

By the end of the 1970s, most young people, and particularly young males, were seen by Somoza and the National Guard as enemies. Hundreds of young people who had no political involvement whatsoever were picked up and held for a day or two, sometimes beaten, other times disappeared or killed. Those who were known to be Sandinistas were often subjected to the most brutal forms of torture.

As a result, many of the women who initially cast their lot against the dictatorship did so out of what were very traditional, socially conservative, motives—first and foremost, they were protecting their children.[28] Many of them came together in AMPRONAC—the Association of Women Confronting the National Problematic (their shorthand for Somoza). Doris Tijerino, first active in the Socialist Party and later in the Sandinista Front, says that initial attempts to create women's organizations linked to these parties were unsuccessful precisely because women's needs and interests were subordinated to those of the given party. While traditional left-wing parties in Nicaragua have historically focused on economic issues and the

25. However, ironically, some mothers experience sons as not being as reliable as daughters. Roger Lancaster quotes one mother as saying, "Daughters are more faithful. They'll stay with you." See *Life Is Hard: Machismo, Danger and the Intimacy of Power in Nicaragua* (Berkeley: University of California Press, 1992), 121.

26. Ibid., 42. Lancaster's study of a working-class neighborhood in Managua is insightful and extremely useful for anyone attempting to unravel the many threads of machismo in Nicaragua today.

27. Ibid., 46.

28. This is not a phenomenon peculiar to Nicaragua, as similar actions have been seen in other countries around the world, with one notable case the Madres de la Plaza de Mayo in Argentina.

public arena—shop floors, the universities, agricultural farms—women's interests tend to be overwhelmingly linked to their experience as mothers or to their needs in the household, a far more private arena. Those interests were given a backseat, when they were discussed at all. But Tijerino calls the AMPRONAC experience "completely different.... Any woman who wanted to participate was welcome... and we discussed the problems in our society, and what we could do as women to deal with those problems."[29]

Esperanza Cruz de Cabrera talks about her own involvement in the Sandinista struggle, spurred on by her son, Ernesto, an FSLN member. She recalls a conversation with Ernesto, in which he reveals his FSLN activity and tells her it is too dangerous for him to continue, as the National Guard are following him. "I don't know if you want to get involved in all this or not," he says. And she relates how, little by little, her house became a safehouse of sorts for Sandinista members passing through Matagalpa: "I delivered messages for my son, we hid arms on our farm, so we could later get them out to the guerrilla column that Ernesto was in charge of."[30] Most of her eight children were involved somehow with the FSLN during the late 1970s.

Women and War: In Their Own Words

The horrors facing any Sandinista who was taken prisoner by Somoza's National Guard were many. Doris Tijerino, today a member of the Sandinista bench in the National Assembly, remembers the torture inflicted upon a number of those taken prisoner.[31]

Tijerino herself spent two years in prison and recounts an incident when a young woman, Yolanda Núñez, was taken prisoner:

> She was pregnant. They had taken her with her comrade. They stripped her and put her in humiliating positions and beat her in front of her companion to make him talk. Elba Campos was also being held there: she too was pregnant but was about seven or eight months along. She had an enormous belly.... She was being held because she was the girlfriend [of a party member] and they assumed she was collaborating or had something to do with the Front. Also, about eight other comrades were being held, three of whom had been raped. In the case of one of those raped comrades, we were able to find out that one of her

29. Margaret Randall, *Todas estamos despiertas: Testimonios de la mujer nicaragüense hoy* (Mexico City: Siglo XXI Editores, 1980), 32. English trans.: *Sandino's Daughters: Testimonies of Nicaraguan Women in Struggle* (Vancouver, B.C.: New Star Books, 1981).

30. Roser Solá and María Pau Trayner, *Ser Madre en Nicaragua: Testimonios de Una Historia No Escrita* (Managua: Editorial Nueva Nicaragua, 1988), 33.

31. Tijerino, *Inside the Nicaraguan Revolution*, 77–78.

rapists was a Security agent named "Alvarenga"; we even learned that Somoza himself had taken part in these rapes.[32]

Sexuality and militarism "have been constructed and reconstructed together," according to Cynthia Enloe.[33] This is underscored by Tijerino's testimony that during her months in jail, she met a number of young women prisoners, many of them prostitutes. She talks about the prostitution rampant under the Somoza dictatorship and the links between that business and *la Guardia Nacional*: "The madams of the houses of prostitution carry on their business together with the Guard and the commanders of the barracks and jails.... When the [girls] became pregnant, they made them abort. They corrupted them to such an extent that when they finally left, it was impossible for them to find a way of remaining in any other environment."[34]

Tijerino remembers her own experience, including being interrogated in a good cop-bad cop routine. One of her interrogators would beat her with a club, insult her, shock her with an electric goad all over her body. Intervention by the "good" guard officer would follow, as he tried to convince the other to stop the beatings. Later, she says, "That fellow proposed that I go to bed with him. He said he was going to protect me—it's all part of the softening-up policy." But the torture continued:

> They made me do squats again, totally naked, and placed [an] object in such a way that each time I squatted it would go into my rectum. They never went so far as to rape me—rather they made use of sex to damage me psychologically and physically. They handled me, tried to put their hands into my vagina. I did everything possible to attack them. They masturbated in front of me and handled me while doing so.[35]

This torture went on for days, and Tijerino spent many more months in prison, including several in solitary confinement.

The Sandinista triumph in 1979 did not bring peace to the country, as the U.S.-funded counterrevolutionary, or contra, war against the Sandinista army and Nicaraguan civilians began shortly thereafter, becoming a source of near daily concern for most Nicaraguans by 1983–84. Former National Guardsmen commanded the contra forces, though many of the foot soldiers were peasants, particularly as the war dragged on.[36] Initially given command of the so-called covert war, the U.S. Central Intelligence Agency (CIA) published a

---

32. Ibid.

33. Cynthia Enloe, *Does Khaki Become You? The Militarization of Women's Lives* (Boston: South End Press, 1983), 18.

34. Tijerino, *Inside the Nicaraguan Revolution*, 108–9.

35. Ibid., 101–2.

36. See Reed Brody, *Contra Terror in Nicaragua: Report of a Fact-finding Mission: September 1984–January 1985* (Boston: South End Press, 1985), appendix 2.

manual, *Psychological Operations in Guerrilla Warfare,* promoting extreme forms of terrorism where deemed necessary, even as it encouraged the contra forces to "regulate their savagery."[37] The human rights agency Americas Watch reported that the so-called Nicaraguan Democratic Force, or FDN, the largest single contra grouping and the one most under the control of the CIA, "systematically engaged in the killing of prisoners and the unarmed, including medical and relief personnel; selective attacks on civilians, and indiscriminate attacks; torture and other outrages against personal dignity."[38]

It is clear that women were not the only, nor in fact the primary, victims of the contra forces. Yet they were often subjected to particularly brutalizing sexual violence. U.S. lawyer Reed Brody led a fact-finding mission in Nicaragua in late 1984–early 1985, compiling a number of affidavits from civilian victims of the contra forces. Time and again, rape is mentioned by the women interviewed by the mission.

One case is that of Digna Barreda de Ubeda, who recounts her story of May 1983. From Estelí, she and her husband were staying with her uncle nearby. He turned out to be a contra collaborator who had denounced Barreda and her husband as Sandinista spies. Several contras showed up at her uncle's house and took Barreda and her husband away. She remembers what happened next: "They beat my husband brutally.... And then, the three... raped me so brutally that I still have scars on my knees. They put me face down. They raped me through my rectum, too. And all this in front of my husband." She and her husband and several other captives were made to walk to a safe house in the mountains—actually a camp of U.S.-made tents. Barreda said that after she was interrogated, they continued to torture her and rape her again during the next several hours. She was subjected to similar treatment every day; on the fourth day she offered to collaborate with the contras if they would let her go. They agreed but still did not release her. The following day, she says, "Five of them raped me at about five in the evening.... They had gang-raped me every day. When my vagina couldn't take it anymore, they raped me through my rectum. I calculate that in five days they raped me 60 times." The contra soldier who was assigned to take Barreda back to the road raped her before releasing her.[39] Her husband was able to escape two weeks later.

A doctor suffered similar agony. Mirna Cunningham, who is from the small northern Atlantic Coast town of Bilwaskarma, served during the first half of the 1980s as the national government's delegate to that re-

37. Peter Kornbluh, "The Covert War," in *Reagan versus the Sandinistas: The Undeclared War on Nicaragua,* ed. Thomas W. Walker (Boulder: Westview Press, 1987), 27.

38. Ibid.

39. From Digna Barreda de Ubeda's affidavit, as reported in Brody, *Contra Terror in Nicaragua,* 119–20.

gion. In December 1981, she was on her way back to the hospital at Waspam (a fairly sizeable town in the region), returning from a visit to Bilwaskarma. When they were some six hundred meters from the hospital gates, Cunningham says,

> The car was attacked by a group of around 20 armed people who started shooting at the car. When the shooting stopped, the hospital administrator was able to jump out and run into the bush.... The rest of us, we were taken out of the car and beaten with rifle butts all over our bodies. And after that they made us get into the car again. They forced the driver to go back into the village at knife point.... [Later] they tied us up, and said they were going to kill us, and they continued to hit us. They held us for several hours.... When it got dark, they separated the doctors, and they took the nurse and myself to a hut, a little house near the river [the Coco River, which separates Nicaragua from Honduras]. At this house, they had us there for seven hours. During those hours we were raped for the first time. While they were raping us, they were chanting slogans like, "Christ yesterday, Christ today, Christ tomorrow" ... although we would cry or shout, they would hit us, and put a knife or a gun to our head. This went on for almost two hours. They told us they were going to kill us, but they wanted to kill us in Nicaragua to leave our bodies as an example to others who work with the Nicaraguan government. They made us walk to the river again and cross the river, on our way back we were raped again, by all the people who were taking us to the village.... [where they were released] We were all bruised for several days, bleeding. The nurse who went through this also was very disturbed emotionally. The hospital had to be closed, because the counterrevolutionaries went in, stole instruments and medicine and terrorized the patients and other health workers, who were afraid to keep working there. So we had to close.[40]

Other affidavits mentioned in the Brody report, as well as many gathered by the Witness for Peace long-term teams who did the most significant on-going reporting from the war zones during the 1980s, point to rape as a common phenomenon for women taken prisoner. A report commissioned by the Washington Office on Latin America in late 1985–early 1986 notes that "the presence of contra troops in a given locale seemed to give rise to a pattern of indiscriminate attacks against civilian targets, kidnappings, rapes,

---

40. From Mirna Cunningham's affidavit, as reported in Brody, *Contra Terror in Nicaragua*, 121–23.

assassinations, mutilations and other forms of violence against the lives and persons of the civilian population."[41]

In addition, in a cruel twist on the concept of "camp followers,"[42] women were often forced to make a horrible choice—"choose" a particular contra in order to avoid constant, gang rapes by the whole group. These women often became entirely dependent on that single contra soldier, knowing that food, water, their very survival, depended upon staying in the good graces of someone who had taken them prisoner and now considered them virtually "his." Women who spent weeks or months in these kinds of situations often emerged psychologically and emotionally confused and troubled, and some who lived with the contra forces for several years were never quite the same. Brody's report highlights the cases of two young girls.

Milyedis Salinas (fourteen) and Ermelina Diaz Talavera (fifteen) were taken from their houses in October 1984 by a group of ten armed contras. Later the group joined forces with another group, for a total of nearly one hundred armed men. The girls were then told that they would have to choose one man to sleep with or be raped by all the men present. The girls said they did so "because that's what had to be done," and that's how they lived for nearly two months. The girls were given rifles but never fought, although the contras took part in nine combats during that time. The girls were forced to carry backpacks with munitions and were given little to eat. They managed to escape after fifty-five days in custody.[43]

Women like Digna Barreda, Mirna Cunningham, Milyedis Salinas, and Ermelina Diaz suffered unspeakable atrocities at the hands of the contra forces. Painful as they are, it is important to tell and retell the stories as one step in preserving the country's historical memory. Hundreds of other women suffered in a very different way during the war—as mothers of the young men and women who put their lives on the line for the Sandinista revolution.

Like many mothers, Esperanza Cruz saw her children fight against the dictatorship and survive the war. And, as happened to far too many mothers, the counterrevolutionary war finally claimed one of her children. Ernesto Cabrera Cruz was killed in a contra ambush in 1984. She talks about dealing with his death in extremely religious terms, the same language of suffering that women in Nicaragua have spoken for generations. "You remember when Christ was crucified," says doña Esperanza, "and the pain, the very same pain that Mary must have felt.... because when you think about Christ and why he died... then we always ask ourselves so many questions: Who did our children die for? What did they die for? For a change in society."[44]

41. See Washington Office on Latin America (WOLA) report, 14.
42. See Enloe's discussion of camp followers, *Does Khaki Become You?* chap. 1.
43. From Brody, *Contra Terror in Nicaragua*, 123.
44. Solá and Trayner, *Ser Madre en Nicaragua*: 35–36.

Too many sons or daughters returned home in simple pine boxes lined with tin. Mothers who lost children suffered greatly, of course, and continue to carry that loss with them. Many houses in Nicaragua that lost a child to the war have small shrines set up to the memories of those children, mementos of youth carefully arranged around the stark, oversized photo of a young man or woman looking far more serious and solemn than the life the mother still celebrates. The graves of the war dead are scattered throughout Nicaragua, and on the anniversary of a child's death, a mother is often found at the gravesite, carefully arranging a bouquet of brightly colored plastic flowers or sweeping away the encroaching underbrush. Many other mothers, however, bear the particular pain of losing their children without ever knowing what happened to them. They are the mothers of the "disappeared" and will never have the kind of emotional closure they so desperately need.[45]

State Policy in the 1980s

Sandinista organizational structure from the beginning was highly militarized, and perhaps logically so, given the tremendously repressive context of the Somoza dictatorship within which all Sandinista political formation took place. While the Sandinista revolution created significant opportunities for women, it also reinforced much in Nicaragua's existing patriarchal, militaristic mold. When power emerges from an armed revolution, it's perhaps inevitable that it continues to be linked to military activity.

While much attention was given to the key military roles played by women during the insurrection against Somoza, in the end the insurrection was several short months, while the contra war lasted nearly a decade. During the contra war, after a brief attempt to deal with the problem through the use of all-volunteer units, a draft was instated. In 1983, the Association of Nicaraguan Women (AMNLAE) fought to have women included in the draft but were voted down in the Council of State, the legislative body at that time. The many battalions that went out during the rest of the 1980s were exclusively male, and where stereotypes had been dispelled during the 1978–79 insurrection,[46] they were often reinforced during the drawn-out war of the 1980s.

---

45. For more on this phenomenon, see the insightful work done by Sheila Tully, "A Painful Purgatory: Grief and the Nicaraguan Mothers of the Disappeared," *Social Science and Medicine* 40, no. 2 (1995).

46. One former army officer who was active in the 1979 insurrection against Somoza remembers that his superiors were women. "It was hard at first," he said, "but we had to change the way we thought about women." From an unpublished interview with this author, Managua, February 1999.

Military activity is not necessarily more important than other tasks under-taken during wartime, and indeed without the so-called rearguard, defense efforts would soon falter. But in the Nicaragua of the 1980s, those who were combatants were awarded a level of prestige and position in society, as well as in the popular imagination. Once the draft took effect, almost all the combatants were men. Women, particularly young women, found themselves blocked from making significant strides up the political ladder. A young woman running for a political post in the student movement or on a shop floor in a given factory, for example, would find it quite difficult to take on a young man who had just returned from the war and proven himself on the battlefield.

In the end, party interests took precedence over women's interests. So, even as women participated in the revolution in enormous numbers, on some fundamental level women were excluded from the revolutionary inner circle—in both a literal and symbolic sense. With the exception of a few women who held positions of power, women were recognized primarily as mothers, or were relegated to being *la mujer de* (woman of) someone who had a certain status himself (a sense of ownership by the male clearly implied).

Postwar Nicaragua

Nicaragua today bears the scars of all these discussed layers of violence. While peace has come to the country in relative terms, violence on an every-day level is soaring. A postwar nation, particularly one that has never come to terms with its legacy of violence, is prisoner on some deep level to that legacy. War veterans from both sides of the conflict spent years carrying guns and now have scant tools with which to reconstruct, carefully and peacefully, their shattered country. In effect, a whole generation of men was profoundly affected by their experience as soldiers. The Sandinista army had the advantage of being an army that came out of a popular struggle in which they were fighting for their own land. Their experience is thus certainly dif-ferent from an invading army or an occupying military force. Nonetheless, they are dealing with serious psychological issues, and there has been very little help available to them.

Women, too, carry their experiences with them, and some today wonder aloud whether it was all worth it. Like men, they have had little time in which to reflect about the war, and they often push their own feelings about that time aside as today's problems become all-consuming. Parallel to the legacy of war is the current reality of neoliberal economic policies. Basic education and health care are now out of reach for many Nicaraguans. The harsher the economic policies, it seems, the more quickly the social fabric unravels, and that is seen in increasing crime, drug use, and domestic violence. As during the war, women are not the only victims of this latest assault on Nicaragua, but they often bear a disproportionate burden in both economic and emotional terms.

Psychologist Martha Cabrera argues that Nicaragua is a nation with so much unresolved trauma at such a widespread level that it has greatly affected the country as a whole. Recent decades in Nicaragua have been convulsive, to say the least, and Cabrera notes that "we haven't had time, as a nation, to really digest what we have experienced."[47] Many people in Nicaragua thought the revolution was going to change the world, Cabrera says, and it has been very hard for some to deal with their sense of loss at seeing those dreams denied.

Today, the "battleground" for many women is in their own homes, as rates of domestic violence continue to soar. The independent women's movement has pushed successfully to pass legislation criminalizing domestic violence—both physical and psychological—but faces an uphill battle in effecting massive changes in attitudes.[48] Like so many other issues in Nicaragua, the bottom line is one of transforming the way in which children are taught, at both the formal and informal levels. While the dictatorship has been accurately charged with leaving the country bankrupt while one family became fabulously wealthy, and its many abuses and crimes have been recorded for history, its longer lasting effects are, perhaps, in more cloaked cultural patterns of behavior. "One of the worst things the dictatorship did was to deny us any true comprehension of democracy, in its truest and fullest sense," says María Teresa Blandón. "We all learned that violence was the only way to solve conflicts." The women's movement may offer an alternative, understanding the need for profound transformations in society but also the imperative of working together for the common good.

Acknowledgments

The author wishes to thank David Gist for his comments. This essay is dedicated to the memory of George Andrew Vukelich, 1927–95.

---

47. Martha Cabera lecture series, Managua, September 1998.

48. This is evidenced by the fallout from the Zoilamérica Narvaez case. She is the stepdaughter of former president Daniel Ortega and in March 1998 went public with accusations that he had molested, raped, and harassed her at different times for some twenty years. Her charges brought support from many within the independent women's movement, most notably the La Malinche Collective and the Women's Network against Violence. Yet many women were fearful of speaking out, and the political structure in the country essentially closed ranks around Ortega.

10

Haiti

Women Speak

YOLANDE
Literary Teacher

When I started to get involved in politics, my mother told me that I shouldn't, that I would get killed. She said I was too young to get involved. So I said, "Mother, it's a matter of will. It's what I want to do. You have to live and die for what you believe in."

At KID we each had specific duties in a poor area. I used to work in Site Solèy. I taught people how to read and write. I taught them so they would know what to do during the elections. Because I was mandated to work in the electoral campaign of President Aristide and my husband was also involved in this movement, they came looking for my husband to kill him. So, we worked in secret. We gave out political tracts in Kalfou, Site Solèy, Lasalin. We mobilized everywhere we could to show we were still standing firm.

They came to arrest me on 27 April 1992. I didn't think they would arrest me because I had kept an eye out in the neighborhood and was working at night so they wouldn't find out what I was doing. At six o'clock they came into my house. I was working and my mother was in her room sleeping. They beat my mother. They took me and pushed me to the ground, handcuffed and kicked me. They hit me on my back with their rifle butts. There were six soldiers and they took me with them. When I was in the jeep, they took turns hitting and kicking me. That's when I told them I was three months pregnant. While they had me on the ground and were kicking me, I had a miscarriage. When I got to police headquarters, they started interrogating me. They asked me where Aristide was and what I thought the poor man could do for me. I said nothing. There were two of them in charge. I couldn't see their faces because they were wearing caps and dark glasses. They put out

These testimonies are taken from *Roots: A Forum of Progressive Analysis and Action on Haitian Affairs* 1, no. 3 (summer 1995): 18–19, and are used with the permission of the publisher, Kalfou Kreyòl, Inc., Washington, D.C. They were excerpted and adapted from Patricia Benoit's film documentary *Courage and Pain*, 1994.

their cigarettes on my arms so I could answer their questions. I didn't say anything and I blacked out. I was bleeding and they put me in a cell.

I found strength in God and in my country's traditions. All countries have their traditions, but in our country we have the spirits. I am always singing. When I was in the hospital, this song came to me: "Help me. Help me with my burden. I am a beast of burden. I have no mother to help me with my burden. I have no father to help me." I kept singing it in the hospital. It's the African gods, the spirits that released me from where I was.

ALERTE
Food Vendor

I was born in Baradè. I am thirty-two years old. I used to sell cooked food—rice, chicken, cornmeal, etc. My husband was mandated under Aristide during the elections. He used to clean up the neighborhood and make it beautiful. He painted the walls and streets with pictures of Aristide. After the coup we left the city and went to the countryside. After things calmed down, we moved back to the city.

On 16 October 1993, we heard a knock at the door, but we didn't answer. Suddenly they started kicking the door. My husband had built a window in the back, and when he heard the knock, he knew there would be trouble, so he left through the window. I stayed behind with the children. They came and asked for my husband. I said he was not at home. They said since my husband was not there, they were going to take me with them.

The first strike of machete hit me on my temple, the next on the side of my face, cutting up my gum and part of my tongue. When I noticed that they were trying to kill me, I lay on my face. I kept blocking machete blows with my elbow. That's how they cut off my arm. My whole body is now covered with scars—my shoulders, my neck, even the back of my neck. I had cuts on my head and scalp. They dragged me, threw me into a ditch, and I spent the night there.

The next morning I dragged myself out to the street. Every time a car passed I would lift my elbow. A piece of it was hanging, but I lifted my elbow anyway. One car backed up, and one of the men said, "This person's not dead; she just lifted her elbow." One other guy got out of the car and said, "What are you doing here?" I said, "I don't know. I just found myself here." He just looked at me and got into the car and left. I just stayed there and said, "Oh God, I guess this is not the person who is going to save me because I know you are going to send someone to save me. Even if I am dying, at least my family will find my body and bury it." So I waited. A little while later, I saw a military car come by, a truck with a bunch of soldiers. They all got out and pointed their guns at me. They asked, "What are you doing here?" I said, "I don't know what I am doing here." They started talking and talking, and one of them said "This is a woman. We are not going to find anyone to take her out of here. Why don't we just take her out; she's a woman."

When my family came, they did not recognize me. The children said, "That's not my mother. You're not my mother." I didn't look like the person I was before. A long time after it happened, the youngest one wouldn't come near me. He would look at my photo and say, "That's my mother. You're not my mother. The person in the photo is my mother."

I have a lot of strength. If I didn't have strength, I wouldn't be here. Some people get a cut on their finger, and they die, but my tongue, my gum, my arm, were cut. I used to be in good shape and now look at me. I have courage. God let me live so I could come here to show people what's going on in Haiti. My tongue was cut, but God left a piece of it in my mouth, and when I went to the hospital, they sewed it back on so I could speak out.

J'Accuse!

LAURA FLANDERS

The woman in the tight, red kerchief opens her eyes wide and spreads her palms across the kneecaps of the women sitting by her side. "Since the Thursday before the arrival, I didn't sleep," she says. In the days after the restoration of ousted president Jean Bertrand Aristide (15 October 1994), Haitians talk of "the arrival" like the second coming: no need to clarify who has arrived. "I didn't expect to eat better or be healthier suddenly, but he'd be back," the kerchiefed woman explains. "It's like my dead brother or my dead father or a whole dead generation returning." Another woman describes the arrival of President Aristide as a birthing: "As I watched TV and waited, I put a belt around my stomach to stop my insides coming out. It felt like labor."

"J'Accuse" is reprinted from Laura Flanders, *Real Majority, Media Minority: The Cost of Sidelining Women in Reporting* (Monroe, Me.: Common Courage Press, 1997), 240–48, and is used with permission of the author. It was first printed in *On the Issues* (spring 1995).

The women are speaking with U.S. visitors in a bright yellow-tiled room in northern Port-au-Prince. Brought together by one of Haiti's largest women's groups, Solidarite Fanm Ayisyèn (SOFA), they are talking about the future for women in wake of the arrival. Their visitors, myself included, are here with MADRE, a twenty-thousand-strong U.S. women's group that has been sending aid to SOFA for the past twelve months.

The Haitians are old and young, from fifteen years of age to over sixty— political activists and friends of activists, market traders, domestic workers, peasants, professionals, daughters, wives—they are fifty of the hundreds of women who were raped by anti-Aristide terrorists in the last months of their country's most recent military regime. It wouldn't be unreasonable to measure the success of the U.S. intervention by the extent to which these women's abusers are brought to justice. But right now, the woman in the kerchief and her friends are celebrating.

A young market trader in a blue-check dress describes taunting an anti-Aristide thug who lives in her neighborhood on the day of the president's return. She dug out of hiding all the photographs of Aristide never found by the Macoutes (a generic term for the agents of the dictators). "I was surprised I was still alive," she said. "But now I told him: You can kill me, but you can't scare me because my husband is coming."

The impossible has happened in Haiti: President Aristide has come home. And like the tiny, wrinkled photos of the ousted president that people here have somehow perilously preserved, the dream of justice that successive military regimes have tried to eradicate is back and, miraculously, alive.

"Our first goal is to bring the men who attacked us to trial," said one of the raped women. "The next is to make sure it never happens again."

SOFA was founded in 1986. At their last public meeting, they estimate that three thousand women from all over Haiti were represented. Since the coup, they've had to work more discreetly, but they've worked. SOFA members in Port-au-Prince help market vendors establish credit collectives. In the countryside, the group tries to offer health care and literacy and political education sessions in the privacy of people's houses, out of sight.

The last time I was in Haiti was in early 1993. Then, the streets were hushed and atypically empty. From my bed, I could hear shooting. Twice in a week the morning revealed dead bodies in the hotel drive.

On this trip in 1994, things are different. Just one week to the day after Aristide flew into Port-au-Prince, the streets of the capital are teeming with recent returnees. Beneath almost every tree, skinny street vendors hawk fruit, fish, shoe leather, or sugarcane. Exiles from the city are gradually reappearing, and after dark, where recently there were only gunshots and their results, now there are young people laughing and bent-over women walking slowly hand in hand.

There's a sense of the extraordinary having happened, a sort of suspension of disbelief. But as the days pass, reality reemerges. In reference to a coup official's comment that the ousted president could no more return to Haiti than a laid egg could be put back inside a chicken, the city walls have paintings of large eggs being inserted into chickens; sometimes the hand doing the inserting is covered with stars and stripes. It's not an image many women would have come up with, but it's a statement about the restoration. Everyone knows the egg can't go back into the chicken, but people are clear there's been a miracle.

In his first public address, delivered from behind a three-inch-thick bulletproof shield on the steps of the presidential palace, Aristide called the women of Haiti "real women" and "queens." "Given all the tribulations of life," said Aristide, "the women of Haiti are always there." The crowd—those crushed against the palace gates to hear and those watching on TVs dragged into dusty neighborhood streets—sent up a cheer. One of those cheering was a powerful, dark-skinned woman in a brilliant blue shiny dress who attended our meeting. In her enthusiasm, she says, she picked up a neighbor and twirled her in the air. "When I heard Aristide talk about the Haitian women, I felt huge inside. I said to myself, yes, we are the Haitian women. We are beautiful and we are strong."

The woman in blue, we'll call her Geraldine, also knows about tribulation. Early in the morning of 4 February 1994, when she was sleeping with her husband, seven men knocked on the door. Two of the raiders appeared to be civilians, but three were dressed in army uniform, and two more wore the blue outfits of the Haitian police. In front of her husband and four of her kids, the soldiers raped her and then raped her daughters. "They put guns to their ears and forced them to lie down...." Among the weapons the men were carrying, she remembers an Israeli Uzi, several U.S. AK47 rifles, and some 45s. "My tongue was filling up my mouth. I was spitting blood, mute."

Geraldine is not mute now. She talks about her thirty-one-year-old niece, a guest, who scrambled out a window when the gang arrived. The young woman's body turned up three weeks later in a common dumping ground. Geraldine's husband has been disabled ever since that night. The beating he received caused permanent damage to his kidneys. But Geraldine is talking about the need for justice. So is the woman in the red kerchief, and the woman in the blue-check dress. Along with the other women of SOFA, the women in the rape group are clear that individual empowerment needs to be followed by social change.

"We feel better, but we're not actually better off," one woman said. "Aristide is a leader and an inspiration," says another. "But he cannot be everywhere. We need to be our own Aristides."

Achieving Justice

One of the priorities for the women in the room is bringing their abusers to trial. Another is changing Haitian law. At present, explained Evelyn, a third-year law school student and one of SOFA's coordinators, "We have no structure for justice for rape." By current law, the punishment for rape is compensation: Offenders are usually required to pay a fine. An alternative is an offer of marriage to their victims. "Rape is still treated as an honor crime," said Evelyn.

In the wake of recent history, it was hoped that Haitian offenders could be tried under an international code. A few years ago the world's attention was drawn to Bosnia, where horrific tales of systematic rape inspired some women to call for war crimes tribunals. At that time, the commander of the Bosnian Serbs, Radovan Karadjic, was charged with international offenses including mass rape because, it was argued, the crimes were committed under his authority and with his implicit consent. More recently, Korean so-called comfort women won compensation from the Japanese government, whom they charged with responsibility for the mass rape and forced prostitution of Korean women during World War II.

Nancy Kelly, part of the MADRE delegation, is a lawyer with the Immigration and Refugee Program at Harvard Law School. "If we can get an international body to recognize rape as an act of torture, it could change things for women all over the world." So far, there has been no action in the Bosnian case. In the case of Haiti, a new initiative has been launched.

On 26 September, a formal "Country Conditions Complaint" about Haiti was presented to the Inter-American Commission of Human Rights of the Organization of American States (OAS) by MADRE, the International Women's Human Rights Law Clinic at the City University of New York Law School, the Haitian Women's Advocacy Network, the Center for Constitutional Rights, and the Immigration and Refugee Program at Harvard Law School, among others.[1]

"What we found, compiling the research of very many groups," said Nancy Kelly, "is a consistent pattern of abuse by members of the Haitian military, the police, and armed auxiliaries." Women of all sorts were targeted "because they were politically involved themselves or because members of their family were or because they were working with women, sustaining civilian life. Others were attacked simply because they were women."

Between February and July of 1994, UN-OAS human rights monitors reported seventy-seven cases of rape, fifty-five of which involved female ac-

---

1. Inter-American Commission of Human Rights, "Affidavits in Support of . . . the Violations of Human Rights of Haitian Women" (Washington, D.C.: Organization of American States, October 1996). —ED.

tivists or close relatives of male activists. Some women's organizations in Haiti reported counting as many as eighteen rapes in a single day. The OAS complaint contains the testimony of over one hundred women, some of whom were forced to witness the rape or murder of their children before being raped themselves. In one case, a fifteen-year-old boy was forced to rape his mother.

A favorable decision at the OAS regarding rape in the case of Haiti could have tremendous repercussions in the legal world. Unfortunately for the women of Haiti, it seems unlikely the OAS will consider the case anytime soon.[2]

But there are, as we go to press, approximately twenty thousand U.S. troops in Haiti. It wasn't totally unrealistic for some women to expect that the armed forces would be used to apprehend abusers. After all, President Clinton did emphasize rape when he addressed the public in a televised speech intended to convince Americans of the need for U.S. military action, after months in which his administration downplayed human rights reports.

"Haiti's dictators, led by General Raoul Cédras, control the most violent regime in our hemisphere," declared the president. "International observers discovered a terrifying pattern of soldiers and policemen raping the wives and daughters of suspected political dissidents."

The "New" Old Police

But a month after U.S. troops descended on Haiti, the women of SOFA see no evidence that the young GIs are intent on bringing murderers and rapists to trial. When the troops first arrived, "the people were very brave and the Macoutes were running scared," explained Anne Marie Coriolon, one of SOFA's directors. "Gradually though, there's been a change. People are beginning to realize that the Macoutes still have arms and they're not about to be disbanded."

"The people turn criminals over to the U.S. troops, and then we see them back on the streets in three days or less," said another woman. "We were told the U.S. troops were here to disarm the criminals, but that's not what's going on."

Spokespeople for the U.S. armed forces acknowledge holding only between thirty and forty men in detention during the period immediately following the Aristide restoration. "It's not our responsibility to judge who's guilty," one young GI from California explained. "We're just here to keep the peace, not to get involved. Unless we see someone committing a crime

---

2. As of August 2000 no one has been charged with the rapes that occurred during the coup. —ED.

in front of us, or doing something to threaten U.S. security, we've been told to leave them alone."

Lunching in a restaurant in Petionville, the wealthy district of Port-au-Prince, we witnessed a crowd growing in front of a nearby police station. An American military police lieutenant, sitting patiently in the cab of a dusty armored transport vehicle, explained that his unit was choosing policemen who were considered eligible for retraining. Under the U.S. plan, the current Haitian army, which includes the police, is to be replaced by an armed force of about 1,500 and a police corps of 7,000 to 10,000. But many men will be the same. A new academy has been established for retraining the "old" police, "professionalizing" them through the U.S. International Criminal Investigations Training Assistance Program (a project funded by the FBI). The "new" police will then be returned to their old neighborhoods.

How many of the Petionville police had been selected for retraining? "Them all," according to the lieutenant. "It will be easy enough to reintegrate the rest," he said. "I've seen them walking in their neighborhoods, smiling and shaking hands with people. I don't think there'll be any trouble."

The SOFA women were not surprised. On the day of Aristide's return a young boy spotted the thug who had forced him to rape his mother and, with the help of a crowd, turned the accused man over to U.S. troops, SOFA's Anne Marie Coriolon remembered. There is no guarantee that man will be held. "If he's released, then what?" asks Coriolon.[3] "That little boy's life is in danger." So far, none of the women in the rape support group coordinated by SOFA has dared come forward to identify their assailants to the U.S. troops.

Another option is to hold the leaders of the anti-Aristide regime accountable for the actions of their men. According to the women who met with MADRE, most of the assailants came masked, but the thugs usually wore recognizable uniforms, or they announced they were with the Front for Haitian Progress and Advancement (FRAPH), a right-wing paramilitary group. "They wanted us to know who they were," one woman explained. "That was part of the point."

But the likelihood of any of the paramilitary leaders being brought to trial in connection with the rapes is slim. On 5 October, the U.S. forces organized a press conference for FRAPH's leader, Emmanuel Constant. "They gave him the sound system, brought him in a U.S. vehicle, protected him while he spoke, and drove him away at the end," said Coriolon. A reporter from *Haiti Info*, a Port-au-Prince-based newsletter, asked U.S. embassy spokesman Stanley Schrager how he (and Clinton) could call FRAPH

---

3. As of August 2000 Emmanuel Constant continues to live in Queens, N.Y., a free man. The U.S. government refuses to extradite him. —ED.

"terrorist" and "antidemocratic" one day and protect their leader the next? "Life's bizarre...things change all the time," said Schrager, explaining that the U.S. now considers FRAPH a legitimate political party. The 24 October issue of the *Nation* was more enlightening: It revealed that the CIA had been instrumental in setting up the paramilitary group and that Constant was on their payroll at the time of the coup.

Business as Usual?

As the news crews started leaving Haiti, businessmen began arriving. At the airport on 21 October, an English engineer was heard explaining to a customs official that his company had plans for him to stay six months. "Haiti's open for business," announced the *Miami Herald* less than a month after 15 October. Haitian commerce minister Louis Dejoie assured U.S. executives that "Haiti is going to roll out the red carpet," at a conference in Miami.

To the women of SOFA, the revival of business as usual in Haiti means a return for women (the majority of industrial workers) to the subpoverty Haitian wage ($.14/hr.). Plans from Aristide's first term in office to double the minimum wage have been abandoned. According to the *Multinational Monitor*, Aristide's administration gave in to pressure from the World Bank and the International Monetary Fund on that issue before August of 1994. Now an estimated $800 million in multilateral (mostly U.S.) aid has been promised to Haiti, and local people suspect there are some strings attached. To Jane Regan of *Haiti Info*, the massive influx of money slated for "selections assistance" and "stability" is tantamount to an "invisible invasion." "The intent of many of these programs," writes Regan, "is to counter the democratic and popular movement's demands for radical economic change and social justice."

It's our responsibility," says Vivian Stromberg, executive director of MADRE, "to not let the U.S. presence redirect Haitian democracy. If we're serious about meeting the needs of people, we have to be serious about supporting the organizations they themselves have set up to respond to those needs. We have to listen to the Haitians."

Listening Up

The day before the MADRE group returned to New York, they listened. At the appointed site for testimony collection, a kindergarten in a popular neighborhood called Martissant, MADRE workers were greeted by dozens of small children in blue-bib uniforms. As they walked into the whitewashed building, Nancy Kelly said she was expecting to see a handful of women, perhaps five or six, inside. But behind the classroom door, on tiny kiddie-chairs, their knees bent almost to their ears, twenty-three women sat waiting.

Kelly reminded the Haitians, again, there was no insurance that adding their testimonies to the OAS complaint would have any direct result. "It's especially unlikely that any damages or compensation would ever come your way.... But the Haitian women have a lot to teach. Women have played a key role here and could play a key role internationally if your cases convince the OAS to recognize the severity of rape."

Despite the risks, the women testified in detail, describing their attackers, streets, dates, times of day. Some had been raped in front of their children, some alone; some in their own homes, some in abandoned shacks. Some had been forced to submit in order to protect their kids. Geraldine told her story, angry but confident that change was on its way. The woman in the kerchief told hers: she hadn't been political, she said, but everyone knew she supported Aristide, "because I talked about him all the time." The last testimony came from a fifteen-year-old with the family name of "Darling"— a tiny, stick-boned child clutching a piece of chalk in her right hand. Her mother, big eyes welling in a smooth, walnut-colored face, leaned toward her, hands reaching out for her daughter's. By the end, both mother and daughter, and also translator, reporter, and all the women from MADRE were in tears. The tragedy of the tale was one thing; more moving even than the stories was the women's courage to talk.

Part Three

WOMEN AND
THE U.S. MILITARY

The question of how in wartime ordinary men become killers and rapists lies behind all of these chapters. Military training is one of the keys. In U.S. military basic training, young recruits are taught marching chants that denigrate women and children; in this way the new soldiers are encouraged to think of themselves as a group apart from civilians and as part of a special, heroic man's world. Typical cadences are:

> Cindy, Cindy, Cindy Lou,
> Love my rifle more than you.

> You used to be my beauty queen,
> Now I love my M-16.

From the Vietnam War came:

> See the women beside the river,
> Washin' clothes and cookin' dinner.
> Pick one out and watch her quiver,
> Yo, Oh! Napalm, it sticks to kids.

> See the baby in its mother's arms,
> Ain't never done no one no harm.
> Barbecue baby ain't got no charm,
> Yo, Oh! Napalm, it sticks to kids.

> A-4 flyin' into the sun
> Droppin' Napalm on everyone.
> If she's pregnant it's two for one
> And Napalm sticks to kids.

Perhaps the best-known chant, based on sexual innuendo, is one that has crossed all service lines:

> This is my rifle; this is my gun.
> This is for fighting; this is for fun.[1]

In chapter 11 a legal scholar investigates what kind of training U.S. military personnel receive that shapes their attitudes toward women. The article concludes that an entire culture of antiwoman references has been created and in a highly nuanced discussion asks if breaking down the all-male nature of the military world would civilize it. Chapter 12 describes in detail the U.S. military's answer to the problem the Japanese solved with comfort stations: in order to satisfy sexual needs, the U.S. government contracted with South Korea to provide the vast official brothels found around U.S. bases there today. Rather than focus on the soldiers, however, this chapter centers on the women themselves—and concludes that there is less difference than one might think between forced and "voluntary" prostitution.

---

1. Carol Burke, "Marching to Vietnam," *Journal of American Folklore* 102 (October/ December 1989): 424–40.

11

In War and Peace

Rape, War, and Military Culture

MADELINE MORRIS

Frequently throughout the history of warfare, widespread rape has been associated with war. It has been alleged in recent years that rape and sexual assault by military personnel in peacetime also constitute problems of substantial magnitude. This article examines the relationship between sexual assault, combat, and military organizations. Toward that end, the article compares military rape rates with civilian rates in peace as well as in war.

The research conducted for this article indicates that the peacetime rates of rape by American military personnel are actually lower (controlling for age and gender) than civilian rates. However, the data also indicate that while military rates of violent crime other than rape are very substantially lower than civilian rates, military rape rates are only somewhat lower than civilian rates. A similar phenomenon is also reflected in the wartime data collected: While military rates of other violent crime were roughly equivalent to civilian rates, military rape rates in the combat theater studied climbed to several times civilian rates. Thus, in both the peacetime and the wartime contexts studied, a rape differential exists: The ratio of military rape rates to civilian rape rates is substantially larger than the ratio of military rates to civilian rates of other violent crime.

The existence of a military rape differential in war and in peace suggests that it may be possible to reduce military rape rates, perhaps bringing them into line with military rates of other violent crime. After demonstrating the existence and magnitude of the military rape differential, this article considers the possible causes of that differential and suggests policy directions that might contribute to a reduction in military rape rates.

Rape by Military Personnel

Rape by military personnel occurs in the two very different contexts of war and peace. It is commonly assumed that the pervasiveness of rape in war results in some way from the nature of war itself: "War is hell," and one of its concomitants is rape. But this *c'est la guerre* view of rape in war may in fact hide more than it reveals. As is examined below, influences particular to military populations appear to affect the incidence of rape by military personnel in peacetime as well as in war.

This article attempts to make some meaningful comparison of the rape incidence of military and civilian populations. Toward that end, this study compares the rates of offenses committed by male U.S. military personnel and civilians in peacetime and during World War II.

To provide a context in which the rape data may be viewed more meaningfully, data on violent crimes other than rape will be considered together with the rape rate comparisons. Thus, the crimes considered in both the peacetime and wartime studies are murder/nonnegligent manslaughter (murder/nn.m), aggravated assault, and forcible rape. The raw data for both the peacetime and wartime studies are drawn from the U.S. Federal Bureau of Investigation's (FBI) Uniform Crime Reports (UCR) for civilian crime statistics and from the archives of each military service for military crime statistics. All crime rate comparisons are for males only and control for the age structures of the civilian and military populations.

The Peacetime Study

The results of the peacetime (1987–92) study are as follows.[1] First, the rates of violent crime are *lower*, controlling for age, among the male military than among the male civilian population. This is true of rape as well as of the other violent crimes studied. Second, however, the difference between military rape rates and civilian rape rates is smaller—*several times smaller*—than the difference between military and civilian rates of the other violent crimes. In other words, military rape rates are diminished far less from civilian levels than are military rates of other violent crimes.

To simplify presentation, I have combined the murder/nn.m and aggravated assault data into an index of "other-violent-crime." (The index is constituted by adding the raw numbers of murder/nn.m and aggravated assault per year in each military service and dividing by the number of male personnel in that service to establish a rate of other violent crime for each service.) Table 1 shows the extent to which military diminution

---

1. The "peacetime" period studied is 1987–92. Of course, that period includes January and February of 1991, during which there was active fighting in the Persian Gulf War. That combat period, however, had no discernible effect on the relevant crime rates.

Table 1
The Peacetime Rape Differential
(yearly averages for 1987–92)

	Army	Navy	Marine Corps	Air Force
Other-Violent-Crime Ratio	.18	.04	.05	.02
Rape Ratio	.47	.19	.20	.20
Rape Differential	2.62	4.95	5.63	10.74

in rates of other violent crime from civilian levels exceeds military diminution in rape rates from civilian levels, controlling for age and gender. The "other-violent-crime ratio" is the ratio of military other-violent-crime rates to civilian other-violent-crime rates. The "rape ratio" is the ratio of military rape rates to civilian rape rates. And the "rape differential" is the multiple by which the rape ratio exceeds the other-violent-crime ratio.

Regression analyses performed on these peacetime data determined that for each military service, the difference between the diminution of rape and diminution of other violent crime was statistically significant. Thus, although the particulars differ among the different services, all of the services show the same overall pattern of diminishing all violent crime rates, including rape, from civilian levels, but diminishing rape rates significantly *less* than the rates of other violent crime.

The Wartime Study

Study of military and civilian crime rates during the World War II period provides a measurement of rape incidence in the combat context.[2] The results of the World War II study suggest that a differential between military rates of rape and of other violent crime exists in war as well as in peace. In the war context, military rape rates in the combat theater studied rose far *above* civilian levels, while rates of other violent crime did not.

---

2. World War II was chosen for study because it is the most recent war, other than Vietnam, for which data were available in which the United States was engaged for a prolonged period *and* in which troops had extensive contact with civilians. The Korean War was not chosen for study because of difficulty in obtaining relevant data. Vietnam was not chosen for study because its levels of low troop morale, particularly during the latter part of the war, would presumably influence crime rates. The Persian Gulf War was not chosen because troops' contact with civilians in the Persian Gulf was limited.

Of course, because rape incidence and reporting are affected by societal factors that change over time, comparisons between 1940s wartime and contemporary peacetime rape statistics would be impracticable. The point of the present study, however, is not to compare rates or measure trends across time. Rather, this study seeks to compare military and civilian rates—first within one time period (1944–45) and then within another (1987–92). Thus, the focus is on the military/civilian comparison within a *given* (1940s or 1980s) time period. For that reason, societal changes over time should not unduly influence the comparison.

Comparisons with U.S. male civilian rape rates were made for U.S. Army forces in the continental European Theater of Operations (ETO). As in the peacetime study, all crime rate comparisons are for males only and control for the age structures of the civilian and military populations.

During the two breakouts in the ETO, in France during August and September 1944 and in Germany during March and April 1945, the incidence of violent crime (murder/nn.m, aggravated assault, and rape) among ETO troops rose dramatically. But the ETO rape rates increased *far* more than the rates of aggravated assault or murder/nn.m.

Specifically, during the breakout across France in August and September 1944, the average monthly ETO murder/nn.m rate was about half (47 percent) of the U.S. civilian rate, and the average monthly ETO aggravated assault rate was about one-sixth (18 percent) of the U.S. civilian rate.

The relative crime rate pattern during the breakout into Germany was very similar to the pattern during the breakout across France. The rates of all three types of crimes examined rose to even higher levels during the German breakout than during the French breakout. But the *relative* relationship of the three crime rates was strikingly similar in the two periods: In each instance, the increase in rape was far greater than the increase in either murder/nn.m or aggravated assault. During the same period, the ETO rape rate was nearly three times (260 percent) the U.S. civilian rate. During the period of the breakout across Germany (March and April 1945), the average monthly ETO murder/nn.m rate was essentially equivalent (102 percent) to the U.S. civilian rate, and the average monthly ETO aggravated assault rate was about one-quarter (27 percent) of the civilian rate. During the same period, the ETO rape rate was nearly four times (366 percent) the civilian rate.[3]

A differential between military rape rates and rates of other violent crime thus exists both in peace and in war. In peacetime, military rape rates are reduced significantly less from civilian levels than are rates of other violent crime. In wartime, military rape rates are increased far more above civilian levels than are rates of other violent crime. The section that follows explores the possible causes of this military rape differential.

The Rape Differential: Causes and Culture

Reporting Factors

In analyzing crime statistics, one must consider the possibility that disparities in reporting patterns and record-keeping practices may distort findings. It

---

3. The figures in these two paragraphs reflect calculations based on data drawn from the UCR and the criminal justice records of the U.S. Army in the ETO. For methodological and source information, see Madeline Morris, "By Force of Arms: Rape, War, and Military Culture," published *Duke Law Journal* 45 (1996): 775–81.

seems unlikely, however, that the rape differential observed in the peacetime or the wartime study is attributable to higher rape reporting rates in military populations than in civilian populations or to record-keeping disparities. As stated in the 1990 *Update Report on the Progress of Women in the Navy,* regarding the authors' study of rape and sexual assault of Navy personnel: "The majority of staff level advisors interviewed perceive that most female victims would not report a rape. In the Study Group survey, only one out of ten females who said they had been raped or assaulted in the past year said they reported it to the police or Master at Arms."[4] Another reason to believe that the military rape figures used in the peacetime study are estimated as conservatively as the civilian figures involves the definition of the crime. The definition of rape applied by the U.S. military until October 1992 *excluded* marital rape while civilian statistics for that time period would have included some marital rapes.

In considering the World War II crime figures, we must bear in mind that they probably do reflect substantial undercounting of all three crimes. There is no reason to believe, however, that the rape statistics are more complete than those for murder or aggravated assault. Indeed, there are reasons to draw the opposite conclusion. Rape is particularly likely to have been undercounted because it is less serious than murder, it is reputedly the most underreported violent crime even in the domestic context,[5] and it was perpetrated in the ETO virtually exclusively against non-Americans[6] who might have been less inclined or less able to report crimes to American authorities. In addition, some substantial number of rapes in the ETO were investigated by agencies other than the Criminal Investigation Branch of the provost marshal's office—for example, by investigating officers appointed by commanders.[7] Reports handled by such other agencies would not appear in official statistics of investigations. Thus, it is extremely unlikely that the ETO rape statistics are more complete than those for the other violent crimes. Therefore, even while acknowledging counting problems, we may still place some reliance on the official counts for purposes of comparing the *relative* patterns or incidence of the three offenses in the ETO.

Demographic Variables

As we consider what factors may contribute to the rape differential, the first point to be acknowledged is that while the peacetime and wartime

4. *Navy Women's Study Group, 1990: An Update Report on the Progress of Women in the Navy* (Washington, D.C.: Chief of Naval Operations, 1991).

5. Ibid., 111–29.

6. Office of the Judge Advocate General, Department of War, *History of the Judge Advocate General's Office in the European Theater, 18 July 1942–1 November 1945* (Washington, D.C.: Office of the Judge Advocate General, 1945), chart 16.

7. Ibid., 249.

studies conducted for this article control for age and gender, additional demographic factors that are not controlled for may account for part of the variance observed. Additional variables that might usefully be controlled for in further studies include race, education, income, social disorganization, and geographic region. The relevant question in connection with those additional variables would be whether any of them *differentially* affects rates of rape as compared with rates of other violent crime so as to account for the military rape differential.

Preliminary examination of the race variable suggests that it would *not* help to account for the military rape differential for the following reasons. African Americans constitute a higher proportion of the American military population than of the civilian population.[8] For the period 1987–92, the rate of arrest for rape for African Americans was 6.36 times that for whites.[9] During the same period, blacks' murder/nn.m arrest rate was 9.37 times that of whites.[10] Therefore, the fact that the military has a higher percentage of African Americans than the civilian population would be expected to increase the military's murder rates somewhat more than its rape rates. Yet the finding to be accounted for is the opposite: Military murder/nn.m rates are *diminished* more than military rape rates. The aggravated assault arrest rate for blacks in 1987–92 was 5.04 times that of whites compared to a rape arrest rate 6.36 times that of whites.[11] A race variable thus might account for some, but very little, of the observed military rape differential with regard to aggravated assault. This preliminary examination suggests that introduction of a race variable would contribute very little to an explanation of the observed military rape differential.

No data comparable to the race data described above are available for the education, income, social disorganization, and geographic region variables. Further research will therefore be required in order to offer even preliminary suggestions regarding the possible effects of those additional variables on the military rape differential.

One additional demographic factor, the percentage of population married, would be of particular relevance to a "sexual deprivation" theory of the military rape differential. The sexual deprivation theory would propose

---

8. Martin Binkin, *Who Will Fight the Next War?* (Washington, D.C.: Brookings Institution, 1993), 61–101.

9. FBI, U.S. Department of Justice, *Crime in the United States: UCR 182* (Washington, D.C.: U.S. Government Printing Office, 1987); *Crime in the United States: UCR 186* (Washington, D.C.: U.S. Government Printing Office, 1988); *Crime in the United States: UCR 190* (Washington, D.C.: U.S. Government Printing Office, 1989); *Crime in the United States: UCR 192* (Washington, D.C.: U.S. Government Printing Office, 1990); *Crime in the United States: UCR 231* (Washington, D.C.: U.S. Government Printing Office, 1991); *Crime in the United States: UCR 235* (Washington, D.C.: U.S. Government Printing Office, 1992).

10. Ibid.

11. Ibid.

that military rape rates are elevated relative to military rates of other violent crime because, whereas military personnel have as much or more opportunity than civilians to express any *aggressive* impulses they might have (for instance, in combat practice), military personnel's sexual opportunities are more limited than those of civilians. Certainly, personnel on ships at sea or in other remote locations may have severely limited sexual opportunities. Moreover, men stationed on military bases on the American mainland—including those who live off base—may have more limited heterosexual opportunities than most male civilians, if only because the sex ratios of the base and surrounding areas are disproportionately male. One might hypothesize that, for these reasons, military populations' rates of sexual aggression would be high relative to their rates of other forms of violent crime. The suggestion here is not the simplistic one that "men must have sex" and will rape if "deprived" of sex. Rather, what is envisioned is a more complex dynamic in which sexual rejection may be more frequent for males in a sex-skewed environment such as would obtain, for instance, around some military bases, leading over time to frustration and anger and to various undesirable outcomes, perhaps including rape.[12]

This sexual-deprivation explanation for the rape differential may account for some of the variance observed, but it seems unlikely to contribute substantially to an explanation of the phenomenon for several reasons. First, the limited research that has been done on the subject does not indicate that skewed sex ratios affect rape rates.[13]

A second factor that detracts from the potential explanatory force of a sexual-deprivation explanation of the military rape differential is the ready availability of prostitution in the vicinity of military installations.[14] The easy

---

12. Related to the "sexual deprivation" explanation for the rape differential is the possible effect on military rape rates of the exclusion of gays from the military. If the percentage of gays is lower in the military than in the civilian population, then perhaps the percentage of potential rapists of women is higher in the military than in the civilian population. (This proposition rests on the untested hypothesis that gay men rape women at a lower rate than do heterosexual men.) The possibly lower percentage of gays in the military than in the civilian population could thus explain some part of the military rape differential. We cannot know, of course, what proportion (if any) of the rape differential is accounted for by this factor because we do not know whether or to what extent the proportion of gay males in the military is actually lower than the proportion of gay males in the civilian population, and we do not know whether or to what extent gay men are less likely than heterosexual men to rape women. Rape of males is excluded from the present study because it was not defined as "rape" under military law prior to 1992 (see 10 U.S.C. §920 [1994]; amending 10 U.S.C. §920 [1988]), and so it does not appear in the available military crime statistics.

13. See, e.g., Manachem Amir, *Patterns in Forcible Rape* (Chicago: University of Chicago Press, 1971), 63–68; Larry Baron and Murray A. Straus, "Four Theories of Rape: A Macrosociological Analysis," *Social Problems* 34 (1987): 481–82.

14. See generally Helen Reynolds, *The Economics of Prostitution* (Springfield, Ill.: C. C. Thomas, 1986); Saundra P. Sturdevant and Brenda Stoltzfus, *Let the Good Times Roll: Prostitution and the U.S. Military in Asia* (New York: New Press, 1992); Charles M. Winick and

access to prostitutes that is typical of the areas surrounding military installations means that an individual lacking other sexual opportunities would have a sexual outlet short of rape that would be preferable to rape both in ease of access and in safety from harsh legal consequences. Still, some proportion of men experiencing a scarcity of sexual opportunity presumably do not go to prostitutes—and some subset of that group may commit rape.

The consistent availability of prostitution together with the lack of support in the research on skewed sex ratios for a sexual deprivation theory of the rape differential suggests that some explanation other than or in addition to sexual deprivation is required to provide a full explanation for the military rape differential.

Male Groups

Another possible explanation for the military rape differential is that all-male groups (especially *young* all-male groups), military or otherwise, have a tendency toward rape proneness. The problem with this avenue of explanation is the apparent existence of counterexamples. There is no evidence that all or most boys' schools, men's clubs, or all-male seminaries and yeshivas have elevated rape rates.[15] While some genres of all-male group may exhibit an elevated tendency to rape (for example, some fraternities or street gangs), it does not appear that all do. Therefore, an adequate explanation of the pattern of military rape rates cannot be based solely on the fact that military organizations have been virtually all-male groups.

Self-Selection

An alternative explanation for the pattern of military rape rates would focus on self-selection. The hypothesis here would be that those who self-select for military service are disproportionately rape prone. This hypothesis too would be flawed. First, it would not explain the patterns of military rape and other violent crime during World War II, when the army was largely conscripted. Second, it would require some elaboration of why individuals who choose to enter military service are disproportionately prone to commit rape as opposed to other violent crimes. Thus, if self-selection contributes at all to the explanation of patterns of military rape rates, it must be as part of a larger explanation.

L. M. Kinsie, *The Lively Commerce: Prostitution in the United States* (Chicago: Quadrangle Books, 1971).

15. Mary Koss, telephone interview by author, July 1994; Susan Roth, telephone interview by author, 17 November 1994; Leslie Lebowitz, telephone interview by author, 17 November 1994.

Biological Factors

Yet another explanation of the military rape differential would rest on the hypothesis that biological factors exert an upward pressure on rape rates but not (or not as much) on rates of other violent crime. The argument regarding military rape rates would be that if there is a particular biological impetus to rape, then we might expect rape rates to be more amenable to increase (such as in war) and less amenable to reduction (such as in peacetime military service) than the rates of other violent crime.

Some sociobiologists do maintain that there is a sex-linked genetic disposition to rape among human males.[16] But sociobiological theories of crime generally posit biological influences underlying a broad range of aggressive behaviors, including not only rape but also, for instance, homicide and assault.[17] Therefore, a view that biological forces reduce the malleability of rape rates *more* than the malleability of other violent crime rates would go beyond the claims currently made even by sociobiology and would be highly speculative at this time.

A related and intriguing avenue of possible explanation for the military rape differential is that there exists a psychosexual linkage—perhaps biologically based, perhaps not—between violence and sexuality, such that training in and focus on deployment of violence, as occur in the military, would tend to foster *sexual* aggression.[18] Again, the state of the science in this area makes this avenue of explanation necessarily speculative.[19] Nonetheless, biological or other psychosexual factors linking sexuality and violence might indeed account for some part of the phenomenon in question.

While biological or related psychosexual factors may account for some part of the military rape differential, it is undisputed that biology is, at most, only one contributing factor determining the rape incidence of individuals, groups, and societies. As sociobiologist E. O. Wilson stated, "[While] genes hold culture on a leash[, t]he leash is very long."[20] Environmental factors bearing on individual psychology, group dynamics, and societal structure and culture all are widely recognized to be influential in determining the rape incidence of individuals, groups, and societies—notwithstanding the

---

16. See Lee Ellis, *Theories of Rape: Inquiries into the Causes of Sexual Aggression* (New York: Hemisphere, 1989), 14–16.

17. See generally John Klama, *Aggression: The Myth of the Beast Within* (New York: Wiley, 1988), 147–48.

18. See Dolf Zillmann, *Connections between Sex and Aggression* (Hillsdale, N.J.: Lawrence Erlbaum Associates, 1984).

19. Ibid., 15–17.

20. Edward O. Wilson, *On Human Nature* (Cambridge: Harvard University Press, 1978), 167.

effects of possible biological influences.[21] While a biological approach may thus partly explain the military rape differential and may warrant further exploration, this approach, like the other explanations discussed above, is unlikely to account for *all* of the variance observed.

Legal Factors

A crucial aspect of an analysis of possible causes contributing to the rape differential is an examination of the law relating to rape by military personnel. If the legal deterrents to rape were different in the military and civilian contexts, then it would not be surprising if there were a resultant differential in the rape rates of those two populations. The following analysis explores whether differences between the civilian criminal justice system and the military justice system may contribute to the military rape differential.

American military law governing the handling of rape by military personnel is comparable to civilian law in its substantive aspects, but possibly less stringent than civilian law in its procedural requirements and actual implementation. Shortcomings in the relevant military procedures and enforcement provisions may be contributing factors in an explanation of the military rape differential. Measures to identify procedural flaws and to bolster enforcement practices are considered below.

The statute under which rapes are prosecuted within the military justice system is similar in its definition of rape to the rape statutes of most American civilian jurisdictions. The military statute provides that "[a]ny person ... who commits an act of sexual intercourse, by force and without consent, is guilty of rape." The sentence provided for rape under the Uniform Code of Military Justice (UCMJ) is "death or such other punishment as a court-martial may direct."[22] By regulation, that UCMJ provision is interpreted to mean *life imprisonment* or such other punishment as a court martial may direct for all rapes, except those in which the victim is under the age of twelve or in which the accused maimed or attempted to kill the victim; the death penalty may be imposed in those cases.[23] The substantive

---

21. See, e.g., Amir, *Patterns in Forcible Rape*, 43–125; A. Nicholas Groth, *Men Who Rape: The Psychology of the Offender* (New York: Plenum Press, 1979), 12–83; Jean S. MacKellar, *Rape: The Bait and the Trap* (New York: Crown, 1975), 68–78, 129–33.

22. 10 U.S.C. §920 (1984).

23. *Manual for Court Martials, United States* (Washington, D.C.: U.S. Government Printing Office, 1984), Rule 1004(c)(9).

Unfortunately, meaningful statistics on the military sentences *actually* imposed for rape are unavailable because of the nature of military sentencing procedures. Military courts do not impose separate sentences for each count of which a defendant is convicted. Rather, one sentence is imposed for all the counts of which the defendant is convicted at a particular trial. For example, in 1991–92, for trials resulting in convictions of which rape was the most serious count, the median sentence in the Navy was five years and in the Marine Corps was thirteen years; however, those number are largely uninterpretable because the sentences might have included

military law defining rape thus is comparable to civilian law on the subject, and the potential sentences are as severe or more severe than those applicable to civilians.

The procedural framework governing the handling of rape by military personnel may be somewhat more problematic. Reports of rape by military personnel are to be forwarded by the military personnel or agency receiving the report to the immediate commander of the suspect (or to a law enforcement or investigative agency if no suspect is identified).[24] That immediate commander is then required to make a preliminary inquiry into the alleged offense.[25] At this stage, the commander generally should refer the case to the service's criminal investigative department (CID) pursuant to a regulation stating that "in serious...cases the commander should consider whether to seek the assistance of law enforcement personnel in conducting any inquiry or further investigation."[26] Assuming that a case is referred to CID, an investigative report is then sent back to the commander who, usually in consultation with Judge Advocate General Corps personnel, decides whether to bring a charge of rape against the suspect.[27] An Article Thirty-two investigation, the military analog to a grand jury proceeding, is then convened to determine whether there is sufficient evidence to warrant referring the charge to a court martial.[28]

Provisions intended to ensure adequate enforcement also are in place. Article Ninety-eight of the UCMJ provides that "[a]ny person...who (1) is responsible for unnecessary delay in the disposition of any case of a person accused of an offense...shall be punished as a court-martial may direct."[29] The UCMJ also provides for the processing and redress of complaints by "[a]ny member of the armed forces who believes himself wronged by his commanding officer."[30] Such wrongs presumably would include failure to process a rape complaint properly.

Notwithstanding these provisions intended to ensure enforcement, there is anecdotal evidence of failure to enforce military rape laws, including fail-

---

punishment for multiple crimes, all prosecuted in the same trial (see Capt. W. F. Grant Jr., Chief Trial Judge, U.S. Navy, letter to author, 15 June 1995 [on file with author]).

24. *Manual for Court Martials*, Rule 301.

25. Ibid., Rule 303.

26. Ibid.

27. Ibid., Rules 306–7.

28. Ibid., Rule 405.

Any plea bargaining with regard to sentencing normally occurs in the period between the conclusion of the Article Thirty-two investigation and the commencement of trial. Plea bargaining as to the *crime charged* is rare in the military justice system, in contrast with the civilian sector where pleas to a lesser charge are common (see Col. Scott Silliman, U.S.A.F. (Ret.), former Staff Judge Advocate, Air Combat Command, interview by author, Durham, N.C., 14 October 1994).

29. 10 U.S.C. §898 (1994).

30. 10 U.S.C. §938 (1994).

ures to investigate, to keep records, and to preserve evidence.[31] Witnesses at Senate hearings in 1992 testified that such failures are common.[32] Other than anecdotal evidence, there are currently no data available to evaluate the nature or extent of failures to enforce military rape law (much less to compare military enforcement with civilian enforcement).

Certainly, commanders have discretion in the processing of rape complaints, especially in the early stages of the process, such as the preliminary inquiry. That discretion could be misused to divert cases from prosecution or otherwise to extend inappropriate leniency. If there is, in fact, a laxity in the enforcement of military laws against rape, then that weakness would be expected to reduce the efficacy of that law in deterring rape. Such a lack of deterrence would be expected to increase military rape rates and therefore could constitute an important element contributing to the rape differential.

Implementation of a thoroughgoing system of record keeping, tracking all military rape allegations from their initial report to final disposition and compiling those data in a central data bank, would be valuable both in encouraging enforcement and in allowing for identification of procedural flaws or enforcement problems in the handling of rape within the military justice system. Careful record keeping and oversight both would tend to improve enforcement directly (simply by increasing the visibility of the handling of cases) and would assist in identification of any problems in enforcement procedures. Legislation instituting such centralized record keeping and oversight of military sexual misconduct cases has been proposed in the past, but none has been adopted to date.

American military law, then, appears to be comparable to civilian law in its substantive aspects but may be less stringent in its actual implementation. If military enforcement mechanisms are in fact comparatively weak, then a resulting reduction in deterrence might explain some part of the military rape differential. Improved oversight in this area is warranted in order to identify and correct any patterns of enforcement failure.

The other body of law governing rape by military personnel is international law. International law clearly criminalizes rape by military personnel.[33] There is, however, evidence that international law's prohibitions of

---

31. See, e.g., Senate Committee on Veterans' Affairs, *The Counseling and Other Needs of Women Veterans Who Were Sexually Assaulted or Harassed While on Active Duty and VA's Ability to Respond, Hearings before the Senate Committee on Veterans' Affairs,* 102d Cong., 2d sess., 1992, Danis at 12–14; Ortiz at 24; Franco at 34; Molly Moore, "Navy Failed to Prosecute in 6 Rapes; Probe Finds Laxity on Sex Offenses at Florida Base," *Washington Post,* 22 October 1990, A1; Jeff Nesmith, "Military Courts Often Fail to Deal with Rape Charges: Leniency Is Common as Commanders Use Their Discretion to Punish Offenders," *Orange County Register,* 4 October 1995, A14.

32. See, e.g., Senate Committee on Veterans' Affairs, *The Counseling and Other Needs of Women Veterans,* Danis at 12–14; Ortiz at 24; Franco at 34.

33. See Morris, "By Force of Arms," 685–86 n. 108.

rape have been even less subject to enforcement than have other provisions of international criminal law.[34] Nonetheless, to date, international criminal law relating to military personnel has been so rarely enforced—whether regarding rape, murder, assault, or otherwise—that it seems unlikely that *differential* enforcement of *international* provisions accounts for any significant part of the rape differential.

The proposition that underenforcement of international criminal law probably contributes little to an explanation of the rape differential should not be taken to suggest that international criminal law could not contribute in the future to a reduction of rape by military personnel. There are indications that the enforcement of international criminal law relating to military personnel may improve considerably in the coming years. Within the past five years, we have witnessed the establishment of international criminal tribunals for the former Yugoslavia and Rwanda, and the establishment of a permanent international criminal court is becoming an ever more real possibility. The establishment of such tribunals for the adjudication of international crimes would be expected to contribute substantially to enforcement of international criminal law, including the enforcement of international law prohibiting rape. Thus, international criminal law may have the potential to become a real factor in the deterrence of crime, including rape, by military personnel. But the influences of international criminal justice probably contribute little to an explanation of the existing military rape differential.

Thus, flaws in the enforcement of domestic law governing rape by military personnel may account for some part of the rape differential and may require the remedial steps discussed above. In contrast, the current shortcomings of international criminal law enforcement probably do not contribute significantly to an explanation of the rape differential observed.

In sum, many of the explanations that might at first appear to account for the military rape differential must be rejected partially or entirely upon closer examination. There is, however, a promising avenue of explanation focusing on environmental factors specific to the military.

Military Culture

This avenue of explanation for the military rape differential rests largely on an interpretation of military culture as follows: There are conditions of military life and lifestyle that inhibit and diminish rates of violent crime including rape, but there are other conditions in military life that tend to re-elevate rape rates. The factors minimizing military violent crime would include a structured and controlled lifestyle, often with greater surveillance of one's

---

34. Ibid., 686–87 n. 109.

activities than in civilian life; fewer opportunities for many kinds of crime (especially for personnel living on base); a population that excludes past felons;[35] a reduced incidence of drug abuse;[36] and a close-knit social organization that generally imparts and enforces anticrime norms. These factors would contribute to a diminution in violent crime by military personnel in peacetime and, to a lesser extent, even in the combat context.

What may explain the lesser minimizing effect of these factors on military rape rates is that even while those crime-inhibiting pressures are being exerted on all violent crime including rape, countervailing factors in military culture tend to push the rape rate—but not the rates of other violent crime—back *up*. The following, in brief, are the cultural influences that may tend to re-elevate military rape rates. When a closely bonded group (a "primary group") shares group norms conducive to rape, the risk of rape by group members is increased. Norms conducive to rape include certain normative attitudes toward masculinity, toward sexuality, and toward women.[37] There exists substantial evidence that primary groups in the U.S. military often do share rape-conducive norms, including norms relating to the meaning of masculinity, and to sexual and gender relations.[38] These features of military culture—primary group bonding and rape-conducive norms—may tend to increase military rape rates but not military rates of other violent crime. These features may, thus, contribute significantly to the military rape differential.

This avenue of explanation for the rape differential may be briefly elaborated as follows. Properly functioning military units are primary groups. They share with other primary groups the central characteristic of personal, affective bonding along with the frequent concomitants of separation from external bonds, initiation requirements, and ideological components.[39] The primary group bonds of the military unit begin forming in basic training and are most intense in the combat context.[40] Because primary groups entail strong bonds that are emotionally central to the individual, primary group norms are particularly influential in shaping their members' attitudes and behaviors.[41]

Social science research conducted over several decades has identified a specific set of gender and sexual norms and attitudes that appears to be

---

35. 10 U.S.C. §504 (1994).

36. Eric Schmitt, "Military Struggling to Stem an Increase in Family Violence," *New York Times*, 23 May 1994, A1, A12.

37. Morris, "By Force of Arms," 701–6.

38. Ibid., 706–31.

39. Ibid., 692–98.

40. Ibid.

41. Dexter C. Dunphy, *The Primary Group: A Handbook for Analysis and Field Research* (New York: Appleton-Century-Crofts, 1972), 40–79.

conducive to rape. This set includes certain attitudes toward masculinity, toward sexuality, and toward women.

Particular attitudes toward masculinity have been found to be related to heightened levels of rape propensity. Standards of masculinity that emphasize dominance, assertiveness, aggressiveness, independence, self-sufficiency, and willingness to take risks and that reject characteristics such as compassion, understanding, and sensitivity have been found to be correlated with rape propensity.[42]

In addition to attitudes toward masculinity, certain attitudes toward sexuality too have been found to be associated with heightened rape propensity. "Adversarial sexual beliefs," the view that sexual relationships are inherently exploitative—that each party seeks to benefit without regard for the other, and will use manipulation and deceit for the purpose—are associated with heightened rape propensity.[43] "Sexual promiscuity," a high emphasis on sexuality and, in particular, a high number of sexual partners, also has been found to be correlated with high levels of sexual aggression.[44] Numerous studies have also found that "rape-myth acceptance" too is associated with rape propensity. Rape myths are "prejudicial, stereotyped, or false beliefs about rape, rape victims, and rapists."[45] Examples of rape myths would include, for instance, the belief that women enjoy being raped. Belief in rape myths has been shown consistently to be strongly associated with sexual aggression and with self-reported likelihood to rape.[46]

In addition to attitudes toward masculinity and sexuality, attitudes acceptant of violence against women also bear a relationship to rape propensity.[47] Finally, not only attitudes specifically toward *violence* against women but also attitudes toward women more generally influence rape propensity. "Hostility toward women" is a measure designed to reflect attitudes of distrust, anger, alienation, and resentment toward women. Such attitudes would include beliefs that most women are deceitful, that women flirt to tease or hurt men, that women will take advantage of men who do not stand up to them, and the like. Several studies have found correlations between hostility toward women and sexual aggression against women.[48]

Similarly, sex-role stereotyping generally—regarding occupational, familial, and social roles—also has been found to be associated with rape

---

42. Morris, "By Force of Arms," 701–6.
43. Ibid.
44. Ibid.
45. Martha Burt, "Cultural Myths and Supports for Rape," *Journal of Personality and Social Psychology* 28 (1980): 217.
46. Morris, "By Force of Arms," 701–6.
47. Ibid.
48. Ibid.

propensity, at least in the contemporary American context. Such sex-role stereotypes would include views that women should not do men's work, nor men do women's work, that a man is the head of the household, that women should take a passive role in courtship, and the like. Numerous studies using a variety of measures of sex-role stereotyping have found a correlation between stereotypic attitudes concerning gender roles and rape incidence or proclivity.[49]

Like other primary groups, primary groups in the military develop and enforce group norms. And, like the sets of norms developed in other primary groups, the sets of norms in military primary groups include norms about gender and sexuality.

The sexual and gender norms imparted to members entering the U.S. armed forces, at present, are inadvertently comprised largely of the sort associated with heightened rape propensity. The rape-conducive attitudinal constellation including elements of hypermasculinity, adversarial sexual beliefs, promiscuity, rape-myth acceptance, and hostility toward women is reflected in various ways in military culture. It is also important to note, however, that the U.S. military is in some ways in a state of transition regarding gender. Women are now participating in greater numbers and in a broader range of roles than has been true traditionally. And, within very recent years (particularly in the wake of Tailhook '91), especial efforts have been made by military leaders to eliminate sexual harassment and assault by personnel. All of these changes have had some influence on the gender and sexual norms extant within military culture. Nevertheless, certain factors that remain within military organizations tend to reinforce and perpetuate the traditional gender and sexual norms of the military. The result is that while the gender norms within military culture have undergone some alteration in recent years, there is strong evidence that much of traditional military gender and sexual norms remains.

The following examination of the gender and sexual norms of military culture will attempt to present a picture of military culture that takes account of the extent of relevant changes in that culture in recent years. Because no systematic study of military culture on these dimensions has yet been conducted, the following discussion is necessarily suggestive rather than conclusive. The analysis that follows is intended to describe central themes within an existing culture of military society.

We may begin by addressing attitudes toward masculinity in military culture. The military traditionally has had, and to a very large extent still has, a central group-identity structure built around a particular construction

---

49. Ibid.

of masculinity.[50] As expressed by David Marlowe, then chief of military psychiatry at the Walter Reed Army Institute of Research:

> In the world of the combat soldier...masculinity is an essential measure of capability. In an interaction between male bonding and widespread cultural norms, the maleness of an act is the measure of its worth and thus a measure of one's ability. While many may disapprove of these norms, they have been and are, as a matter of ethnographic fact, the operative ones in much of military society and particularly in the combat group.[51]

General William Westmoreland made explicit the traditional link between military service and masculinity in his testimony to Congress that "[n]o man with gumption wants a woman to fight his battles."[52] Or as General Robert Barrow, former Marine Corps Commandant, testified to Congress on the prospect of women in combat, "When you get right down to it, you have to protect the manliness of war."[53] As summed up by David Marlowe: "The soldier's world is characterized by a stereotyped masculinity. His language is profane, his professed sexuality crude and direct; his maleness is his armor, the measure of his competence, capability and confidence in himself."[54]

While such a vision of masculinity as a basis for group identity or individual worth is not now officially a part of formal military training or socialization (and while statements like those made by Generals Westmoreland and Barrow more than a decade ago presumably would not be made by military leaders now), this aspect of military culture continues to be of considerable vitality. As personnel at Parris Island Marine Recruit Training Depot told me in interviews in 1993 and 1994, the value of "manliness" is heavily impressed upon (male) recruits.[55] This "manliness," as one stated, means

> a warrior spirit that is based upon a sense of brotherhood, fraternalism—which, obviously, excludes women.... When a military

---

50. Kathryn Abrams, "Gender in the Military: Androcentrism and Institutional Reform," *Law and Contemporary Problems* 56 (autumn 1993): 217.

51. David H. Marlowe, "The Manning of the Force and the Structure of Battle: Part 2–Men and Women," in *Conscripts and Volunteers,* ed. Robert K. Fullinwider (Totowa, N.J.: Rowman & Allanheld, 1983), 194.

52. Jeanne Holm, *Women in the Military: The Unfinished Revolution* (Novato, Calif.: Presidio Press, 1982), 384.

53. Michael Wright, "The Marine Corps Faces the Future," *N.Y. Times Magazine,* 20 June 1982, 74.

54. Marlowe, "Force and the Structure of Battle," 194.

55. Marine Corps Drill Instructor, name withheld, interview by author, Parris Island, S.C., Marine Recruit Depot, 22 October 1993; Marine Corps Public Affairs Officer, interview by author, Parris Island, S.C., 22 October 1993; Marine Corps Drill Instructor (Ret.), name withheld, telephone interview by author, 2 October 1994.

organization is called to war, the mission is to kill and to dominate the opposing force. And domination is generally associated with a masculine thing. There's very little remorse. That's where the manliness thing comes into play.[56]

The normative elements of hypermasculinity are strikingly reflected in these descriptions.

In addition to the attitudes toward masculinity just discussed, the attitudes toward sexuality embodied in military culture also largely partake of those found to be conducive to rape, including both adversarial sexual beliefs and high valuation of promiscuity. Within traditional military culture, women are cast largely as the sexual adversary or target while men are cast largely as promiscuous sexual hunters. These themes remain rather prevalent in military culture currently.

To understand better the military construction of female as sexual adversary and male as promiscuous, we should meet "Suzie." "Suzie Rottencrotch" is the name that has sometimes been used by military men to refer to women (other than close relatives of the men present).[57] One drill instructor had the following to say about her in the course of a training lecture on the use of hand and arm signals:

If we get home with little Suzie...we're in a nice companionship with little Suzie and here you are getting hot and heavy and then you're getting ready to go down there and make that dive, privates, and Suzie says...Suzie says it's the wrong time of the month. Privates, if you don't want to get back home and indulge in this little adventure, you can show your girlfriend the hand and arm signal for "close it up."

And you want her to close up those nasty little thighs of hers, do you not, privates?[58]

The same training lecture included the following aside: "Privates, if you don't have a little Suzie now, maybe you're going to find one when you get home. You bet. You'll find the first cheap slut you can get back home. What do you mean, 'No'? You're a Marine, you're going to do it."[59] Together with the intended humor of the presentation, other messages inhere. These include the intimation that for a Marine, the female is the sexual adversary or target and is without other value—that what a Marine is looking for in women is "the first cheap slut he can get." The attitude is thus conveyed

56. Marine Corps Drill Instructor (Ret.), telephone interview.
57. Gwynne Dyer, *War* (New York: Crown, 1985), 123; Robert J. Lifton, *Home from the War* (New York: Simon & Schuster, 1973; Boston: Beacon Press, 1992), 243.
58. Dyer, *War*, 123.
59. Ibid.

that a Marine's only relationship to women is the pursuit and acquisition of sex—a relationship that both casts the Marine as promiscuous and women as prey.

The status of "Suzie Rottencrotch" is perhaps emblematic of the partial changes that have occurred in military culture. In October 1993, I asked a female drill instructor at Parris Island Marine Corps Recruit Depot whether the name "Suzie Rottencrotch" was still in use. She had never heard of the name but asked her male counterpart who was standing nearby. He replied that the name was still used but "not officially."

Events at the 1991 and earlier Tailhook conventions reflect similar themes. There, according to the Department of Defense inspector general, "[i]ncidents related by witnesses included a high ranking Navy civilian official dancing with strippers in hospitality suites, the throwing of flaming mannequins from rooftops, [and] earlier gauntlets and strip shows."[60] Nor are these events limited to convention weekends. As one Army combat engineer stationed at Fort Bragg related to me in 1994:

> You'd be amazed. Most people have no idea what goes on. The talk is "down." The whores and sluts are circulated between the guys. (They go for pay, for no pay, for drinks, whatever.) Those women actually go into the barracks. The guys talk and brag about it and share it with each other. You pull out of it once you've found a good woman (like my wife). It's a lot of contempt toward the women plus bragging about what studs they [the guys] are.[61]

Without providing a systematic or scientific comparison of military and civilian sexual attitudes, the foregoing discussion does suggest the continuing presence within military culture of adversarial sexual beliefs and normative promiscuity. (Because no information on rape-myth acceptance by military personnel is currently available, no comparison of military and civilian populations on that dimension is possible.) Suzie Rottencrotch, Tailhook, and remarks from Fort Bragg each reflect—without, of course, providing a systematic measure of—those attitudinal elements of military sexual culture. While recent military policy changes are presumably effecting some change in military gender and sexual norms, such a transition is, based on the available evidence, far from complete.

Along with the attitudes toward sexuality just discussed, also reflected in military culture are attitudes toward women—hostility toward women and possibly also acceptance of violence against women—that are associated

---

60. U.S. Department of Defense, *Tailhook '91, Part 2: Events at the 35th Annual Tailhook Symposium* (Washington, D.C.: U.S. Government Printing Office, 1993), X-1.

61. Army Combat Engineer, name withheld, telephone interview by author, 25 September 1994.

with rape propensity. The masculinity that is definitive of the military in-group is, not surprisingly, defined in *contrast* to the "other"—in particular, in contrast to women.[62] An unmistakable hostility is directed toward this other. A typical method of ostracization, particularly in basic training, is to refer to a male group member as a female. For instance, male recruits are called "ladies" or "girls" as well as more vulgar names for women when they perform poorly in training.[63] As Randy Shilts recounts,

> The lessons on manhood...focus less on creating what the Army wanted than on defining what the Army did not want. This is why calling recruits faggots, sissies, pussies, and girls had been a time-honored stratagem for drill instructors throughout the armed forces. The context was clear: There was not much worse you could call a man.[64]

While the practice of this particular type of gendered name-calling is not now officially sanctioned, it still does occur with continuing frequency in practice.[65]

Perhaps the most straightforward expression of hostility toward women is found in the T-shirt worn by several male officers at the 1991 Tailhook convention. The back of the shirt read "Women Are Property," while the front read "He-Man Woman Hater's Club."[66]

In addition to general attitudes of hostility toward women, attitudes accepting of violence against women *may* be heightened in military society. Direct measures comparing military and civilian attitudes regarding violence against women are lacking. However, recent studies conducted by the Army do suggest elevated rates of domestic abuse of the female partners of Army personnel as compared with rates of abuse of the female partners of civilian men.[67] This heightened rate in the Army population of violent abuse of women may (though it does not necessarily) reflect underlying attitudes in

---

62. See generally Georg Simmel, *Conflict* (Glencoe, Ill.: Free Press, 1955).

63. Christine L. Williams, *Gender Differences at Work* (Berkeley: University of California Press, 1989), 69; Cynthia Enloe, *Does Khaki Become You?* (Boston: South End Press, 1983), 14.

64. Randy Shilts, *Conduct Unbecoming* (New York: St. Martin's Press, 1993), 133.

65. Former Army Captain, name withheld, telephone interview by author, 22 September 1994; Army Enlisted Legal Specialist, interview by author, 1994; Marine Drill Instructor, telephone interview.

66. U.S. Department of Defense, *Tailhook '91, Part 2*, X-3.

67. Eric Schmitt, "Military Struggling to Stem an Increase in Family Violence," *New York Times*, 23 May 1994, A1; Mark Thompson, "The Living Room War: As the U.S. Military Shrinks, Family Violence Is on the Rise: Can the Pentagon Do More to Prevent It?" *Time*, 23 May 1994, 48; see also William A. Griffin and Allison R. Morgan, "Conflict in Maritally Distressed Military Couples," *American Journal of Family Therapy* 16 (1988): 14.

the Army population that are more accepting of violence against women than are the attitudes in the civilian population.

In sum, there is substantial evidence—though, as yet, no systematically collected data comparing military and civilian populations—of themes of hypermasculinity, adversarial sexual beliefs, promiscuity, hostility toward women, and possibly acceptance of violence against women within current military culture.[68] The norms and normative attitudes toward gender and sexuality that are prevalent in military culture thus appear to partake largely of the set of attitudes that have been found to be associated with heightened rape propensity. These norms and attitudes are in turn imparted to new members as they are socialized into their new primary groups within the military. Even while the services institute policies of "zero tolerance" of sexual harassment and assault, and provide formal training pursuant to those policies, informal socialization continues to perpetuate group norms inconsistent with those formal policies and goals. The result is that even while the U.S. military is in some ways in transition regarding gender, military units' normative attitudes toward gender and sexuality continue in part to be those associated with heightened levels of rape propensity.

We have seen evidence, in the discussion thus far, that there exists a differential between military rapes rates and military rates of other violent crime. We have considered the possibility that the military rape differential may be attributable in part to the norms and attitudes extant within military organizations. If that causal analysis is at all accurate, then it suggests that we may be able to reduce military rape rates—in peace and perhaps also in war—by altering the norms that are conveyed within the military.

The potential for reducing military rape incidence provides an additional perspective from which to evaluate policies affecting military culture. The possibility that certain aspects of military culture contribute to the military rape differential would weigh as a factor favoring policy choices that foster change in those aspects of military culture. Thorny questions, however, remain. In particular, we must ask what sorts of policy choices would foster the cultural change in question, and we must ask whether the contemplated cul-

---

68. Clearly, systematic research comparing military and civilian populations' attitudes on gender and sexuality would be most valuable. While the Department of Defense (DOD) has conducted extensive personnel attitude research on other topics (see, e.g., U.S. DOD, Defense Technical Information Center [DTIC], *Technical Report Summaries, DTIC Bibliography* [17 May 1993]; on file with the author), virtually no DOD research has been done on the attitudes toward gender and sexuality discussed here. The Army did collect some data relevant to personnel's attitudes toward sexuality in a survey conducted by the Army Senior Review Panel on Sexual Harassment in 1997 (see Dana Priest, "Army Destroyed Data on Sex Survey," *Washington Post,* 27 June 1997, A21). However, that data was suppressed and, according to Army sources, destroyed (ibid.). The Army's stated reason for destroying the data was that the survey questions at issue were "inflammatory and offensive" (ibid.).

tural change can occur while also maintaining military effectiveness. These are the issues to be addressed in the following sections.

Changes in the Content of Military Culture

There is reason to believe, as we have seen, that change in the gender and sexual norms of military culture could contribute to a reduction in the rape incidence of military organizations. Such cultural change could very likely be fostered through gender integration of the military, from basic training through combat, as shall now be discussed. Such thoroughgoing integration of the military would be importantly facilitated by further narrowing or eliminating the female combat exclusion and by accession of a greater proportion of female personnel.

We might expect that a truly thoroughgoing integration of women throughout the services would do much to undermine group norms featuring the constellation of attitudes comprised of hypermasculinity, hostility toward women, adversarial sexual beliefs, and the like. The presence of women as full members of the fighting forces would be inconsistent with a military culture in which women are viewed as the "other," primarily as sexual targets, and in which aggression is viewed as a sign of masculinity. The very presence of women as military equals would call into question those views.

There has been, in recent years, considerable movement toward integration of women into the American military. The gender integration of some military units may already be having an effect on gender attitudes. As a female Army sergeant interviewed in 1994 put it, "The idea that being a soldier means being masculine is changing because of more women coming into the services. The fact that there are now female fighter pilots, for example, helps a lot."[69] One enlisted woman perhaps summed it up, saying, "The units that work with females every day seem to be able to relate better."[70]

While we have seen movement toward integration of women into the services in recent years, however, that movement has been within limits. Those limits on gender integration of the military appear also to limit the extent of change likely to occur in military gender and sexual culture. It seems improbable that we will see a full transition in the gender and sexual norms of the military so long as there remain rules excluding women from a range of combat positions and low proportions of women accessed for military service. A change in gender and sexual norms, and a resultant reduction in the

---

69. Army Sergeant, name withheld, interview by author, Fort Bragg, N.C., 23 September 1994.

70. Monica Krause, telephone interview by author, 23 September 1994.

incidence of rape by military personnel, may be a previously unconsidered benefit that would result from a further narrowing or elimination of female combat exclusions and a further augmentation of the proportion of females accessed for military service.[71]

The rules excluding women from combat have been narrowed considerably in recent years. However, the remaining exclusions of women from combat positions still limit the potential for change in the gender and sexual culture of the military. Women in positions of military leadership would affect military gender norms both at a symbolic level and in very concrete ways. To the extent that women are, because of remaining combat exclusions, less likely to become military leaders and more likely to remain in lower echelons, their value in changing the gender norms of military culture is thereby limited.

But it is not only the *rank* held by women but also the substance of their military roles—their job duties and fields—that would be expected to affect military gender norms. The combat exclusions contribute to a powerful symbolic message about the appropriate roles of men and women. Only men and not women are deemed suitable for ground and certain other forms of combat—arguably the very positions that have been considered the most prototypically military. In this way, the continued exclusion of women from certain combat roles may actually reinforce and reaffirm traditional military gender norms—the view that to be a "real soldier," a fighter, means to be a man.

In addition to the effects on military culture generally of the symbolic message carried by the remaining combat exclusions, we must consider also the particular effects of the exclusion on those occupational fields from which women are actually excluded. Units from which women are excluded may well elaborate "macho" norms (norms consisting of the constellation of rape-conducive gender and sexual attitudes discussed earlier) even more intensively than we have seen before, as all-male composition now becomes a distinguishing group feature even within the broader military. We would expect for that tendency toward masculinist group identification to be heightened yet further as individuals attracted to that group image self-select into the remaining all-male occupational fields.

---

71. In the fall of 1996, it was revealed that extensive and severe sexual harassment was occurring at Aberdeen Proving Ground and several other Army institutions. Some commentators have pointed to these events as indicating the inherent impossibility of successfully integrating women throughout the military. But such a conclusion is unwarranted by the evidence. It is at least as plausible an explanation that the ongoing problem of sexual harassment by personnel is attributable to a need to change attitudes toward gender and sexuality within military culture that may be fostering harassment. As shall be discussed in this section, such a change in military culture would be fostered by increasing, not by decreasing, the integration of women in the services.

While important progress has been made in reducing the range of combat positions from which women are excluded, reform has been limited in ways likely also to limit effects on military culture. The remaining combat exclusions may tend, in both concrete and symbolic ways, to reinforce the traditional military gender and sexual norms that may be contributing to the military rape differential.

Related to but distinct from the issue of combat exclusion rules are the services' policies on accessions of service members. No matter how many military positions are "open to women," unless the services' accessions policies contemplate actually placing women in some substantial proportion of those positions, military occupations will not become substantially integrated, and resultant change in military gender and sexual culture will thereby be limited.

Each year, each service produces a personnel management plan for the next year including projected accessions, promotions, and discharges.[72] These plans set numerical goals for accessions on a variety of bases including prior service experience, job specialty, geographical district, race, and ethnicity.[73] The Army and Marine Corps also have set minimum female enlisted accessions goals (18 percent and 6 percent, respectively).[74] Informed sources within each of these services state that they intend to meet but do not expect to exceed their minimum goals for female accessions.[75] The Navy and Air Force now have gender-neutral accessions policies (in the sense of having no stated gender goals or quotas),[76] but both still have projected or predicted numbers of females expected to be accessed (18–20 percent for the Navy).[77]

The planned or projected number of women to be accessed is not simply a function of the number of jobs open to women in each service (i.e., jobs not restricted to men under a combat exclusion and not "reserved" to men for other policy reasons).[78] Rather, each service considers a variety of factors, including the service's needs, potential availability of female recruits, and costs, in identifying the number of females to be accessed.[79] That number may bear only a very distant relationship to the number of jobs open to women in the service.[80] For instance, while 62 percent of Marine Corps

---

72. Judith H. Stiehm, *Arms and the Enlisted Woman* (Philadelphia: Temple University Press, 1989), 155, 158.
73. Ted Triebel, Capt. U.S. Navy (Ret.), telephone interview by author, 2 November 1994.
74. Ibid.
75. Ibid.
76. Ibid.; Stiehm, *Arms and the Enlisted Woman*, 155.
77. Triebel, written communication with author, 18 August 1994. A predicted percentage for the Air Force was not available.
78. Stiehm, *Arms and the Enlisted Woman*, 157, 165, 175.
79. Triebel, written communication.
80. Stiehm, *Arms and the Enlisted Woman*, 157.

positions are "open" to women (in the sense that women are not excluded on the basis of the job description), the current Marine Corps minimum goal, or floor, for female enlisted accessions is 6 percent.[81] And the Navy prediction for female enlisted accessions is 18–20 percent,[82] even while 94 percent of Navy positions are open to women.

For gender integration to be effective in changing gender and sexual norms in the military, women must be present in sufficient numbers to be perceived as more than tokens. Two decades of research in commercial, educational, and military contexts indicate that when women are introduced into a previously male environment, the *proportions* of male and female in the newly integrated environment are crucial in determining the outcome of integration. Where women remain a small minority, stereotyping and negative reaction are perpetuated, and women remain isolated within the group.[83] As Rosabeth Kanter has observed, "[A]s long as numbers are low, [organizations] will consider any disruptions involving the 'token' women as a huge deflection from central purposes, a drain of energy, leading to the conclusion that it is not worth having people like tokens around."[84] The presence of women in small numbers dispersed throughout the military creates, in some ways, the worst of both worlds. As Judith Stiehm puts it, "Because the women remained a small percentage both of the whole and of any unit to which they were assigned, were dispersed through a variety of noncombat jobs, and were integrated into many previously all-male units, their presence disturbed without altering."[85] Thus, the gender ratios of accessions are a very important factor in determining what effect the presence of military women will have on the gender and sexual norms of military culture.

Accessions policies exert a strong influence on accessions results. Recruiting commands in each service pursue recruiting strategies targeting particular populations (defined by factors including age, region, race, and gender) in their advertising, and in high school recruiting visits and the like. While accessions policies and resultant recruiting strategies surely do not fully determine the proportion of recruits who are female (broader societal gender roles, for instance, may more narrowly limit the number of

---

81. Triebel, written communication.
82. Ibid.
83. Ross A. Webber, "Perceptions and Behaviors in Mixed Sex Work Teams," *Industrial Relations* 15 (1976): 121–29; Diane N. Ruble and E. Tory Higgins, "Effect of Group Sex Composition on Self-Presentation and Sex Typing," *Journal of Social Issues* 32 (1976): 125–32; James H. Thomas and Dirk C. Prather, "Integration of Females into a Previously All-Male Institution," in *Proceedings of the Fifth Symposium on the Air Force 8 April–10 April* (U.S. Air Force Academy, Department of Behavioral Sciences and Leadership, 1976), 100–101.
84. Rosabeth M. Kanter, *Men and Women of the Corporation* (New York: Basic Books, 1977), 239.
85. Stiehm, *Arms and the Enlisted Woman*, 152.

females than the number of males that are "recruitable"), those policies do exert a considerable influence on the proportion of female accessions. For that reason, accessions policies are crucially important to the future of women's military participation and, thus, to the potential effects of gender integration on military culture: "Accessions are at the heart of the women-in-the-military matter. If women are not accessed, all other considerations become moot."[86]

Accessions policies have to date been formed on the basis of numerous factors including military readiness, force diversity, and cost. Military cultural change and the potential resulting reduction in military rape rates are yet another factor that might valuably be taken into account in the future formation of accessions policies regarding gender.

A detailed analysis of the considerations for and against thorough gender integration of the military is beyond the scope of this article. However, in suggesting that considerations of rape reduction may weigh in favor of policies that will render change in military gender and sexual culture, it will be worthwhile to explore the feasibility of such change at the broad conceptual level. In particular, it will be important to ask: Can military gender and sexual culture be changed more thoroughly than has occurred to date without degrading military effectiveness? That is, does the traditional gender culture of the military itself contribute in necessary ways to military readiness? That question shall now be addressed in the next and final section.

Functions of and Alternatives to a Masculinist Military Identity

We have seen that a certain constellation of attitudes toward gender and sexuality—in particular, toward masculinity, toward sexuality, and toward women—has been found to be associated with heightened rape propensity. For ease of exposition, I will refer to this attitudinal constellation as "masculinist."[87] We have also seen evidence suggesting that this masculinist constellation of normative attitudes toward gender and sexuality is prevalent within military culture as currently constructed.

We now must ask, in contemplating a change in those gender and sexual norms of military culture, whether such a change can occur while also maintaining military effectiveness, or, put differently, whether traditional military

---

86. Ibid., 174.

87. I add the "ist" suffix to "masculine" to indicate "one who practices or is occupied with, or a believer in" a particular construction of masculinity (*Webster's New Twentieth Century Dictionary of the English Language*, 2d ed., s.v. "ist"). Thus I do not intend for the word "masculinist" to carry a particular evaluative valence. Rather, I aspire for it to take its place among the multifarious group of "ist" words such as herbalist, specialist, feminist, dermatologist, racist, therapist, capitalist, somnambulist, sexist, proctologist, economist, criminalist, cultist, novelist and, of course, the Shootist.

gender culture contributes in necessary ways to military effectiveness. For that reason, it will be valuable to explore the reasons for and the functions of a masculinist military identity and to consider whether functions now served by a masculinist military identity can be fulfilled through alternative means.

Certainly, the phenomenon of linking military identity with masculinity has been longstanding and widespread. The pervasiveness of a masculinist military construct raises the question of the reasons for its widespread popularity and the functions that the construct may serve. While no definitive explanation for the pervasiveness of the masculinist military construct is possible, five elements are likely contributing factors. The first two, as we shall see, may be waning in their causal vitality at this moment in history. The latter three continue to be causally efficacious, but because of the availability of suitable alternatives, may not represent an insurmountable barrier to change, as shall be discussed.

The first and rather obvious explanation for the linkage of military service and masculinity is that, historically, success in combat depended heavily upon the physical strength of the combatants. Combat would have been a male domain so long as strength was largely determinative of combat's outcome. Now, of course, with the advent of increasingly lighter and more effective firepower, this basis for linking combat and maleness has become much more tenuous.[88]

But the historical importance of strength for combat, while addressing the linkage of combat and maleness, does not satisfactorily explain the more complex linkage of combat with the particular construction of masculinity (and attendant attitudes toward sexuality and toward women) that I have termed "masculinist," or the significant emotional energy invested in that link. The second explanation of the linkage between military service and masculinity addresses the issue on that more complex dimension. Here, at the level of psychosexual causes, explanations necessarily become more speculative.

One psychoanalytic explanation for the linkage of military service and a particular, "masculinist" construction of masculinity is that young males, unlike young females, utilize institutions like the traditional military as the means through which to affirm their gender identities. The reasoning is that young males gravitate toward opportunities to affirm their masculinity (in a way nonanalogous to the behavior of young females) because of gender

---

88. A broader version of the physical-suitability-for-combat explanation for the link between combat and maleness would address not only the strength differences between men and women but also the fact that males are not subject to pregnancy and lactation as are women. Technological progress including the availability of contraception and of bottle feeding lessen the import of these additional physical factors favoring males as fighters, just as the advent of lighter firepower reduces the import of the strength differences between the genders.

asymmetry in parenting that makes the psychosexual development of girls and boys fundamentally different. In essence, the argument here is that in a society where girls and boys are both primarily parented by women, girls never have to shift away from their primary attachment (mother) to develop (female) gender identity, while boys have to separate psychologically from the primary bond with mother to establish identification with a male figure to develop male gender identity. This more problematic male course of development, it is argued, creates a variety of psychological differences between the sexes including a continuing need in many young (and some older) men to separate, distance, and distinguish themselves from the feminine, the (m)other, and to affirm their masculine identification in sharp contradistinction to femininity.[89] Methods for such affirmation of maleness include, presumably, bonding with father figures as well as with all-male "hyper-masculine" groups. One such group would be, of course, the traditional armed forces.[90] Viewed in this light, we can perhaps make sense of the Army National Guard advertisement that shows a group of young men wading through high water and bears the caption "Kiss your Mama goodbye."[91]

To whatever extent the psychoanalytic view, just described, of the reasons for a masculinist military is accurate, trends toward more shared parenting would reduce the power of young males' need for participation in masculinist groups defined in distinction to the feminine (m)other. At the same time as technology currently plays a part in weakening the link between maleness and combat (by making successful use of violence less dependent on physical strength), technology and other, social, factors also weaken the link between femaleness and primary parenting. Both of these historical changes make more possible and more likely a movement away from the traditional masculinist military and toward a desegregation of military culture.

The first two reasons for the masculinist military construct may be waning in their causal efficacy as just discussed. As mentioned above, the other three likely bases for that linkage, now to be considered, are of continuing vitality.

The third factor contributing to the masculinist military construct relates specifically to the particular *vision* of masculinity as dominance, aggressiveness, and toughness embraced in military culture. Presumably, idealization of those characteristics is highly functional in an organization whose raison d'être is combat. It therefore is unsurprising that those characteristics would be highly valued in military organizations. Nevertheless, there is no reason that the high valuation of those attributes cannot be retained while simul-

---

89. Nancy Chodorow, *The Reproduction of Mothering: Psychoanalysis and the Sociology of Gender* (Berkeley: University of California Press, 1978), 13–15.

90. Williams, *Gender Differences at Work*, 15, 32, 66–67, 134–35.

91. Ibid., 47.

taneously dissociating them from masculine gender. They may be valued, instead, as important attributes in a good soldier regardless of gender.

Nor need the celebration of a certain steeliness exclude the approval also of compassion and understanding (as it does in the hypermasculinity aspect of the masculinist construct). Indeed, it is that very combination of aggressivity with compassion that is required for compliance with the laws of war that require humane treatment of prisoners, civilians, and the wounded.[92] Compassion, understanding, and "taking care of your troops" also are important attributes in officers and unit leaders, as is taught in, for example, the Navy's Leadership Management Education Training classes.[93] Thus, in this regard, there is much to be gained and little to be lost by changing this aspect of military culture.

The two final factors contributing to the masculinist military construct arise from the benefits of that construct for group cohesion. First, a masculinist group identity may provide a basis for group cohesion between group members who may otherwise share little common ground. The group of individuals composing a military organization is often quite diverse in terms of race, ethnicity, religion, region, education, class. and the like. This is especially true under conscription but remains somewhat true even with an all-volunteer force. Because, until recently, military organizations *have* been virtually all male, a focus on masculinity or "manhood" may well have served as a handy and powerful basis for group identity, allowing for a stable definition of group and other. Moreover, embracing a particular vision of masculinity that is defined in part by eschewal of the feminine may further aid group cohesion by defining an "other" that is constant over time: Even while the "enemy" changes, the *sexual* other does not change.

Given the importance of group cohesion for military effectiveness especially in combat units, we must ask, in contemplating changes to the military's traditional masculinist group identity, what alternative bases of group identity and cohesion could successfully replace the existing gender-based structure. Group identity and cohesion in ideological primary groups can be effectuated around themes that are religious, political, moral, and the like, and nonideological primary groups can bond on the basis of not much more than the merest assertion of a "we/they" divide such as gang or fraternity or team membership. There thus exists a range of possible bases for group identity and cohesion to be considered.

---

92. *Geneva Conventions*, 1949: "Convention for the Amelioration of the Conditions of the Wounded and Sick in Armed Forces in the Field," 6 U.S.T. 3114, 75 U.N.T.S. 31; "Convention for the Amelioration of the Condition of Wounded, Sick, and Shipwrecked Members of Armed Forces at Sea," 6 U.S.T. 3217, 75 U.N.T.S. 85; "Convention Related to the Treatment of Prisoners of War," 6 U.S.T. 3316, 75 U.N.T.S 135; "Convention Related to the Protection of Civilian Persons in Time of War," 6 U.S.T. 3516, 75 U.N.T.S. 287.

93. Triebel, written communication.

Appropriate and effective bases for military group identification other than gender could incorporate both ideological and nonideological elements. Ideological bases could include an identification of the group as just warriors, protecting democracy and the decent lives of decent people, while the "other" (always important for group identity) could be defined as those who would be oppressors, the unjust. Such visions of just warriors on an honorable mission can be mightily motivating.

One may have certain misgivings about such a basis for military group identity. Group identification as an armed band on a righteous mission can be powerfully motivating—intoxicating—and, for that reason, dangerous. Certainly, people who believe that they are justified in using violence for a righteous cause often are dangerous. As Myriam Miedzian well states: "Cossacks, whose pogroms against Jews terrorized my father and his family... believed that they had God and virtue on their side.... [T]he Germans who threw my aunts and uncles... into gas chambers... believed they were serving the higher cause of purifying the Aryan race."[94]

The use of violence in the pursuit of good, then, is always something to be suspicious of, but so is pacifism in the face of atrocity. Short of adopting a position of thoroughgoing pacifism, the merits of which I will not debate here, some basis for military group identification must exist. Surely, if armed force is ever to be deployed, then idealism and moral conviction are preferable motives to macho posturing. Examples of cohesive groups centered on ideological rather than gendered bases for bonding include some religious orders, the French resistance underground, and even Alcoholics Anonymous. Each of these types of groups has based a high degree of cohesion on an ideological basis, a shared cause, without utilizing gender as a basis of group bonding.

Nonideological bases for military group identification also are available. Those bases could include such basic definitions of group and other as national identification and, of course, unit and buddy identification.[95] The readiness with which formation of group identification occurs even in the absence of shared ideology or other apparent basis is remarkable. As Donald Horowitz has described,

There is now a rapidly accumulating body of evidence that it takes few differences to divide a population into groups. Groups can form quickly on the basis of simple division into alternative categories. Once groups have formed, group loyalty quickly takes hold....

---

94. Myriam Miedzian, *Boys Will Be Boys* (New York: Doubleday, 1991), 275–76 n. 76.
95. Frederick J. Manning, "Morale, Cohesion, and Esprit de Corps," *Handbook of Military Psychology* (New York: Wiley, 1991), 453, 456–65.

The tendency to cleave and compare . . . forms the theme of a series of experiments . . . [which demonstrated] a marked propensity to form groups on the basis of the most casual differences and then to behave in a discriminatory fashion on the basis of the new group identity. There are many variations on the experiments, but they generally involve subjects assigned to a category on the basis of trivial differences, no differences, or a conspicuous toss of a coin. Once assigned, group members experienced no face-to-face interaction with other ingroup or outgroup members, and there was no effort to instill ingroup loyalty or outgroup hostility. Given the opportunity to apportion rewards, subjects nevertheless discriminated so as to favor ingroup members and disfavor outgroup members.

The minimal basis of group differentiation needs to be underscored. What produced group feeling and discrimination is simple division into categories. . . .

These findings have now been replicated and have a solid basis in the experimental literature.[96]

There thus exists a range of bases for group identity and motivation that would be suitable alternatives to the traditional masculinist military identity. Indeed, new bases for military identity may actually be more sustaining for soldiers' morale over time than the masculinist identity. William Manchester has argued, for instance, that while the "macho" image provides initial attraction, soldiers faced with the tragic realities of combat may reject that vision as false, and may feel duped and betrayed by the leaders who fostered that image.[97]

Thus, while masculinist images may be potent motivators for young men, their productive effects may be short-lived and followed by counterproductive ones. Alternative bases for group identification might, thus, be not only equally but actually more efficacious than the traditional masculinist construct.

To recognize potential alternative bases for military group cohesion is not in any way to underestimate the power of gender as a basis for group bonding. Prudence requires clear recognition that gender-based bonding has served well to foster unit cohesion in the past. At the same time, though, we must acknowledge that utilization of that basis likely comes at a price. A balancing of factors may therefore be required: Loss of cohesion resulting from a shift away from gender as a basis for group identity may be at

96. Donald Horowitz, *Ethnic Groups in Conflict* (Berkeley: University of California Press, 1985), 143–46.

97. William Manchester, "The Bloodiest Battle of All," *New York Times Magazine*, 14 June 1987, 84.

least minimized by the development of other bases for cohesion, as just discussed. A policy decision then is required as to whether, if any residual loss in cohesion remains, the benefits in military cultural change are worth that loss in cohesion. We have accepted marginal losses of cohesion in choosing to integrate units by race, ethnicity, class, region, religion, and the like.[98] A similar weighing of costs and benefits would be required as to any loss in cohesion that could result from further change in military gender and sexual culture.

Finally, in considering the functions of a masculinist military identity, it is important to note that an exclusively male heterosexual group identity may serve to minimize sexual tensions between group members. (Of course a male heterosexual group identity may exist even with homosexual group members, particularly if their presence is unacknowledged.) Sexual loyalties as well as sexual rivalries or jealousies pose a potential threat to primary group cohesion. The maintenance of an all-male, ostensibly all-heterosexual military would be expected to minimize those threats to cohesion within military primary groups. Sexual desires or relationships would be minimized within the group, thus minimizing threats to cohesion. Moreover, if those outside the group were viewed primarily as sexual targets (or even adversarial sexual targets), then this would tend to minimize even threats to group cohesion coming from the formation of bonds and loyalties from relationships outside the group. Given this cohesion-protecting function of a masculinist group identity, we must ask, in considering amending such a basis for group identity, whether there are alternative means to minimize sexual tensions within the military group.

All primary groups develop sexual norms—sometimes specialized sexual norms—to control the potentially destructive effects of sexuality on group cohesion. The specialized sexual norms best suited to the military would appear to be much like those of the family (just as the military unit replicates many of the other psychological functions of the family). For example, a military "incest taboo" would strictly prohibit sexual relationships between members of the same military units. The level of unit (squadron, platoon, etc.) to which the incest taboo would apply would need to be defined—and might vary depending on the functional needs of the different components of military organizations (for example, the cohesion needs of combat versus noncombat groups). Presumably, an essential criterion for defining "unit" for purposes of the incest taboo would be whether and to what extent the grouping in question is intended to have primary group characteristics. Another important criterion would be based on practicability: the narrower the definition of "unit," the smaller the range of potential relations would be

---

98. Manning, "Morale, Cohesion, and Esprit de Corps," 462.

prohibited and, in turn, the greater the likelihood that the taboo would be observed in practice.

The minimization of sexual relationships within military units has been accomplished historically through the exclusion of women and the ostensible exclusion of gays. The full inclusion of women would require some adjustment of mechanisms for enforcement of the military incest taboo. Just as military units have traditionally been "a band of brothers," gender-integrated units will have to be carefully shaped and defined as a band of brothers and sisters, between whom sexual relationships would be unacceptable.

The incest taboo approach would amount to a broadened fraternization policy, prohibiting not only inappropriate relationships between rank but sexual relationships regardless of rank within functionally defined units. Currently, the antifraternization rule as a criminal prohibition applies only to inappropriate relationships between officers and enlisted personnel.[99] In addition, however, each military service has promulgated regulations governing fraternization and professional relationships. These tend to cover a broader range of relationships than only officer/enlisted. Air Force regulations, for example, provide that "unprofessional relationships can develop between officers, between enlisted members, and between officers and enlisted members. Such relationships create the appearance that personal friendships and preferences are more important than individual performance and contribution to the mission.... Any relationship that harms [a] unit's morale, discipline or efficiency requires action."[100] We might realistically expect that an incest taboo regularizing the prohibition of certain "unprofessional relationships" within rank, like the fraternization policy prohibiting sexual relationships between ranks, would be less than completely enforceable but nevertheless sufficiently effective to minimize the potential problem.

Results of a large-scale study on gender relations in mixed-gender military units support the validity and potential efficacy of this family-analogy approach. The study observes that, in fostering positive gender relations that minimize sexual tensions,

---

99. U.S.C.A. §934 (1994); implemented by Executive Order No. 12473, 3 C.F.R. 102 (1985); amended by Executive Order 12767, 3 C.F.R. 334 (1991).

100. Air Force Regulation 36–2909, Fraternization and Professional Relationships, Attachment 1.1995.

Regarding the need for an adapted antifraternization-type policy in a gender-integrated military, see William J. Davis Jr. (LCDR, USN), "Nobody Asked Me, But...," in *Naval Institute Proceedings* 105 (September 1994): 120/9/1,099 (Annapolis, Md.: U.S. Naval Institute): "Currently stated Navy policy fails to address the issues that must be resolved for a commanding officer to lead a gender-integrated wardroom. The Navy's fraternization policy, for example, does not address the particulars of intra-wardroom relationships among peers."

[w]omen may . . . rely on societal roles in which men and women are not sex objects for one another, such as sibling, parent, and child. Common during interviews were sentiments similar to this one heard in Somalia: "We're just like brothers and sisters out here." Women often note that harassment tends to come from outside the unit—from men who do not know them personally and especially from men who do not work with women regularly. A "brother" may stick up for a "sister" he feels is being discussed disparagingly behind her back.[101]

The taboo against within-unit sexual relationships could be intensified in units, such as combat units, where cohesion is particularly crucial. Impressing upon troops that their lives may depend upon group cohesion in combat may cause units to develop mechanisms for enforcing the sexual-relationships prohibition for purposes of self-preservation.

Thus, there are methods available to minimize the disruptive potential of sexuality other than through the maintenance of a masculinist military. Certainly, other cohesive groups such as zealous political, religious, and self-help organizations have, without gender exclusions, maintained strong group cohesion.[102] And, as the report of the Presidential Commission on the assignment of women in the Armed Forces states,

A review of the psychological literature and post-integration studies and testimony before the Commission indicates situations have existed in which women were able to bond with men in various noncombat environments. Also, noncombat mixed-gender units seemed to communicate and work better than single gender units performing similar tasks.[103]

Moreover, group cohesion has been strong in the gender-integrated combat units of the past including those of Russia, Israel, North Vietnam, and others.[104]

---

101. Laura L. Miller, "Creating Gender Detente in the Military," (paper written for then Army chief of staff, Gen. Sullivan, and also distributed to Navy flag officers, 1994), 2.

102. John M. Brownlee, "Toward Diversity in the Local Church" (doctoral dissertation, Columbia Theological Seminary, 1993), 76, 88, 116–17, 184; Marc Galanter, *Cults: Faith, Healing, and Coercion* (New York: Oxford University Press, 1989), 176, 187.

103. Presidential Commission on the Assignment of Women in the Armed Forces, *Report to the President, November 15, 1992* (Washington, D.C.: Presidential Commission on the Assignment of Women in the Armed Forces, 1992): 47–48.

104. Anne E. Griesse and Richard Stites, "Revolution and War," in *Female Soldiers— Combatants or Non-Combatants?* ed. Nancy L. Goldman, (Westport, Conn.: Greenwood Press, 1982), 61–85; Anne R. Bloom, "Israel: The Longest War," in *Female Soldiers— Combatants or Non-Combatants?* ed. N. L. Goldman, 137–62; William J. Duiker, "Vietnam: War of Insurgency," in *Female Soldiers—Combatants or Non-Combatants?* ed. N. L. Goldman, 107–22.

Even so, the presence of both men and women within a unit surely creates some potential for sexual tensions that would not exist in an all-male group. And, indeed, some loss of cohesion may result at the margin. The question is whether the benefit is worth the cost. As discussed earlier, marginal losses in cohesion have been accepted for purposes of racial, ethnic, class, regional, and religious integration of the armed forces. The decision whether any loss in cohesion that does result from gender integration is warranted by the benefits of integration is a policy decision. Rape incidence considerations are among those that should be taken into account in that weighing.

In sum, while the masculinist military identity has served important functions as a basis for military group cohesion and identification, it would appear that viable alternative bases for military group identity are available. Masculinist military identity, then, is not inevitable or indispensable to military effectiveness but, rather, is a matter of choice.

Of course, altering the masculinist basis of military group identification may raise important concerns: What if there are important functions of the masculinist identity that we have not accounted for? What if the new basis is therefore less powerful, leads to less cohesion, less motivation, less effectiveness in combat? These are crucial questions requiring careful address. Certainly, experimental programs to test rigorously the viability of a fully integrated combat force, for instance, should be earnestly pursued.[105] The exploration undertaken in the present section suggests that the prospects for military cultural change consistent with military effectiveness are promising—and identifies reduction in military rape incidence as one potential benefit of such change. The factors that have been considered to date in the policy debate regarding women in the military have been primarily equal employment opportunity and military readiness.[106] The present article points to yet another, previously unconsidered, factor—the reduction of rape by military personnel—that should be taken into account in future consideration of policies, such as integration of women, likely to influence and to shape military culture.

Conclusion

This article has presented evidence of a military rape differential, has explored in some depth the possible explanations for the existence of that differential, and has considered methods of addressing the differential. The evidence considered suggests that the gender and sexual norms of military

---

105. Binkin, *Who Will Fight the Next War?* 59–60.
106. See, e.g., ibid., 26–47; Martin Binkin and Shirley J. Bach, *Women and the Military* (Washington, D.C.: Brookings Institution, 1977), chap. 4.

culture may be contributing causal factors. The foregoing consideration of the functions of and possible alternatives to a masculinist military culture suggests that changes in the military's gender and sexual norms, which may help to reduce military rape incidence, may be effectuated without unduly degrading military effectiveness.

Beyond indicating the need for further research, the present article also points to the appropriateness of presently taking into account rape incidence in making policy decisions affecting the gender and sexual norms of military culture. While more information will be extremely useful in this area, we may begin to act upon the indications that we do already have of the sorts of cultural changes that could contribute to reducing rape incidence in the military. The benefits of any such reduction are great, not only for potential rape victims in war and in peace, but also for those personnel who may thus be spared from becoming rape perpetrators. Both further research and present action are warranted. To do less would be a betrayal both of potential future victims of rape and of the men and women who serve in the military.

Epilogue

In 1997, in the wake of the sexual misconduct scandals at Aberdeen and other U.S. Army bases, I was appointed special consultant to the secretary of the U.S. Army, Togo West. One responsibility of the consultancy was to keep closely abreast of the activities of the Secretary of the Army's Senior Review Panel on Sexual Harassment (the body created by Secretary West in 1996 to conduct a study of sexual harassment in the Army) and to advise the secretary on the panel's work.

At first, it appeared that the panel was moving toward fulfillment of its mandate to do a thorough study of all the possible causes of sexual harassment in the Army, with an eye to considering a full range of possible remedies for the problem. However, in February 1997, I became aware that the panel had abandoned one area of inquiry. The questionnaire initially used by the panel for its survey research contained seven questions relating to attitudes toward gender and sexuality. But, after the questionnaire had been administered to nine thousand troops, those seven questions were deleted. This deletion occurred after preliminary analyses of the data from those nine thousand questionnaires already administered revealed strong statistical correlations between sexual harassment within Army units and the subjects explored in those seven questions (i.e., attitudes toward gender and sexuality). Secretary West was made aware of this turn of events but took no corrective action.

Several months later it was disclosed that not only had the Senior Review Panel deleted the seven questions, but it had also destroyed the data in question.[107] In the aftermath of the data destruction, the Army issued a memorandum to all relevant personnel threatening severe penalties for failure to hand in any copies of the data in their possession.

It is particularly unfortunate that the Army saw fit to suppress its own findings on this subject. The data constituted a potentially promising contribution to our understanding of this issue and to informed and intelligent policy making on this subject. At the time of this writing, certain members of Congress are inquiring into the matter.

---

107. Priest, "Army Destroyed Data on Sex Survey."

12

Militarized Prostitution

The Untold Story (U.S.A.)

JENNIFER S. BUTLER

I can't say my work [in the club] is bad . . . but it was bad. What I mean to say is that in other people's eyes, people who are not understanding, this work is bad. But they don't understand the reasons why the women do this.

—MADELIN in *Let the Good Times Roll: Prostitution and the U.S. Military in Asia*

Listening Is Political

In the wake of sexual assault allegations at the U.S. Army's Aberdeen Proving Ground, growing alarm at the number of rapes in armed conflict situations, and increased awareness of the connections between militarism and sexual exploitation, the Advocacy Committee for Women's Concerns (ACWC) of the Presbyterian Church (U.S.A.) asked me to help prepare a report for the church on the military and the sexual exploitation of women.[1] The ACWC presented its report at a church meeting and received a largely positive response. After many of the participants responded in support or with earnest questions, a former military officer stood up to make a few pointed remarks. He commended the committee for having adopted the report, but then he told a disturbing story. He recounted an incident in the Philippines during his military service in which he and a buddy were propositioned by two Filipina women at a restaurant. He described the women as taunting them, saying their husbands were not home and they wished to have a good time. He then proceeded to explain to the committee that in his view many of "these women" were flocking into the cities, even the young girls, because they enjoyed sex and could make lots of money doing what they were doing.

---

1. "The Military and Sexual Exploitation and Abuse of Women," in *GA Minutes* (Louisville: Presbyterian Church [U.S.A.], 1998).

They often seduced what he described as poor, innocent young recruits into betraying their values or even marrying them so they could get their money. Seeming to contradict his statement, he concluded by congratulating the Advocacy Committee on a sound report. His comments placed the blame for U.S. servicemen's involvement in prostitution on the women working as prostitutes. The intent of his anecdote was to evoke sympathy for the servicemen at the expense of the women who are, in many cases, forced to serve as prostitutes.

There was an uncomfortable silence after his monologue until the moderator of the gathering rose to bring the meeting to a close. Our initial elation at the group's positive response to the report was dampened by this participant's comments. Several members of the committee sensed that we had failed to accomplish our most important goal—that of illuminating the impact of militarism on women and girls. Our report focused on establishing military complicity and devoted only a short paragraph to describing the lives of women in the sex industry. The retired officer's comments made us realize that what had been missing in our presentation to the group and even in the report itself were the voices of women abused by the sex industry around bases.

Violence against women during wartime in the form of rape, sexual slavery as in the case of the Korean comfort women, harassment of female soldiers, or the commodification of women's bodies in brothels around military bases has until recently not received sustained national or international attention. Often female victims of wartime violence have been further victimized as they are blamed, stigmatized, or ostracized from their communities for the violence done to them. Women who are forced by a variety of dynamics into selling sex to servicemen around military bases are further stigmatized by the perception that, as adults, they have the ability to choose whether or not they sell sex and that to choose to do so is immoral. Since their stories are seldom part of the public discourse, these women's realities are not reflected in the shared public reality. Their suffering is denied.

Throughout history, women's identities and lived realities have been defined for them by males in society who have controlled the public discourse. One of the greatest contributions of the feminist movement has been its success in enabling women to tell their stories so that male representations of women in society and culture might be challenged and problematized by women's realities. Feminists have asserted, as Cynthia Enloe puts it, that "listening is political."[2] It naturally follows that telling is also political. In telling their stories, women define their reality, sometimes becoming fully

---

2. Cynthia Enloe, *The Morning After: Sexual Politics and the End of the Cold War* (Berkeley: University of California Press, 1993), 160.

aware of their true selves for the first time rather than their selves as defined by media, literature, and histories that do not reflect their experiences of life. Systems of oppression are usually well maintained by blaming their victims for their own abuse and exonerating evil. By telling their stories, prostitutes take a step toward dismantling the complex, interlocking systems of sexual abuse of women around military bases.

The purpose of this article is to dispel the myths and examine the realities of the sex industries that develop around U.S. military installations by listening to the perspectives and stories of women who have earned a living selling sex to U.S. servicemen. While prostitution is ubiquitous around military installations in many countries, this article focuses on U.S. military bases in Asia, where the most research and advocacy have been done. It presents excerpts from the recorded interviews of women living around U.S. bases in Korea and Okinawa, Japan. It examines the impact of Subic Naval Base and Clark Air Force Base in the Philippines, which occupied Subic Bay and Pampanga respectively until 1992, spawning the sex industries of Olongapo and Angeles. This article also touches on Thailand as a rest and recreation spot developed for U.S. servicemen during the Vietnam War and still frequented by the U.S. military.

Military Prostitution in Asia

There are many different and interrelated types of prostitution in the sex industry, of which military prostitution is one (sex tourism, sex trafficking, and child prostitution are others).[3] Military prostitution refers specifically to the establishment of brothels around bases to provide entertainment and sexual "services" to occupying soldiers. Brothel owners usually either buy women and children from sex traffickers or recruit those who are desperate because of poverty, war, or violence to sell their bodies to military servicemen. During war women and young girls who are displaced from land and family support are often forced to sell their bodies to survive or to support their families. Sometimes they are the victims of rape during war and deemed unworthy of the protections of marriage by a patriarchal culture. They are often uneducated because of poverty or because they are female and barred from the jobs that pay a living wage. Occupying soldiers have access to hard currency and may even offer escape through marriage from the woman's war-torn country.

---

3. Rita Nakashima Brock and Susan Brooks Thistlethwaite, *Casting Stones: Prostitution and Liberation in Asia and the United States* (Minneapolis: Fortress Press, 1996). Vern Bullough and Bonnie Bullough, *Women and Prostitution: A Social History* (Buffalo: Prometheus Books, 1987).

South Korea by the 1960s was known as the "GI's heaven." Over 20,000 prostitutes were available to "service" approximately 62,000 U.S. soldiers.[4] In 1977 South Korea's Ministry of Health and Social Welfare reported 36,924 prostitutes.[5] Today Osan, American Town in Kunsan, Tongduch'on, and Uijongbu are the only major rest and recreation areas left. However, according to My Sister's Place, a Christian outreach ministry to prostitutes, in 1990 there were still 18,000 women registered as prostitutes in the bars and clubs outside U.S. bases in Korea and at least 9,000 unregistered.[6]

Before the 1992 closing of Subic Naval Base and Clark Air Force Base in the Philippines, bars and clubs in Olongapo and Angeles employed approximately 55,000 registered and unregistered prostitutes. While the sex industry may have diminished in size due to a decrease in demand after the closing of U.S. bases, it still thrives and finds new markets. Sex tours, mainly men from Australia, Europe, and Japan, have filled some of the gap left by the U.S. military. The sex tourism industry in this and other towns has been encouraged or even courted by local officials as a way of bringing large amounts of money into the local economy to replace the income lost when the military bases closed.[7] Sex industries functioning around former U.S. military bases are still used for rest and recreation. During the Gulf War the Seventh Fleet docked in Subic Bay and Pattaya, Thailand.[8] Thailand, currently a site for international sex tourism as well as an R and R station, has an estimated 800,000 to 2 million prostitutes.[9] In March 1996, 2,500 to 3,000 GIs took shore leave in Angeles and Olongapo, creating such a high demand that the mayors of the cities got together to work out how to find more women.[10] The Department of Defense is also negotiating a Status of Forces Agreement (SOFA) that would include the ability to use its former bases in the Philippines for R and R.[11]

Women living in areas formerly occupied by the U.S. armed forces are often trafficked to brothels around other bases. Since the withdrawal of the U.S. military, many Filipinas have been trafficked to military bases in Ok-

---

4. Katharine Moon, *Sex among Allies: Military Prostitution in U.S.-Korea Relations* (New York: Columbia University Press, 1997), 30.

5. Ibid., 24.

6. Brock and Thistlethwaite, *Casting Stones*, 74.

7. Ibid., 55.

8. *New York Times*, 25 March 1991.

9. *A Modern Form of Slavery: Trafficking of Burmese Women and Girls into Brothels in Thailand* (New York: Asia Watch, 1993), 49.

10. Gwyn Kierk, Martha Matsuoka, and Margo Okazawa-rey, "Women and Children, Militarism, and Human Rights: International Women's Working Conference," *Off Our Backs* (October 1997): 9.

11. Roland Simbulan, "The SOFA Draft: A Wholesale Abdication of Our Country's National Sovereignty, Self-Respect, and Dignity" (Manila: Nuclear Free Philippines, 4 December 1997). Also written communications with Norma Nacaytuna with GABRIELA-Philippines.

inawa, South Korea, and Guam to meet the demands of the sex industries there.[12] Since the numbers of brothels decrease only because of the withdrawal of U.S. troops, not because of a change in the attitudes of the U.S. military that encourage such prostitution, the sex industry will simply ebb and flow and shift according to the presence and size of bases, not disappear entirely. During the Gulf War the U.S. military demonstrated that it was possible to implement strict policies prohibiting soldiers from patronizing prostitutes. It did so because engagement in prostitution in an Islamic setting would have jeopardized its mission. Such policies have not yet been enforced for other locations.

As foreign occupation continues and the national economy is rebuilt, the economic situation of the poor, especially poor women, improves much more slowly than that of the rest of the country. Poverty drives many women to sell their bodies. Women are usually held in debt bondage and receive little of the earnings from their labor. Ironically, women's sexual labor is used to rebuild their countries after wars while they gain little in return. In Okinawa during the early 1970s, women's sexual labor directly or indirectly was a primary source of income that fueled much renewed economic activity.[13] Shimabukuo Hiroshi, an Okinawan writer, calculates that the annual income from the labor of prostitutes during the early 1970s would be about $50,400,000. The income from the largest industry, sugarcane, was $43,500,000.

Military prostitution in Thailand and the Philippines, which helped lay the foundation for modern-day sex tourism, has had a significant impact on rebuilding those economies as well.[14] The UN Educational, Scientific, and Cultural Organization (UNESCO) reports that "the major impetus of the growth of commercialized prostitution among Thai women took place in the 1960s during the Vietnam War. The so-called 'hired wives' for American soldiers stationed in Thailand was a new social phenomenon in the country. Many resort areas of the country also became major recreation areas for the American soldiers on leave."[15] Thanh-Dam Truong documents the development of Thailand's sex industry. The effects of rest and recreation tourism on Thailand's balance of payments was so substantial that when this market declined after U.S. withdrawal, alternatives had to be found.

---

12. Kierk, Matsuoka, and Okazawa-rey, "Women and Children, Militarism, and Human Rights," 9.

13. Saundra Pollock Sturdevant and Brenda Stoltzfus, eds., *Let the Good Times Roll: Prostitution and the U.S. Military in Asia* (New York: New Press, 1992), 251–52; and Moon, *Sex among Allies*, 32.

14. Moon, *Sex among Allies*, 32–33; also Sturdevant and Stoltzfus, *Let the Good Times Roll*, 251.

15. Suchart Prasithrathsin, *Child Prostitution and Education: Thailand* (Bangkok: UNESCO, April 1992), 1.

R and R tourism was adapted to sex tourism, which capitalized on the geographical mobility of corporate professionals, technicians, and military servicemen and the growth of the leisure industry in the First World. According to Truong's research, since the mid-1970s, tourism, of which sex tourism is a major component, has been a major foreign exchange earner, overtaking rice in 1982.[16]

The sex industry's role in rebuilding the economy of Korea was openly acknowledged by officials. During every "Etiquette and Good Conduct" lecture, sponsored monthly by local camptown officials to train prostitutes on how to treat GIs, "the local mayor or public information officer or public peace officer would...give the introductory remarks. They would say, 'All of you, who cater to the U.S. soldiers, are patriots. All of you are working to increase the foreign exchange earning of our country.'"[17] Of course, the prostitutes saw only a small fraction of that foreign exchange.

Those who have studied brothels around military bases equate military prostitution with rape and sexual slavery. More than one military officer has connected the existence of brothels around bases with rape. Napoléon Bonaparte said that "prostitutes are a necessity, without them men would attack respectable women in the streets."[18] In the wake of a rape by U.S. Marines of a twelve-year-old in Okinawa, the chief of the U.S. Pacific Command, Admiral Richard Macke, told reporters, "I think it was absolutely stupid, as I've said several times. For the price they paid to rent the car, they could have had a girl."[19] Pimps often "initiate" kidnapped women for prostitution by raping them or having them gang-raped.[20]

There are historical connections between the prostitutes who serviced U.S. soldiers after World War II in Okinawa and Korean comfort women. The Japanese government, in an effort to protect "pure" Japanese women, established brothels for occupying U.S. soldiers. Many of the women conscripted by the Japanese government to serve U.S. troops occupying Okinawa were Korean comfort women.[21] In addition to this historical connection, many assert that there is little difference between the Japanese military that forced Korean women into sexual slavery and the American soldiers who paid cash for a truckload of impoverished women and girls instead of giving them room and board. Many Korean activists view the prostitutes around U.S. military bases as a contemporary form of *jungshindae*, or comfort women.[22]

16. Thanh-Dam Truong, *Sex, Money, and Morality: Prostitution and Tourism in Southeast Asia* (Atlantic Highlands, N.J.: Zed Books, 1990), chaps. 3 and 5.

17. Ibid.

18. Bullough and Bullough, *Women and Prostitution,* 188.

19. Cynthia Enloe, "Spoils of War," *Ms. Magazine,* March/April 1996, 15.

20. Moon, *Sex among Allies,* 23.

21. Ibid., 46. See also Sturdevant and Stoltzfus, *Let the Good Times Roll,* 251.

22. Moon, *Sex among Allies,* 47.

Myths

Myths about prostitutes and the sex industry cloak the true nature of the global sex industry. Such myths perpetuate the sex industry by obscuring or justifying its existence to society and to individuals that participate in it as consumers, procurers, pimps, or apathetic government officials. They hide the true causes and hence solutions from law enforcement, governments and even advocacy and outreach organizations.

Most often prostitution is seen as something that is done by "bad girls." While johns are rarely stigmatized, prostitutes are seen as immoral and deviant. Categorizing some women as "bad" allows others to be "good" so long as they don't step outside strictly prescribed social roles. The label creates a class of women—bad women—who are viewed to be sexually available commodities and who are outside the protection of the law. The behavior of good women is circumscribed by threats of being labeled "bad women" and placed outside the structures (such as marriage) that guarantee them a limited amount of security. Such categories also drive a wedge between women in opposing categories.[23] Katharine Moon in her study of military camptown prostitutes in Korea points out that moralistic stereotypes of Korean prostitutes as "bad girls" initially distracted peace activists and women's groups from a political analysis of prostitution as a form of U.S. colonization and an outcome of militarization.[24] In the United States, peace and social justice communities have also not traditionally seen prostitution as an issue of peace and justice.[25]

Popular culture often makes prostitution seem appealing. Such portrayals help justify the use of women's bodies as sexual commodities by depicting prostitution as enjoyable, romantic, rewarding, and exciting. *Miss Saigon* romanticizes militarized prostitution. The American experience in Vietnam with militarized prostitution helping to define masculinity and U.S. domination has even been portrayed in pornographic films. Cynthia Fuchs describes a whole genre of Vietnam War porn films that portray Asians as prostitutes by nature (reaffirming the U.S. ideology regarding race). These films "collapse sex and violence where white male transcendence and self-redemption are established over bodies that are feminized, Asian, duplicitous and penetrated, and use intercourse as a conspicuous metaphor for the war."[26]

---

23. See Laurie Bell, *Good Girls, Bad Girls: Sex Trade Workers and Feminists Face to Face* (Toronto: Women's Press, 1987).

24. Moon, *Sex among Allies*, 9–10.

25. Brock and Thistlethwaite, *Casting Stones*, 324.

26. Cyntha J. Fuchs, "Sex Acts," in *Vietnam Generation Journal* (Charlottesville, Va.: Vietnam Generation, 1993), 2.

One of the oldest myths is that prostitution is unremarkable because it is ubiquitous, part of the human landscape, or the "oldest profession." Similar phrases dismiss prostitution as unworthy of concern or attention: "Boys will be boys," "War is hell," or Spike Lee's "It's a dick thing."[27] These statements legitimize prostitution by saying it needs no legitimization. They claim that the purchase of women's bodies is simply natural and unworthy of comment or closer examination.

Partly because of such attitudes, scholars, until recently predominantly male, have generally neglected the political import of militarized prostitution just as they have overlooked women's lives as important in critical discussions of imperialism, interstate relations, or the global political economy. As Enloe puts it, scholars have never examined "what the connections might be between international debt, foreign investment and militarism on the one hand and rape, prostitution, housework and wife battering on the other hand...the former are inherently 'serious' and the latter are 'private' and probably trivial."[28] Enloe reflects that war museums are unrealistic when they leave out the sex, prostitution, Amerasian offspring, VD policies, dating, interracial marriage, and immigration of GI wives and families to the United States.[29] What little scholarship does exist on prostitution carries a masculine bias.[30]

When prostitution does become part of public discussion, it is usually addressed in terms of the needs and concerns of those who use prostitutes. Prostitutes are then discussed as vectors of disease or as manipulative women trying to take advantage of young innocent soldiers. Most militaries, including the U.S. armed forces, have historically been concerned with the prevention of sexually transmitted disease (STD) and have established monitoring systems to limit the spread of venereal disease and HIV/AIDS among their troops. Such systems rarely if ever involve monitoring U.S. military personnel to insure they do not spread such diseases to prostitutes.[31] There is a perception among advocates for women and children in prostitution, although it is difficult to substantiate, that U.S. military personnel introduced HIV/AIDS to the Philippines and Thailand.[32]

---

27. Bruce Cumings, "Silent but Deadly: Sexual Subordination in the U.S.-Korean Relationship," in *Let the Good Times Roll*, ed. S. P. Sturdevant and B. Stoltzfus, 170.

28. Enloe, "Spoils of War," 104.

29. Ibid., 142–43. See also Moon, *Sex among Allies*.

30. Bullough and Bullough, *Women and Prostitution*, xiii.

31. Ibid., 194; Sturdevant and Stoltzfus, *Let the Good Times Roll*, 310–13; and Moon, *Sex among Allies*, chap. 4.

32. Truong, *Sex, Money, and Morality*, 161–67; and Sturdevant and Stoltzfus, *Let the Good Times Roll*, 311. Also Sister Mary Soledad Perpinan, "Militarism and the Sex Industry in the Philippines," in *Women and Violence*, ed. Miranda Davies (London: Zed Books, 1994), 149–55.

Recent efforts by the Department of Defense (DOD) to address the issue of child prostitution around U.S. bases have had the same tendency to ignore the effect of the U.S. military presence on the lives of women and girls in prostitution around bases. While the DOD has recently been willing to conduct anti–child prostitution briefings to prevent servicemen from engaging in child prostitution, it is significant that they do not have briefings aimed at preventing their involvement in prostitution with both adults and children. Their concern in addressing child prostitution is primarily for diplomacy and the safety of U.S. servicemen, not for their inappropriate behavior or for the impact of U.S. military presence on the communities that surround their bases. For instance, the stated goals of an Army Anti–Child Prostitution Briefing designed in 1997 are "to protect soldiers, our national interest, and in the process save the lives of children."[33] Saving children is expressed as an indirect outcome of protecting soldiers and national interests, not a goal. Yet history has demonstrated that protection for women and children is not always an indirect income of protecting national interests, and rarely an outcome of protecting soldiers.

Securing the lives of women and children in occupied countries is not a high priority among those who define and enforce national security interests. The low priority of women and children is reflected by the remarks of a Marine chaplain who was asked by the Pentagon to help design a training module to educate servicemen about child prostitution. Rather than expressing any concern for the sexual abuse of children, he wondered anxiously how he might help "his boys" avoid sex with minors when so many of the young prostitutes used makeup and clothing that could "trick" servicemen into believing they were adults, especially young servicemen who tend to be "juiced up." He asked anti–child prostitution advocates if they had any tips he could give the servicemen to help them identify minors so that he could protect the men from prosecution under the new U.S. anti–child prostitution law. It never occurred to him to question the involvement of U.S. servicemen in prostitution of any kind.[34]

Prostitutes around bases must be aggressive and flirtatious with servicemen if they are to make a living. One U.S. Army chaplain commented that "in Korea, the guy is inundated with prostitutes."[35] An Army captain who served in the 1980s noted that young enlistees were susceptible to getting "duped" into serious relationships with prostitutes who sought to "exploit the boys for money."[36] Servicemen rarely see the inside story of what mo-

---

33. Army Office of the Deputy Chief of Staff for Personnel, Human Relations Directorate, Department of Defense, script of "Anti–Child Prostitution Briefing," 22 January 1998.

34. Marine chaplain, this author's interview, January 1998.

35. Moon, *Sex among Allies*, 20–21.

36. Ibid.

tivates the women's outward behavior, nor do they reflect upon their own exploitative practices.

Posters and souvenirs denigrating women and the culture of the occupied country are ubiquitous in the bar areas, creating a climate that enables individuals and institutions to justify exploitative, even violent, behavior. T-shirts and hats sold around the clubs display messages such as, "Women are angels in the street, but devil in bed," "I may not go down in history, but I will go down on your little sister"; and "I love you no shit, but buy your own fucking drink."[37] One poster displays a long poem about a sexual encounter with a prostitute that concludes, "and as you dress and put on your hat / you look back and say ... / did I fuck that????!!!!"[38] Women in the Philippines are referred to as "little brown fucking machines powered with rice," or LBFM for short. In Korea, GIs during and after the war referred to all indigenous women as "moose."[39] For selling their sexual labor, women are objectified in ways that men who buy the labor are not.

Stereotypes of prostitutes from developing countries as exotic and submissive expose global racism as being instrumental in perpetuating systems of sexual exploitation. Because of several wars between the United States and Asian countries and heavy U.S. occupation of those areas, American GIs have had extensive experience with Asian prostitutes, experiences that they often share with other males. Rita Nakashima Brock, a scholar who spent her childhood on U.S. military bases in the United States, Germany, and Okinawa, writes that "most of my life, I have faced assumptions made about me based on sexual stereotypes of Asian women. 'Geisha girl' and 'Susie Wong' are two common examples. Perceptions of me based on such stereotypes plagued me throughout my teens, twenties and thirties."[40] Many Asians report similar experiences of being stereotyped as sexually available. Japanese women who married soldiers, especially after World War II, were immediately suspect as prostitutes.[41]

Such racial stereotypes, while obviously misleading, simultaneously reveal the connections between racism and sexual abuse. Many feminist studies of the sex industry argue that "the exoticization of the Third World 'other' is as equally important as economic factors in positioning women in sex work."[42] Sex tour operators take advantage of these stereotypes as well as perpetuate them. For instance, a tour magazine in Switzerland carried an advertisement

---

37. Sturdevant and Stoltzfus, *Let the Good Times Roll*, 326.
38. Ibid., 287.
39. Ibid.
40. Brock and Thistlethwaite, *Casting Stones*, 324.
41. Maxine Baca Zinn and Bonnie Thorton Dill, *Women of Color in U.S. Society* (Philadelphia: Temple University Press, 1994), 281.
42. Kamala Kempadoo, *Global Sex Workers* (New York: Routledge, 1998), 10.

which read, "Slim, sunburnt and sweet, they love the white man in an erotic and devoted way. They are masters of the art of making love by nature, an art that we Europeans do not know."[43] Many servicemen who would never dream of buying sex from a Caucasian child in the U.S. rationalize sex with children in other countries based on myths that sexualize people of color. Some even allow themselves to believe they are helping the children because they would otherwise starve. It is no mistake that in most parts of the world, those outside the dominant race are found in disproportionally large numbers among the ranks of sex workers and are the lowest paid. Racism and sexism join with economic forces to produce a cadre of people who can be commodified.

Dispelling Myths: Telling Is Political

What is presented here is a synthesis of common themes in the stories of women working as prostitutes as gleaned from the records of advocates for prostitute rights and scholars. Such records are unfortunately scarce. Researchers rarely privilege prostitutes' experiences in research on this issue. The literature usually provides an economic, political, or social analysis of prostitution rather than record the experiences of prostitutes. Also, much of militarized prostitution, like most illegal activities, is hidden from view by organized crime. In many cases prostitutes can jeopardize their jobs or safety by speaking about their work to outsiders. It is often painful for those who have left or escaped from the sex industry to tell their stories. Many are deeply ashamed even though they have been victimized.

Many women working in military prostitution cite that they chose to do this work to keep themselves and/or their children, parents, and siblings alive. In the words of one woman, "It was then I realized that life is like this. When you have no money—you agree to anything. In the end I said yes."[44] Women often "choose" this work, if this can be called choice, because it is the only or best way to make money. Sometimes it is no less dangerous or painful than other options.

Lita from the rural province of Samar in the Philippines tried many strategies before she resorted to prostitution. Working as a maid at the age of ten with her mother in Manila, she was nearly raped by her boss's son. After fleeing this job, they worked scavenging in a trash dump until Lita and her father were nearly buried to death by bulldozers in two separate incidents. After migrating to two other towns looking for a way to support themselves, and after the family home was destroyed by a typhoon sending the family

---

43. Truong, *Sex, Money, and Morality*, 178.
44. Sturdevant and Stoltzfus, *Let the Good Times Roll*, 158.

into debt, Lita went to Olongapo, the site of a U.S. naval base until 1992, to make a living as a maid. Unable to find work, she decided to work in a bar. She was fourteen when she took her first customer. Her first experience was terrifying. "I cried. I said, 'Don't have sex with me.' " The word she uses for sex is *galawin*. Women in the Philippines often use the word *galawin* to refer to the sexual intercourse they have with servicemen. This word can mean sex or rape and is never used to refer to consensual sex.[45] He offered to pay what looked to her like a lot of money. "I agreed because he gave me money.... I really didn't want to but he forced me. It was very painful. I bled.... I sent the money to my mother."[46]

After a typhoon destroyed her community in the Philippines, Janet applied to an agency that told her she would be a dancer in Japan. Instead, she found herself selling sex in a bar near the American base in Okinawa. Hearing that Corazon Aquino might stop Filipinas from going or being trafficked into Japan for sex work, she responded: "How will these women who have worked here earn a living? Will Cory [Aquino] give them work? The news I heard was that women from Korea would replace them. We wouldn't work in a club anymore if we were given work that's adequate." Her comments reveal the fact that removing the industry of prostitution is not in itself a solution to these women's oppression: "I wouldn't have made myself strong inside to come here if we had had enough to live on, but we really didn't."[47]

Most of the brothels work on a system of debt bondage that creates slave-like conditions. The brothel systems are similar in Korea, Japan, Thailand, and the Philippines. Job placement agencies (usually illegal ones) that specialize in bar and brothel prostitution place women in a club and charge the club owner a fee. This fee is charged to the new employee's account at usurious rates. Women have to work off this "agency fee," plus fees for items required to attract soldiers, such as makeup, stereo equipment, and clothes; their room and board; and other expenses they incur, such as medical bills to treat VD, abortions, bribes for law enforcement, bail money, and emergency expenses.[48] Often, the owners find ways to increase the women's debt or lie about how much debt a woman has incurred. Nan Hee says: "If you had no debt they see to it that you incur some.... Escaping from a club isn't easy to do."[49]

To work as a prostitute around U.S. military bases, a woman must be registered in order to work legally. To complete the registration she must

---

45. Ibid., 80.
46. Ibid., 70–94.
47. Ibid., 282–98.
48. Moon, *Sex among Allies*, 19–23; and Sturdevant and Stoltzfus, "Olongapo: The Bar System," in *Let the Good Times Roll.*
49. Sturdevant and Stoltzfus, *Let the Good Times Roll*, 203.

have a chest X ray, a VD smear, an AIDS test, and a blood test and give a stool sample. She receives a card stating she is clean and is required to report back for checkups to renew the registration. If she is found to be unclean, the bar is contacted and she must stop work until she is cured. She must, of course, pay for the test and treatments herself. Women have often been stopped by local and military police to show their cards. Customers may ask to see her card as well, although they are not commanded to show one themselves. If men are found to have a sexually transmitted disease, they are not allowed to leave the base, although some servicemen get treatment in clinics outside the base in order to avoid restrictions. Historically the clinics where women are registered have been joint projects between the local health departments and the U.S. armed forces. In Korea the clinics are now run by the Korean government.[50]

The club requires a club worker to sell as many drinks as possible— alcohol for the men and "ladies drinks" (usually soft drinks) for herself. The woman receives a small amount of income from the drinks she sells— in Korea it has historically been 10 to 20 percent. To sell drinks she must flirt with soldiers. Selling drinks, however, has never been the mainstay of women's earnings in the club. Women must have sex with soldiers for the bulk of their income. In Korea in Uijongbu in the mid-1980s, "long-time" (overnight) was twenty dollars, while "short-time" (hourly rate) was ten dollars. Owners and pimps generally take 80 percent of the earnings per trick. If a customer is not satisfied with a woman, he may ask for his money back. If the bar owner agrees, his fee is charged to the woman. In Korea in the mid-1990s, clubs were paying a hostess $250 a month.[51] In Olongapo, Philippines, say Saundra Sturdevant and Brenda Stoltzfus in one of the most detailed accounts of camptown life, "the level of income of the women is difficult to determine, but it is a myth that they earn a lot of money."[52]

Usually the women live in crowded conditions behind the club or in a rented apartment. Another type of arrangement is that of a "kept woman." A serviceman may pay for an apartment and send money to a woman on a regular basis. She then serves him full time, or in the case of a Navy base such as Olongapo, the woman stops working when her serviceman's ship comes in. Some of these arrangements lead to marriage. Many more do not.[53]

Yoon Hee's account of her life includes many of these elements. She had moved to Tongduch'on, Korea, and sold her body for room and board at the Five-Star Club for American GIs. She met Charlie, who worked as a fuel handler on the base. He promised to bring back three thousand dollars to

---

50. Moon, *Sex among Allies*, 18–19.
51. Ibid., 19.
52. Sturdevant and Stoltzfus, *Let the Good Times Roll*, 47.
53. Sturdevant and Stoltzfus, "Olongapo: The Bar System," in *Let the Good Times Roll*.

pay off her debt. Her debt was especially high because she did not want to flirt with customers to get them to buy drinks and did not want to sleep with them. Her boyfriend promised to pay off her debt but was unable, driving Yoon Hee into near despair. In a rare stroke of luck, the club owner fired her because he said he was losing money on her and allowed her to leave without paying the debt. Relieved, she moved in with Charlie and found a job at a clothing factory, making three hundred dollars a month working twelve hours a day, including holidays, and only resting on Sundays. With his added income, she was able to survive. Despite communication problems, Yoon Hee was satisfied to be out of the club and able to buy things she couldn't previously afford. Charlie was overcoming a recent divorce and seemed to prefer "a woman who because she cannot talk back to him in English keeps silent."[54]

While many are pressured by economic necessity to enter prostitution, still others are physically forced or tricked into prostitution by sex traffickers who either recruit young girls from rural areas or look for women as they get off trains fleeing economic depression in the countryside in the hopes of finding a job in the city. Others have been abused by family members, spouses, acquaintances, or strangers. Katharine Moon in her study of Korean camptown prostitution summarizes: "The overwhelming majority of the prostitutes have experienced a combination of poverty, low class status, physical sexual and emotional abuse even before entering the kijich'on world."[55]

A Human Rights Watch report tells the story of "Chit Chit," a young Thai woman who left her village in 1990 at the age of eighteen. She was taken directly to a policeman named Bu Muad in Mae Sai, who himself was the brothel agent. The policeman raped Chit Chit and warned her that if she ever told anyone, he would beat her. She was afraid of him because he always carried his gun. According to Chit Chit, this policeman was a regular visitor to the brothel in Chiangmai, beating girls for the owner if they did not cooperate.[56] It is not uncommon for police to be involved in the sex industry.

Women in many cultures face a double jeopardy with rape, since a woman who is no longer a virgin cannot get married or must marry her rapist. Kim Yonja describes being raped when she was eleven years old by her cousin as one reason she became a prostitute. She believed the rape would not have happened had her mother been home, but her mother had to work because her father had abandoned them.[57] Kim Sun-Ok was raped by a date. After

---

54. My Sister's Place, *Newsletter* no. 10 (February 1992).
55. Moon, *Sex among Allies*, 23.
56. *A Modern Form of Slavery*, 49.
57. Moon, *Sex among Allies*, 23.

the rape, Kim was forced by cultural expectations to live with her rapist. He beat her and drove the family into poverty. Fearing for her life, she ran away to Seoul, where she was recruited to work in one of the brothels around the American base of Uijongbu. The recruiter told her: "Anyway, you'll have a hard time getting married to another Korean man. You have a baby, you're uneducated, you have no money, you're not especially pretty.... If you want to change your fate, you'd better go and meet an American soldier and marry him." She quickly went into debt as most club women do, since the system is stacked against them. Ironically, her only hope at that point was to meet an American soldier who would pay off her debt to the club owner and marry her.[58] Few of these marriages work out. By several estimates, the failure rate is 90 percent.[59] Often women end up in abusive situations in marriages to American men.[60]

Women who enter militarized prostitution are clearly victims of poverty, abuse, and their low status as women in patriarchal societies that are economically and militarily dominated. However, within their limited range of options many demonstrate a great deal of agency. They demonstrate courage and altruism. They often see themselves and are seen by others as family breadwinners, caretakers, committed daughters and mothers, and ambitious women.[61]

In most parts of Asia, the basic unit of society is the family, not the individual. The self exists within social relationships. Girls and young women in many cultures take on more responsibilities earlier than do boys and are socialized to make greater personal sacrifices to take care of their families. This leads many girls and women to enter prostitution out of a sense of family duty. When commercialized prostitution in Thailand increased dramatically during the Vietnam War, recruiters largely forced and tricked young women and girls from rural areas into prostitution. These women were able to send money back to their families and increase their standard of living. As word got out about this, the jobs in brothels became much sought after. Some girls and women began to chose to enter prostitution to alleviate the humiliation and suffering of their families. Families found that by selling their daughters, they could support themselves or drastically improve their standard of living. When women and girls enter the sex industry, their choice was understood, not as a moral flaw, but as bad fate or karma. Their sacrifice

---

58. Kim Sun-Ok, "Only One Hope: To Marry an American Soldier," in *Once I Had a Dream*, ed. Marion Kennedy Kim (Hong Kong: DAGA, 1992), 41–48.

59. Moon, *Sex among Allies*, 35.

60. Faye Moon and former staff at My Sister's Place, my interview, 15 August 1998. See also Bok-Lim Kim et al., *Women in Shadows: A Handbook for Service Providers Working with Asian Wives of U.S. Military Personnel* (La Jolla, Calif.: National Committee Concerned with Asian Wives of U.S. Servicemen, 1981).

61. Prasithrathsin, "Child Prostitution and Education"; see also *A Modern Form of Slavery*.

is considered to have meaning to others and was believed to improve the women's karma, especially since to be born female indicates bad karma.[62]

Nan Hee, a Korean prostitute, relates: "Mother didn't think that everyone working in the clubs was bad. What could she say? I was helping the family out, after all."[63] Madelin, a Filipina, in summarizing the reasons women enter prostitution states, "They want to help their families."[64] Sung Ae fled an abusive husband. She never wanted to "lower herself" to be a waitress in a bar, but when her mother got sick, she says: "I finally decided I would sell my body for a living. When I started work, I got a lump sum from the pimp and helped my mom to get treatment."[65] Families often have mixed feelings about their daughters working in prostitution. Lita in the Philippines reports that her family was initially angry and upset, telling her she did not have to do "this kind of work" to pay off their debt. They seem to know, though, that the truth was that she did. Her mother says: "She ended up in Olongapo in this work. Never mind. I'm not ashamed." She described the family debt and concluded: "If it hadn't been for our children, we would not have survived. No matter what we thought to do, nothing worked."[66]

Often the women sell their bodies to provide for or keep their children. After being forced to perform oral sex on servicemen in Subic Bay, Glenda reports thinking, "If I don't earn this way, my children and I will go hungry." Linda similarly says, "If it weren't for them [the children] I wouldn't be doing this—going with Americans." Johnston's Mom in Songt'an, Korea, tried to give up her sons for adoption but could not bear to do it, so she went back to prostitution to keep her boys.[67] Many of the women try to hide their work from their children to protect them. Some women stay in prostitution not only to be able to feed their children but to make sure they can get an education and get out of the cycle of poverty.

Even if a woman's work as a prostitute doesn't curtail her chances at marriage, having an Amerasian child might.[68] An Amerasian child is living proof of the woman's occupation as a prostitute. Once a woman has a child by an American, well-founded concerns that she and her child won't be accepted by their community keep her in the brothels in hopes that she might marry an American who would bring her and her child to the United States or at least support them financially. The withdrawal of U.S. naval bases

---

62. For a full discussion of the Christian concept of sin and Buddhist understandings of karma in relation to perpetuating patriarchal cultural perceptions that perpetuate the sex industry, see Brock and Thistlethwaite, *Casting Stones*, chap. 8.

63. Sturdevant and Stoltzfus, *Let the Good Times Roll*, 191.

64. Ibid., 64.

65. My Sister's Place, *Newsletter* no. 11 (August 1992).

66. Sturdevant and Stoltzfus, *Let the Good Times Roll*, 107–8.

67. Moon, *Sex among Allies*, 35.

68. Sturdevant and Stoltzfus, *Let the Good Times Roll*, 88–89.

from the Philippines in 1992 left behind a legacy of about fifty thousand Amerasian children in the Philippines, with an estimated ten thousand living in Olongapo. Many of these children are placed for adoption or abandoned. Many end up working as prostitutes serving American pedophiles or are sold to sex traffickers; others end up as street children.[69]

Those who have "chosen" from a limited range of options to sell sex are often demonstrating the ability to take charge of their lives by removing themselves from a worse form of abuse or poverty. Many of the women take care of others even at great sacrifice to themselves, a role that women are uniquely socialized to play. Many working as prostitutes around bases have fled husbands who were abusive or neglectful. For some, selling their bodies is safer, or at least not any worse, than what they experienced in their marriages. Many women actually end up in prostitution because they refuse to accept the limitations of their situation, because they are enterprising, courageous, and willing to take risks for their families. Janet, who works in a brothel in Okinawa, sees herself as courageous. She relates, "I made myself strong inside" to go to Japan.[70]

Although it is sometimes difficult for many women working as prostitutes to reconcile their sense of integrity and spiritual lives with formal religious or moral teachings, they often think deeply about the consequences of their actions and try to make a moral decision under difficult circumstances. Lita says about her choices: "I pray to God because I have committed many sins. We sell our bodies. That's a sin. I decided in order to lessen my sin I would go to church. I think God understands why I am here."[71] Similarly Glenda goes to church but worries sometimes that God won't accept her. At other times she thinks that God may understand her situation. She has observed that the priests don't help the women in the bars. She often feels ashamed of herself: "It's as though I'm not needed in the world. Maybe now that I'm like this, the One above will understand."[72] In contrast, when Linda was told by family members that she was sinful, she responded: "That's okay if it's only you, but what about those you are feeding and putting through school?"[73]

Many have thought seriously about the ethics of what they do for a living. Nan Hee reflects that it meant something to her to be a good daughter while her parents were alive by supporting them financially with her earnings from prostitution. She doesn't think people in the business are "bad." She says they are there because of family circumstances. She is not ashamed of herself,

---

69. Moon, *Sex among Allies*, 35.
70. Sturdevant and Stoltzfus, *Let the Good Times Roll*, 299.
71. Ibid., 93–94.
72. Ibid., 130.
73. Ibid., 164.

although she knows others look down on her: "It doesn't matter what others say if our hearts are clean." Janet used to think that if you had sex outside marriage, you were a bad woman, "repulsive to look at." Although she still sees herself as conservative, the way she sees it, the women don't work at the clubs because they want to. They work because they need money.[74]

Faye Moon, the cofounder of My Sister's Place, a Korean Presbyterian ministry to camptown women, remembers one woman who went to the market to buy a quilt for her child. She paid far too much for the quilt. When Moon asked her why she paid such a price rather than bargaining, the woman responded that she was thinking about how hard it was to make those quilts. For Faye Moon this woman was truly living out the Christian calling. Another woman had lots of boxes of noodles in her home. Moon asked her why she had so many noodles. The woman responded that the woman who was selling the noodles needed the money.[75] This isn't to say that prostitutes are saintly (lest we fall into the myth of the "whore with a heart of gold"), but that like most people, they run the gamut.

While the views of the U.S. servicemen toward the women who sexually service them are made rather clear through tour brochures, club advertisements, posters, and souvenirs sold around the bases, we rarely hear the women's opinions of those who buy their sexual services. The women often see servicemen as exploitative, ugly, manipulative, and immoral. Says Ms. Pak: "I've met many Americans in this business. All of them are good liars."[76] Lita says: "In my eyes Americans treat Filipinas like toys. The women, like myself, need money so they go along with it."[77] Many dislike or are disgusted by Americans because they demand sexual services that are outside the norm for the women. They view these men as perverts. Madelin says: "Most of the U.S. Navy are wild. They think that as long as they have paid they can get whatever they want."[78] Lita complains that "they make you do blow jobs and get in different positions that they like."[79] Many of the women have had their lives threatened or have been forced into sex acts that they tried to refuse. The women are often anxious about learning the sexual habits of men from different cultures and races. Ms. Pak expressed fear at beginning work at a GI club in Osan, Korea, because Americans were so big and she worried how she would handle their large bodies.[80] Some of the prostitutes have neutral or even sympathetic views of servicemen. Says

---

74. Ibid., 180.
75. Faye Moon, interview, 28 July 1998.
76. Sturdevant and Stoltzfus, *Let the Good Times Roll*, 237.
77. Ibid., 93.
78. Ibid., 62.
79. Ibid., 92.
80. Ibid., 230.

Nan Hee: "I dislike American GIs being in Korea, but they are human beings. They've also left their homelands and must be lonely." She says that,
"The American GIs treat us better than Korean men."[81]

Violence is common for women working as prostitutes around bases.
As mentioned, they are often forced into sex acts besides vaginal intercourse. Many are raped by their managers/pimps, who sometimes consider
the women to be sexually available to them at any time. Manager/pimps
often lock the women in the brothels in the evening to prevent their escape.
Others are found and beaten if they try to leave before paying off their club
debts. At worst, a woman encounters a GI who tortures and murders her,
as Yun Kumi did in Korea in 1992. Private Kenneth Markle was convicted
of killing her. She was found naked with a coke bottle embedded in her
uterus and the trunk of an umbrella driven twenty-seven centimeters into
her rectum.[82] Women in camptowns and brothels report that many crimes go
unprosecuted, sending a clear message that their lives aren't worth much to
law enforcement, the military, or the government. Ms. Ch'oe reported that
she had been beaten by a U.S. serviceman and had reported the incident to
the Korean and U.S. military police, but the soldier was not prosecuted.[83]
Ms. Pak recounts that her sister was mutilated and murdered allegedly by
a U.S. serviceman in the early 1970s, but he was never turned over to Korean authorities to be tried in their legal system, and she never received an
apology or financial compensation.[84] The Korean National Police reported
that in 1989, of 819 incidents involving U.S. military personnel and Korean citizens, not even one case was prosecuted.[85] Advocates for prostitutes
rights in Okinawa have compiled a list of crimes against local women and
girls, including those who work in the sex industry, that spans from 1945
to 1997. Many of the cases have gone unsolved, or suspects have not been
prosecuted.[86]

Brothel managers make it difficult for women to develop any solidarity.
Often the women working in bars and brothels are not allowed to speak to
one another. Brothel owners keep them isolated, and the only outside news
they may get is from customers. Recent attempts by feminist activists in
Thailand to organize prostitutes have been halted by entrepreneurs and the
state.[87] Women must compete with one another for customers and potential
American husbands. In some bars, the competition is quite literal. One petite

81. Ibid., 203.
82. Moon, *Sex among Allies*, 21.
83. Ibid., 153.
84. Ibid., 145.
85. My Sister's Place, *Newsletter* no. 8 (July 1991).
86. Suzuyo Takazato, Harumi Miyagi, and Carolyn Francis, "Postwar U.S. Military Crimes
against Women in Okinawa," unpublished manuscript.
87. Truong, *Sex, Money, and Morality*, 187.

woman tells the story of having to box other women for the entertainment of U.S. servicemen. Those women who are registered in clubs often have conflicts with those who are unregistered. Some women manage to move up the hierarchy of sex work and can become club managers themselves. They do not necessarily treat the prostitutes with compassion.[88] Still, many women are supportive, teaching each other such survival skills as how to recognize potentially violent customers and how to protect themselves from STDs, how to fake orgasms, and how to remain appealing to customers when they are older.

Katharine Moon has documented that prostitutes have managed to galvanize as a political force at times despite the tight control exerted by pimps and the state. During the early 1970s in South Korea, the U.S. armed forces, the Republic of Korea, and the Korean government jointly initiated a "Clean-Up Campaign" to alleviate racial tensions exacerbated by club interactions and to reduce rates of venereal disease.[89] Clubs not complying with regulations would be shut down by base authorities for a period of time. Moon examines the impact of this campaign on Korean prostitutes' lives as well as their responses. She demonstrates that Korean prostitutes, although powerless in many ways, did not remain passive during political maneuvering that impacted their lives during the 1970s.

Moon documents how a protest by 100–150 prostitutes against the decision of the Camp Humphreys command to close its main gate and put the town of Anjongni off-limits grew to a crowd of approximately six hundred prostitutes and three thousand other villagers. The prostitutes and others demanded that the base authorities open their gates. Waitresses who worked on the base and who were blocked from entering the compound hurled stones at military personnel, overturned a Korean police car, and demanded to meet with the base commander. The crowd, led by prostitutes, held six U.S. soldiers hostage and demanded to speak with the commander. They were granted an audience. Ms. Yi Chongja, the representative of the village's "Girlie Club," was invited with other village leaders and a national assemblyman to have lunch with Colonel Best to discuss the lifting of the off-limits ban. The event was significant not only because of its success but because the prostitutes were supported by local villagers.

Camptown prostitutes also staged demonstrations on behalf of their human rights when U.S. airmen launched a boycott to lower prices in the P'yongt'aek region. The boycott was also a protest against local Koreans' discrimination against black soldiers (camptown prostitutes were considered by Korean and base authorities to be a crucial link in controlling racial ten-

---

88. Moon, *Sex among Allies*, 21.
89. Prostitutes who had sex with black soldiers often faced retaliation by white soldiers.

sions and racially sparked riots in the camptowns). Kim Yonja, who helped lead the protest, demanded to know, "How is it possible that someone can set the same price for a pair of shoes and a woman's body, then print the prices and circulate them?" The boycott ended partly because of lack of participation and partly because of the public protests. Moon reflects that although the prostitutes are the most despised of camptown residents, they represented the vulnerability of Korean residents to U.S. power and were therefore able to lead other villagers to challenge that power. The prostitutes understood their powerlessness before the bases to be a violation of their human rights and as a symbol of U.S. domination over the Korean people. However, as the Clean-Up Campaign progressed and U.S. and Korean control over the camptowns increased, such protests became rare.

Violence against the women working in prostitution by U.S. servicemen has also sparked protests. In Korea, increasing resistance to U.S. dominance in camptown life reached a critical mass with the murder of Yun Kumi, a camptown prostitute, in the fall of 1992. Thousands of Koreans from outside the camptown again joined with prostitutes to publicly protest U.S. crimes against Koreans. Rather than seeing this crime as one committed by an individual soldier, they viewed it as an example of how American soldiers treat Korean women. Prior to this time, prostitutes had held small demonstrations against GI violence against women, especially murders, but did not receive as much public support. Growing outside support for such demonstrations seems to indicate a growing anti-Americanism among Koreans, especially the younger generations. The plight of camptown prostitutes is symbolic of the problems associated with U.S. military presence, which is increasingly being viewed as U.S. imperialism.[90] Prostitution around bases in the Philippines has also become symbolic of U.S. domination, and prostitutes were part of the movement to close U.S. bases there. The aforementioned 1995 rape of the twelve-year-old Japanese girl by Marines touched off similar protests in Okinawa.

While constraints are placed on women by pimps, legal and law enforcement systems, and a society that ostracizes them, making political action difficult, women in brothels form political perspectives based on their experiences of abuse and neglect. Katharine Moon's interviews with camptown women reveal that they define national security differently than do national and foreign elites: "All of the women I interviewed stated that their greatest need for Korean government protection [after the Korean War] was not from North Korean threats but the exploitation and abuse of club owners/pimps, local Korean police, and VD clinic officials, and the power of US

---

90. Moon, *Sex among Allies*, 32.

bases."[91] The women interviewed by Moon felt betrayed by both Korean and U.S. authorities.

Moon found that Korean prostitutes' most common complaints about the United States were that Americans considered the women to be mere sex toys, that the U.S. military was concerned only with the health and well-being of the GI, and that there was little legal accountability on the part of military authorities for the soldiers' criminal behavior. Women in camptowns often expressed ambivalence toward the U.S. presence. Ms. Pak, interviewed in *Let the Good Times Roll*, asks: "Isn't it true that the Americans and Russians are playing with us by placing us in the middle?" She observed that the Americans are needed to protect South Korea from North Korea, but if it weren't for that, "it would be a hundred times more profitable for our country if the Americans left." She once had an argument with a GI about U.S.-Korea relations. She told him: "You are in Korea to make money, not to help us."[92] Katharine Moon was told by Bakery Auntie, an uneducated former camptown worker in South Korea, that Japan got rich off the Korean War and that South Korea did the same off the Vietnam War. She also asserted that the United States had fought Iraq in the Gulf War because the United States had amassed too many fancy weapons that had to be used.[93]

Moon documents that Korean camptown women feel betrayed by their government because it has done little to improve their welfare and has seemed impotent or unwilling to help them leave prostitution. The women in her interviews ridiculed the Korean government's efforts to label their selling of sex as patriotic service. They did believe, however, that their role as camptown prostitute served to protect "normal" Korean women from being raped by U.S. soldiers. One woman interviewed by Moon complained: "So why does the society call us *yanggalbo* [Western whores]? We've played our part—if it weren't for us, where would 'normal' Koreans be?"[94] There is an awareness among at least some of the women that they have been used to further their government's political and economic ends but given little protection or economic benefit in return. Ms. Chang even asserted that in the worst case "if the Korean government wanted to continue using women's sexual labor to keep US soldiers happy, then the government should take over the prostitution system...to benefit the women."[95] The comments of those Moon interviewed expressed a deep desire to be embraced by their

---

91. Ibid., 153.
92. Sturdevant and Stoltzfus, *Let the Good Times Roll*, 209.
93. Moon, *Sex among Allies*, 6.
94. Ibid., 156.
95. Ibid., 157.

nation-state and included in the rights and privileges that would empower their lives.

Developing a Framework for Understanding Military Prostitution

A division in the feminist movement's view of prostitution tends to over-simplify the experiences of women working in military prostitution. The feminist movement is currently divided in its analysis of prostitution between a liberal feminist view that seeks to legalize prostitution and a feminist view that takes an abolitionist approach. Each side of the debate accuses the other of believing myths about prostitutes. Both views seem unable to capture the diverse opinions and interpretations that prostitutes offer about their work.

Liberal feminists see prostitution as being like any job for which feelings are required and commodified, jobs such as airline service, acting, psycho-therapy, child care, and massage. Liberal feminists therefore prefer the term "sex worker" to "prostitute" and advocate for the legalization of prostitution, which they believe will alleviate, if not eliminate, discriminatory and exploitative aspects of the industry. For liberal feminists, sex workers' problems are labor related: workers lack legal protection, have no rights, do not have the ability to unionize, and are not subject to wage laws.[96]

The abolitionist feminist perspective views all prostitution as a form of violence against women that perpetuates and stems from patriarchy and misogyny.[97] Kathleen Barry, whose book *Female Sexual Slavery* sparked a renewal of concern about prostitution and sex trafficking during the 1980s, situates the sex industry along a continuum of female sexual slavery that includes such forms of sexual control and violence as forced marriage, domestic violence, incest, rape, female genital mutilation, and veiling.[98] Barry believes that men control and dominate women by controlling their sexuality.[99] For Barry, prostitution is sexual slavery and must be abolished, not regulated.

Both liberal feminists and abolitionists use the stories of prostitutes to back up their own theoretical claims and claim to represent the voice of

---

96. For a full discussion, see Kemala Kempadoo and Gail Pheterson, *Vindication of the Rights of Whores: The International Movement for Prostitutes' Rights* (Toronto: Seal Press, 1989).

97. This perspective is characterized by Kathleen Barry and the Coalition against Trafficking in Women (CATW) and WHISPER (Women Hurt in Systems of Prostitution Engaged in Revolt), Global Alliance against Trafficking in Women, and UNESCO and by organizations to end child prostitution such as ECPAT.

98. For a full discussion of this viewpoint, see Kathleen Barry's *Female Sexual Slavery* (New York: New York University Press, 1979); and *The Prostitution of Sexuality* (New York: New York University Press, 1995).

99. Barry, *Female Sexual Slavery,* 194.

prostitutes. Liberal feminists see prostitutes as agents, making a valid professional choice. Abolitionists tend to see prostitutes as victims of sexual exploitation. These conflicting conclusions indicate just how difficult it is to hear the varied experiences of women who are working as prostitutes. Advocates and researchers must be cautioned that in searching for the right theoretical framework it is easy to forget that reality seldom fits neatly into either framework and theory often reflects more about the theorist than those who are being studied. In identifying main themes running through interviews with women who have worked in brothels, this article, rather than seeing victimization and agency as mutually exclusive categories, has seen both of these aspects as characteristic of the lives of women working in brothels. Thanh-Dam Truong and Katharine Moon provide research and more complex theoretical frameworks that help move the debate beyond the polarized debate over whether prostitutes are victims or agents and the attendant theoretical stances.

Both Truong and Moon make the helpful observation that thinking in dualistic terms such as victim/agent does little to illuminate the complex systems that lead to the development of sex industries. Moon observes: "We need to begin viewing even the most dispossessed women as 'players' in world politics; without jumping back and forth from two opposite poles of self-agency and victim-hood, a middle ground must be found."[100] While she stresses that the camptown prostitutes she studied were definitely not autonomous actors; neither were they simply recipients of governmental actions. Her case study of the experiences of camptown prostitutes during the U.S. armed forces, Korea, and the Republic of Korea government joint Clean-Up Campaign of the 1970s demonstrates that women played a significant role in camptown politics.

Truong similarly observes that "the dualistic approach to prostitution bypasses complex social processes. It is the dualistic approach to prostitution shared by many feminists which enables the shift of the argument from victimization to glorification."[101] Truong suggests that feminists look even deeper than liberal and sexual slavery perspectives to see "deeply-rooted dimensions of social inequality exacerbated by social change such as agrarian change, urbanization, foreign currency crisis, international labor mobility and militarization."[102] She points out that methodological gaps in the study of prostitution surface in the tendency of feminists "to add prostitution to the range of social issues which are pertinent to social movements emerging in defense of a particular interested position (labor emancipation, national

---

100. Moon, *Sex among Allies*, 52.
101. Truong, *Sex, Money, and Morality*, 55.
102. Ibid.

emancipation, sexual emancipation or autonomy)."[103] This leads her to question how far the voices expressed through prostitutes' organizations actually reflect the consciousness of the majority of prostitutes. While each side in the feminist debate makes important observations, each appears to be fitting data about the lives of prostitutes into their own agendas and theoretical frameworks rather than listening to the complexity revealed in the stories of prostitutes.

Truong explores the complex role of the international political economy, and Moon the complex impact of interstate relations on the creation of prostitution to service military interests and ultimately national and international interests. Truong critiques the sexual politics position and the liberal position as failing to conduct a thorough analysis of the global political economy. Abolitionists, focusing on sexual politics, overload the concept of patriarchy and neglect analysis of other aspects of the problem. The liberal perspective fails to address coherently the issue of exploitation. Truong views prostitution as the result of disruption in kinship patterns caused by increased human geographical mobility and dislocation, of which militarization is one cause (urbanization, migration, and commerce are others). The biological and social aspects of reproduction, normally structured by the institutions of family and kinship, are then placed in the market system. This phenomenon is hidden by belief systems (such as religion and cultural value systems) and institutional structures governing sexuality that pretend prostitution is unacceptable (such as police enforcement and the law), when it is in reality tolerated and even promoted for economic gain. This concealment enables an intensification of accumulation of capital in the sex industry, since prostitutes with no legal rights can be easily exploited. Women's sexual labor is a commodity that requires little overhead and capital investment and is easily exploited for economic gain by First World investors, national governments, and national as well as foreign militaries.

While Truong focuses on prostitution as the outcome of interests and interactions between governments, international organizations, and multinational corporations of wealthy countries, Moon takes this a step further by analyzing the role of the residents and authorities of specific localities who actually maintain the daily operations of the sex industry. Where Truong focuses more on economic relationships, Moon reveals the interstate relations that lead to prostitution. She claims that women's relationships with soldiers "personify and define, not only underlie, relations between governments." She documents how the South Korean government attempted to mobilize camptown prostitutes as "personal ambassadors" to secure foreign policy objectives that involved keeping the U.S. armed forces in Korea dur-

---

103. Ibid., *Sex, Money, and Morality*, 193.

ing the 1970s. Moon carefully documents the importance of the camptown prostitutes in interstate relations. She points out that many variables affect the creation of militarized prostitution to serve international interests. Dispossessed women need to be viewed as one of the variables affecting world politics. Further, players such as "strong state," "the military," or even "capitalist interests" cannot be viewed as monoliths. Researchers and advocates should also be aware that the national elite use different groups of individuals according to class, local culture, and race to pursue national interests. Therefore, not all women are affected by interstate relations in the same way.

Pointing to these other variables, Truong and Moon observe that while gender analysis is central, it alone does not illuminate the causes of militarized prostitution. For Moon, "the gender lens alone fails to address the political context in which international institutions—alliances, military assistance programs and military bases—seek to control women and gender constructs for the sake of pursuing their 'militarizing objectives.' "[104] For Truong the problem of prostitution "cannot be tied to the male-female relationship alone but must take into account the process of internationalization of production in the area of leisure and entertainment facilitated by state and capital intervention."[105]

In examining the causes of violence against women in wartime, feminists need also to examine the connections between economic and military violence and the theoretical linkages between militarism and modern economic theory. Bakery Auntie and Ms. Pak both point out that war and militarization can improve the economic situation of elite groups of society. Marilyn Waring, a member of the New Zealand Parliament from 1975 to 1984 and author of *If Women Counted: A New Feminist Economics*, asserts that war making is the basis of modern economics. John Maynard Keynes based much of his economic theory on finding a way to pay for World War II. Waring writes, "The current state of the world is the result of a system that attributes little or no 'value' to peace. It pays no heed to the preservation of natural resources or to the labor of the majority of its inhabitants or to the unpaid work of the reproduction of human life itself not to mention its maintenance and care. The system cannot respond to values it refuses to recognize." Naturally such a system cannot define national security in such a way as to include women and children.[106]

The stories of the lives of women working in brothels illustrate the complex dynamics that create and sustain militarized prostitution. As Janet from

---

104. Moon, *Sex Among Allies*.
105. Truong, *Sex, Money and Morality*.
106. Marilyn Waring, *If Women Counted: A New Feminist Economics* (San Francisco: Harper and Row, 1988), chaps. 3–4; cited in Brock and Thistlethwaite, *Casting Stones*, 111–13.

the Philippines pointed out, simply abolishing prostitution does not abolish the sex industry or address the root economic causes of the problem. She makes it clear that once the industry is abolished for a certain group of people, in her case, Filipinas, it finds another source of cheap labor, in Janet's context, Korean women. If Janet is no longer able to work in the sex industry, she will not have any means of supporting herself. But how can Janet be given work if her nation's development strategy or interstate relations are in part built upon the sexual labor of women or if the needs of women and children are ignored by developers? Trying to legalize sex work, however, would not resolve the economic disparities that drove Janet into sex work. It is naive to believe that legalization will terminate exploitative conditions, given the oppressive factors that drive many women into prostitution, especially militarized prostitution. As Truong points out, legalization fails to examine closely the social context of "free choice" or "full consent"[107] and to realize the impossibility of separating in most cases "free choice" and coercion.[108]

Clearly, militarized prostitution cannot be reduced to economic factors alone. The experiences of prostitutes show that in a patriarchal society men dominate women in part through controlling their sexuality, in particular through sexual violence. Mainly men benefit from militarized prostitution, both nationally and internationally, though how much they benefit depends on nationality, race, and class. The continuum of sexual violence (from rape to marriage to prostitution) that Barry speaks of is expressed in Nan Hee's story as well as the stories of Kim Sun-Ok and Yoon Hee. Women's sexuality is usually defined in terms of male ownership. Once a woman has lost her virginity to one man, she is considered to be his property—whether she was forced or not. She usually cannot then become the property of another male through marriage. Sometimes the only option left is to become the shared property of many men—brothel owners and those seeking to buy sex. Most women, especially poor women, are given few choices in a patriarchal world and often must move from one abusive, male-defined institution to another in hopes of a better life. They are refugees of wars waged between nations and political factions as well as wars waged by men against women in every part of the world.

Researchers and advocates must also examine the motivations of men who use and abuse women as sexual objects. Researchers have begun to examine the expression of male dominance as it occurs in hypermasculine contexts. Brock, Thislethwaite, Enloe, Sturdevant, and Stoltzfus have examined the construction of militarized masculinity in relation to sexuality

---

107. Truong, *Sex, Money, and Morality*, 49.
108. Ibid., 50.

and prostitution.[109] Military training and socialization are often riddled with misogynist messages about gender relations. At military initiation and training camps (boot camps) across the United States, military recruits were taught this marching chant throughout the seventies and eighties: "This is my weapon, this is my gun, One is for shooting, the other's for fun."[110] Slogans and other expressions of aggression often equate sexual prowess with dominance and military strength. A soldier's honor is tied to his ability to prove his masculinity. Masculinity is defined as a disdain for feminine aspects, which are considered to be weak, unmanly, and contemptible. The denigration of female traits and hence women is an integral part of the military construction of both masculinity and aggression against the enemy. The bodies of women become a means by which men can prove their strength and dominance, especially if the "enemies' women" are defiled or dominated. Rape and prostitution can become a part of a soldier's proof of masculinity and success, even a hallmark of success in battle. Racism and xenophobia encouraged in wartime propaganda also help to justify rape and prostitution. Sexual exploitation of women then becomes an integral part of the military construction of masculinity and aggression against one's enemies.

Conclusion

To begin to understand militarized prostitution, we must first start with the stories of women who have directly experienced selling sex to U.S. servicemen. Much difficult work remains to be done in this area. Saundra Sturdevant and Brenda Stoltzfus have provided one of the best examples of such work in *Let the Good Times Roll: Prostitution and the U.S. Military in Asia*, which is one of the largest (if not largest) collections to date of the stories of women in Korea, Japan, and the Philippines. Ministries such as My Sister's Place in Korea have documented the stories of women that come to them for support. Still, many voices have yet to be heard. Even less is known about militarized prostitution in other regions, such as Latin America.

As Sturdevant and Stoltzfus point out, until women who have sold their sexual labor around bases can participate in this discussion as theorists, our analysis will be incomplete. However, scholars and advocates are often in a position to break the silence around militarized prostitution. They are also able to access information that is difficult for those working in prostitution

---

109. See Brock and Thistlethwaite, *Casting Stones*, 75–78 and chap. 2; and Enloe, "Spoils of War," chap. 3.

110. Brock and Thistlethwaite, *Casting Stones*, 75.

to access, such as information about Status of Forces Agreements, interstate negotiations, corporate business dealings, and the dealings of local politicians. Scholars need to be careful, not to fit prostitutes' experiences into theories, but to base theories on these stories. Together, women working in militarized prostitution and scholars can uncover a complex picture of the causes and solutions to militarized prostitution as a part of the sex industry. That complex picture must include a close examination of male dominance and oppression, as well as many factors including race, class, culture, government economic policies, corporate practices, international development policies, social disruption, and military culture.

For the past two decades the voices of women abused around bases have increasingly been heard by the public. Continued efforts must be made to bring forth those voices so that reality will no longer be defined as though violence against women in wartime does not exist or is trivial or irrelevant. When women tell their stories of servicing soldiers in brothels, and when others listen, they dispel myths that describe prostitutes as immoral, as "asking for it," or as mere victims. Instead, they are seen as women surviving against all odds in a sexist and racist global political economy structured to exploit, oppress, or neglect them to serve the ends of those who are more powerful.

Part Four

THE INTERNATIONAL RESPONSE

13

The United Nations' Role in Defining War Crimes against Women

ANNE LLEWELLYN BARSTOW

In February 1992, when Etsuro Totsuka went to Geneva to introduce the comfort women's issues to the UN Commission on Human Rights (CHR), she was backed by a growing movement to make the world aware of and responsive to the suffering of women in wartime.[1] Still, she faced formidable obstacles. Even in sophisticated international circles, sexual assault was still considered "a private matter," and the female victim was often blamed. There was not even an agreed-upon vocabulary with which to discuss these matters: use of the term "gender," for example, long a staple of feminist discussion, was still hotly debated in these arenas.

There was a long list of questions that could be used to obstruct any discussion of women's rights. Was forced prostitution really sexual slavery? Was rape in conflict situations truly a war crime? And if it was, how could it be tried in courts that had no precedent for dealing with rape as a war crime? There was little agreement on or even awareness of rape used as a systematic military strategy. Even as basic a question as the relation of women's rights to human rights was open to debate. People questioned: Are there such things as universal human rights? There was virtually no awareness that being female required its own definition of rights. Human rights were still thought of chiefly as protection of the individual from state coercion and of the family as an entity to be preserved at all costs. In fact, both of these rights could be interpreted to work against women's needs.

Yet when Totsuka asked the CHR for justice for comfort women, the matter was not dismissed or swept under the rug. At this point the case entered the mainstream of world debate. In the following two years, a hundred or more interventions were made to the CHR by governmental and nongovernmental groups, all demanding that the surviving comfort women

---

1. Etsuro Totsuka, "Military Sexual Slavery by Japan and Issues in Law," in *True Stories of the Korean Comfort Women,* ed. Keith Howard (London: Cassell, 1995), 193–200.

be compensated. The Japanese government fiercely defended its position that it had settled all monetary claims from World War II in 1965 and that it owed nothing to the survivors.[2]

Meanwhile, the struggle for women's rights was being broadened. Women's NGOs had been exceedingly active. The fruit of their efforts was a remarkable series of presentations at the UN Conference on Human Rights, held in Vienna in June 1993.[3] In local, national, and regional groups, women had prepared agenda and testimonies for Vienna.[4] In the process, they formed local networks and cooperative agencies that had never existed before.[5] When the Vienna Conference threatened to split along North-South lines, the women were well positioned to survive the split: *their* organizing had already built coalitions across those lines.

At Vienna, the caucus got women assigned to all of the NGO working groups; they in turn secured a place for gender issues in all NGO presentations. Most effective of all was the Tribunal for Women's Human Rights, held on the two days preceding the conference. Women from all parts of the world came to give personal testimony to the violence they had endured, from domestic violence and economic discrimination to war crimes and global trafficking. The severe impact of war was documented by women from Korea, Palestine, Peru, Somalia, Bosnia, Croatia, Serbia, and Russia.[6]

As women victims and those representing them told of the suffering of individuals, a powerful picture emerged, a picture that touched on many aspects of wartime atrocities: torture, the loss of children and husbands, forced pregnancy, starvation, and of course rape. A form of psychological torture was documented by Asha Samad of Somalia:

Men and women are born into a clan ... and they stay in that clan. However, women quite often marry into another clan, which is fine in peace time. But when there's war, they have to choose between the clan of their birth or the clan of their husband and children. What a hor-

---

2. Ibid., 194.

3. Charlotte Bunch and Niamh Reilly, *Demanding Accountability: The Global Campaign and Vienna Tribunal for Women's Human Rights* (New Brunswick, N.J.: Center for Women's Global Leadership, 1994). The following discussion is based largely on this account.

4. Among the many groups in the Vienna coalition were the Asian Women's Human Rights Council, Center for Women's Global Leadership, Church Women United, MADRE, Women against Fundamentalism, Women in Black, Women in Law and Development, Women's International League for Peace and Freedom (WILPF), Third World Movement against the Exploitation of Women, and UNIFEM.

5. Women had, of course, worked together before at the international level, perhaps most effectively at the three UN conferences on women (Mexico City, 1975; Copenhagen, 1980; and Nairobi, 1985).

6. *Testimonies of the Global Tribunal on Violations of Women's Human Rights: At the UN World Conference on Human Rights, Vienna, June 1993* (New Brunswick, N.J.: Center for Women's Global Leadership, 1994).

rible choice!... [Women] are considered a fifth column, spies within the homes of their husbands, who are told to divorce them and send them out [without their children]... so women have more at stake in wanting peace and lose more in terms of war.[7]

But, as Samad pointed out, women in Somalia are excluded from decision-making processes. When war or peace is being debated, they have no say.

One of the most disturbing reports at the tribunal came from Bosnia, where social workers were just beginning to see the results of the Serbian army's campaign of forced pregnancies. Aida Zaidgiz reported on the Muslim women she worked with who had been deliberately impregnated by Serbian soldiers:

Ayse... was eight months pregnant (as the result of rape).... All the time she felt she would go crazy, that she was half crazy. She said that she would give the baby away, she didn't want to have anything to do with it and so forth. And then when she was delivered, the child was born dead. I talked to her and she was really depressed. I tried to tell her "somehow you didn't really want it." But she responded, "Aida, I carried it for nine months under my heart."

... there is a lot of sorrow in the world and we have to start doing something about it... we're always talking about the victims. But all of us avoid naming the perpetrator. Because it is against the perpetrator we have to fight. The perpetrator—do I really have to say this?—is the Serbian soldier.[8]

The judge appointed to hear the cases at the tribunal said in conclusion:

I am deeply saddened, almost beyond description, because as one of those who spoke said, 'those making the war are not women, those doing rapes are not women, however those being raped, yes, we are women....' These unspeakable acts... are the results of not years but centuries, not of one culture, but of almost all cultures around the world, of patriarchy.... These acts we've heard about in times of war... are breaches of the Fourth Geneva Convention. That is a formal way of saying that rape, forced prostitution, and forced pregnancy are forms of torture. We must understand legally and morally that they are forms of torture, and we must respond that way.[9]

---

7. Bunch and Reilly, *Demanding Accountability*, 45.
8. *Testimonies of the Global Tribunal*, 42.
9. Honourable Ed Broadbent of Canada in *Demanding Accountability*, ed. C. Bunch and N. Reilly, 45–46.

And the conference did so respond. In its final declaration, it specifically called for punishment of systematic rape, sexual slavery, and forced pregnancy as violations of women's human rights.[10]

What emerged from all the testimony was that women's bodies are used as the site of combat, both figuratively and actually. In particular, the witness of the Korean and Bosnian women made it clear that rape is often carried out in a systematic way, planned at high levels of military or governmental command, intended to destroy enemy morale and cause chaos in communities.

The tribunal drew major attention before the conference even began. It made further impact when six of the witnesses were able to give their testimony again—this time before the main forum. The effect of women describing their own victimization could not be dismissed. The delegates were prepared to listen because for several years they had heard the comfort women's stories and the press reports of the "rape camps" in Bosnia and the Serbian ethnic cleansing policies; now the conference acted.

The final Vienna Declaration included major gains for women: statements that women's rights are human rights, that they must be taken into account in all parts of the United Nations' work, that UN personnel must be trained to recognize violence against women, and that systematic rape, forced pregnancy, and genocide must be condemned. The declaration however left much undone: the legal definition of rape in wartime (systematic rape) was not exact, and no court was set up to deal with gender-related crimes. But there was no turning back: war crimes based on sexual assault had been acknowledged. It remained for future conferences and committees to carry out what is in fact a revolution in international law and understanding.

The Beijing Conference

When the comfort women were denied any recompense by the Japanese government, their supporters tried another tack: they called for punishment of the perpetrators as war criminals. Again Japan denied them; indeed, it had not investigated any person, military or civilian, in connection with sexual slavery. The CHR, however, sent the charges to its Sub-Commission on Protection of Minorities, and it was before this group that Japan formally acknowledged in August 1993 the enslavement of the comfort women by the Japanese Imperial forces; some NGOs labeled this as a crime against humanity.[11] The same subcommission appointed Linda Chavez to investigate further wartime sexual slavery and systematic rape.

---

10. Bunch and Reilly, *Demanding Accountability*, 150, 152.
11. Totsuka, "Military Sexual Slavery by Japan," 195.

Despite the efforts of the UN Working Group on Contemporary Forms of Slavery to bring Japan to the negotiating table, the Japanese government refused. Instead, in August 1994, it called for Japanese citizens to donate money to the victims, a move widely seen as an evasion of its own responsibility.[12]

In December of that year the United Nations further acknowledged the continuing urgency of the assaults on women by adopting a Declaration on the Elimination of Violence against Women, which specifically condemned "Physical, sexual and psychological violence perpetrated or condoned by the State, wherever it occurs."[13] The United Nations put teeth into the declaration by appointing a special rapporteur on violence against women, Radhika Coomaraswamy.

This was the situation in August 1995, when almost fifty thousand women gathered in Beijing for the UN's Fourth World Conference on Women. An idea of how the women's movement had grown at the global level can be seen by comparing the attendance at the three previous women's conferences: Mexico City 1975—three thousand; Copenhagen 1980—five thousand; Nairobi 1985—twelve thousand to fifteen thousand. It was a movement whose time had come.

Of the Beijing Conference's twelve themes, the dominant one was that of violence against women. While the official delegates debated in Beijing, almost thirty thousand women met an hour away at Huairou in a huge, free-wheeling gathering called the Forum. As at Vienna, women used the strategy of the public hearing—this time, two tribunals—at which women gave evidence of what militarism does to them: women from Algeria, Uganda, Palestine, Tahiti, Fiji, Croatia, Chiapas, Rwanda, and comfort women from Korea and the Philippines spoke at the hearings.

The word from Rwanda was the most shocking because it was both the newest and the most devastating in numbers. We learned that in previous outbreaks of violence between Hutus and Tutsis, men had been the targets, but in the massacres of 1994 women were not spared. Most Tutsi teenaged girls were raped. Many bore babies, who have been abandoned. Like the Serbs, the Hutus intended these rapes as a form of ethnic cleansing, but in a reversal of the Serbian strategy, the Hutus expected the rapes to destroy the ability of the girls to have Tutsi children (because no Tutsi man would marry a woman who had been raped by a Hutu). Both cases were a deliberate strategy of genocide.

---

12. Almost all comfort women rejected this money for this reason. See chapter 2 for the strong rejection of this move by many Japanese women.

13. Amnesty International, *It's About Time! Human Rights Are Women's Rights* (New York: Amnesty International, 1995), 148.

Violence against women in war was the theme also in many of the smaller workshops. Women from Sudan, Sierra Leone, Liberia, Eritrea, Ethiopia, Mozambique, Haiti, Azerbaijan, Cambodia, and Nepal, among others, told of their lives as refugees from conflict. Refugee women, often widowed or separated from their men, are particularly vulnerable to kidnapping, rape, and extortion. Many told of how they have banded together as women to help each other when their communities were destroyed.

And many national groups sponsored workshops on women as peacemakers. From Burundi, Zambia, Sierra Leone, the United States, South Africa, the Netherlands, among others, women gave amazing accounts of their ingenuity in lessening violence. It became clear that if it were left to these women, the endless cycles of violence in many of these countries would be ended. Those who suffer most from war—and who gain least from it—are quite willing to work to end it.

Most memorable of all were the street events, especially those highlighting the plight of the comfort women. Many Japanese women joined their Korean sisters in calling for the Japanese government to meet the comfort women's demands, not only for recompense but to include their story in the history texts of World War II. The Women in Black led street demonstrations in memory of all women who are victims of violence.

The greatest tension came from the delegates from countries where conservative religious forces are dominant. The movement for women's human rights had received a setback at the UN Cairo Conference on Population, a gathering that suffered from too little input from women both before and during the meetings. A powerful opposition emerged as the Vatican, nations with a strong conservative Catholic presence, and a number of conservative Muslim nations joined forces. Insisting on maintaining their own cultural integrity, the Muslim nations defended the rights of husbands over wives, a position that leaves the women defenseless against domestic violence. With the same opposition coalition active at Beijing, it wasn't clear until the last day whether the conference would be able to issue a statement of achievements. But through extraordinary diplomatic persistence, the majority was able finally to convince the conservative minority to go along on most issues. As a result, the conference passed a remarkable series of motions on violence against women in armed conflict:[14]

It condemned murder, systematic rape, sexual slavery, and forced pregnancy.

---

14. United Nations, *Platform for Action and the Beijing Declaration: Fourth World Conference on Women* (New York: United Nations, 1996), 73–93.

It specified that rape during war is a war crime and that its perpetrators should be tried as war criminals.

It condemned violence perpetrated or condoned by the state, wherever it occurs. Pointing out that even the threat of such violence is a way of keeping women subjugated, it called for a new respect for women's human rights.

It condemned blaming and shaming women for acts perpetrated against them by men.

It singled out policies of genocide, ethnic cleansing, mass removals of populations, and mass rape as special threats to women.

It reiterated the conclusion of the Vienna Conference that such violations are violations of the fundamental principles of international human rights and humanitarian law.[15]

Recognizing that women together with their children make up 80 percent of the world's refugees, the Beijing Conference called for giving these displaced women a voice in the rebuilding of their communities. It praised the role that women play maintaining families in the midst of war and the contributions they make to conflict resolution.

The Test

Yet despite the overwhelming energy and determination expressed at Beijing, the conference actually made painfully clear what women were *not* achieving. Doubt was expressed at Beijing about the UN's ability to do more than talk. When Charlotte Bunch said, "It is the UN that is now on trial; shall women have to turn elsewhere?" she was applauded. The special rapporteur on violence against women, Radhika Coomaraswamy, placed the blame on the states:

In recent years there has been a general phenomenon of the creation of international norms, an acceptance of these norms at a rhetorical level by states, but a failure with regard to their actual implementation within the countries concerned. This...is a new kind of international hypocrisy.[16]

The first and most crucial test of the acceptance of these new norms after Beijing would be the conviction of those responsible for the Bosnian rape camps and Rwandan rapes/massacres. The United Nations had established

---

15. United Nations, *Platform for Action*, 83.
16. *Unifem in Beijing and Beyond* (New York: UNIFEM, 1996), 37.

an international criminal tribunal at The Hague in 1993 to try war criminals from the former Yugoslavia and in 1994 had set up a similar tribunal at Arusha, Tanzania, to try Rwandan perpetrators. Both, however, were ad hoc courts with limited jurisdiction—they could neither compel nations to hand over accused persons nor hand down the death penalty. As such, they had far less power than the Nuremburg and Tokyo courts had had. And they had an insufficient grasp of what would be involved in trying sexual crimes. As a result, the trials began at an agonizingly slow pace.

The very definition of rape was itself problematic. Rape was seen as a crime, not of physical violence, but against honor: either as dishonoring the man who possesses the woman or as damaging the woman (that is, destroying her "purity") in the eyes of her man.[17] These old definitions, although improved upon at Vienna and Beijing, still influenced jurists. They rendered rape a less serious crime than other crimes against humanity. What in fact was needed at The Hague and Arusha, in order to break the old patterns of seeing gender crimes as "secondary," was nothing less than

gender sensitivity training of all personnel,

women represented at all levels of the court,

female investigators trained to get information in a way that respects the woman's privacy and feelings,

and court procedures that spare the victim a face-to-face confrontation with her attacker and protect her life after she gives testimony.[18]

But neither tribunal fulfilled these criteria. Underfunded and occupied with working out procedures among lawyers from many countries, both began with handicaps.

The first trial charging rape at The Hague, which did not take place until 1998, showed much that was wrong with a traditional court setup. A Bosnian Muslim woman gave evidence against four Bosnian Croatian soldiers for repeated rape. Just as the judges were ready to give their verdict against one of the accused, the defense lawyer called for a mistrial on the following grounds: after release from the rape house, the victim had had nightmares and stomach pains, for which she had consulted a psychologist, and these facts had not been made known. Therefore, the defense claimed that her testimony could not be trusted. The judges agreed—meaning that the case would have to be tried again, and the victim would have to give

---

17. Rhonda Copelon, "Surfacing Gender: Reconceptualizing Crimes against Women in Time of War," in *Mass Rape: The War against Women in Bosnia-Herzegovina*, ed. Alexandra Stiglmayer, trans. Marion Faber (Lincoln: University of Nebraska Press, 1994), 197–218.
18. Copelon, "Surfacing Gender," 210.

her painful testimony a second time, which is called "retraumatizing the witness." One official said, "This is shocking. Of course the rights of the accused must be protected. But the witness must not be made to suffer over and over again. It's what rape victims call feeling raped again in court."[19]

With "justice" like this, women might well feel that their former neglect in the courts had been merciful. Meanwhile, however, in Arusha, the court learned from the mistakes of The Hague. In the beginning the Rwandan tribunal had failed to prosecute sexual crimes, despite the very high rate of rape during the Rwandan genocide. In June 1997, however, the International Centre for Human Rights and Democratic Development, based in Montreal, urged that sexual crimes be included. The case against the tribunal's first defendant, Jean-Paul Akayesu, was rewritten to include rape. History was made on 2 September 1998 when Akayesu was found guilty on nine counts; he was given three life sentences. It was the first time an international court found rape to be an act of genocide and punished sexual violence committed during a civil war.[20]

The Hague tribunal finally retried its first rape case, rejected the argument about flawed testimony, and on 10 December 1998 sentenced the commander who had allowed the rapes to take place to ten years in prison.

While these convictions set a very important precedent, the two tribunals have so far dealt with only a handful of cases. The Rwandan situation is especially pressing since the jails in Rwanda are crowded with men and a few women awaiting trial. The slowness and awkwardness of the trials prove the difficulties of getting justice for either rape or genocide. These experiences demonstrate the necessity for a strong, permanent international court, one that uses sophisticated gender techniques.

The UN's response to this need was the Rome Conference of 1998, attended by 156 nations, to set up a permanent International Criminal Court (ICC). In order to get gender issues onto the agenda from the start, women's NGOs set up a Women's Caucus.[21] A network of 350 organizations and individuals came together to send advocates to the Preparatory Committees. They lobbied not only to get feminist items on the agenda but to influence the very language to be used at the conference.

During the five-week conference, the Women's Caucus kept the global women's movement informed. When a crisis arose because the Vatican delegates rejected the terms "enforced pregnancy" and "gender," the Women's

19. Marlise Simmons, "Landmark Bosnia Rape Trial: A Legal Morass," *New York Times*, 29 July 1998.

20. "Human Rights Watch Applauds Rwanda Rape Verdict," New York: Human Rights Watch, 2 September 1998, e-mail.

21. Wahida Naimar and Eleanor Conda (of the ICC Woman's Caucus), interviewed by this author, New York City, 11 February 1999.

Caucus rallied support around the world. It brought in piles of faxes supporting feminist language. The gender analysis that made it into the report would not have happened without this advocacy.

Since Beijing we have succeeded in getting women's issues into the plans for the ICC. The tribunals now sitting are changing their procedures so that women will not be revictimized when they use the courts. Now the challenge is to educate women about the possibilities and to enable them to use these new resources.[22] To do this, we will need a large core of women to work in every part of the world.

---

22. Mandy Jacobson reports from Rwanda that communication between the Arusha tribunal and Rwandans is so poor that there is "a serious breakdown of trust in the judicial process.... Extraordinary precedents have been set in ICTR courtrooms but they are not well documented by the tribunal staff" (personal communication with this author, 9 August, 2000). For Jacobson's efforts to get the word out, see the African section of the "Resources" section of this book (p. 249 below).

Conclusion

The United Nations had condemned sexual slavery in 1993. Yet at the Beijing Conference in 1995, we saw that the Japanese had been frustrated because their government still did not accept the term "sexual slavery" for what they had done to comfort women. This long struggle ended in Geneva in March 1996.[1] There, before the UN Commission on Human Rights (CHR), a group of North and South Korean, Japanese, and Filipino women presented the comfort women's case. It was the first time that women from the two Koreas had worked together. Radhika Coomaraswamy, who had told the CHR several months before that the Japanese brothels of World War II must be called "military sexual slavery," announced that the CHR had indeed ruled that Japan's actions were sexual slavery.

The audience would not stop clapping; the Korean women were crying for joy. One Japanese woman said, "I felt a new power growing—now we are participating in decision making." Yet when the women called for blocking Japan's application to join the Security Council until Japan made full recompense to the survivors, they received little support.

Since then, women in the "justice for comfort women" movement report that it is difficult to maintain momentum. The elderly victims are dying, and their supporters are worn down by the obstinacy of the Japanese government. In Korea strong, early support had come from Christian women, but these women have found themselves marginalized by their churches; many Korean men, Christian or other, do not want to be reminded of what they consider a sordid event in their country's history.[2]

Women still hold a vigil every week in front of the Japanese Embassy in Seoul, the longest-running protest in Korean history. But some are beginning to despair of gaining the full recognition that the comfort women long for: their rightful place in the histories of World War II.[3] President Kim Dae

---

1. Aiko Carter (of the Japan Women's Christian Temperance Union, a translator at the Geneva hearing) interview by author, 15 January 1997.

2. David Suh and Sonia Strong, conversations with author, January 1997.

3. The Netherlands set an example that one wishes had been followed: in 1948 in Batavia (Jakarta), Java, the Dutch colonial government tried a number of Japanese military for having used Dutch women in comfort stations. One officer was condemned to death, several were imprisoned, and one committed suicide. But other nations that had proof of the Japanese military brothel system (such as the United States) did nothing: the subject was mentioned,

Jung gave up on winning compensation for them; in April 1998, he instead awarded each survivor $22,700 and promised to continue to press Japan for a full apology and acceptance of legal responsibility.[4]

We have seen the breakthroughs to justice at the level of international courts for Bosnia and Rwanda. But what of cases left to be tried by state judicial systems? In other venues justice is being slowly and unevenly applied. In Guatemala, some of the killers at the 1982 massacre at Río Negro were finally brought to trial in 1998. In the first war crimes convictions following Guatemala's long civil war, three paramilitary fighters were sentenced to death for the killing of women and children.[5] It is hoped that the UN Truth Commission's report there will lead to many more trials. In Haiti, where the justice system is barely functioning, no one has been convicted of any of the rapes and murders committed in 1991–94, although the Center for Constitutional Rights (U.S.A.) is attempting to pursue justice in several cases.[6] For crimes such as rape or murder carried out by U.S. soldiers around army bases in Okinawa and Korea, military courts prosecute some offenders, but many go unsentenced.[7] The demand of Okinawan women that the bases be removed from their country has received no response.

At the end of this decade so important for women's legal rights in armed conflict situations, two facts are clear: (1) women's groups must continue to press for changes in law so that at every level of justice crimes against women are recognized and (2) women's groups must continue to press for changes in procedures so that women believe that the courts will give them a fair hearing. We have a long way to go in both areas.

Yet how can we not go forward? At the conference "Men, Women, and War" held in Derry, Northern Ireland, in 1997, we began deliberations by hearing the testimony of two comfort women, one Korean, the other Dutch. When they had finished speaking, Aida Zaidgiz, who was working with Bosnian victims of the rape camps, said: "This testimony fills me with sadness. Because what happened then has happened again, this time in Bosnia. We are repeating what should never have happened at all." Another conference member thanked the comfort women for their courage in speaking of such painful memories. Then she asked them, "If anyone would have lis-

---

but dropped, at the Tokyo war crimes trials. See George Hicks, *The Comfort Women: Japan's Brutal Regime of Enforced Prostitution in the Second World War* (New York: W. W. Norton, 1995), 168, 269–70.

4. *New York Times*, 22 April 1998.

5. *Boston Globe*, 1 December 1998. I have not been able to learn if the rapes were included in the charges.

6. Interviews by author with Tom Driver and with Gabor Rona of the Center for Constitutional Rights, New York, 22 December 1998.

7. "Final Statement," International Women's Working Conference, Naha City, Okinawa, 4 May 1997.

tened to you in 1945, would you have told your stories then?" Both were silent for a moment, weighing the consequences. Then both said, "Yes." The questioner replied, "If you could have spoken in 1945—and been heard— the world might have begun to respond. And the Serbs might not have dared to build rape camps in 1993."

It is in order to tell these stories, and to respond, that this book has been written.

Resources

General

Amnesty International. *It's About Time! Human Rights Are Women's Rights*. New York: Amnesty International, 1995.

Olivia Bennett et al., eds. *Arms to Fight, Arms to Protect: Women Speak Out about Conflict*. London: Panos Publications, 1995.

Brownmiller, Susan. *Against Our Will: Men, Women, and Rape*. New York: Ballentine Books, 1975.

Clinton, Hillary Rodham. "Words to Break the Silence." *Women's Studies Quarterly* 24, nos. 1–2 (spring–summer 1996): 42–45. Speech to the Beijing Conference Forum.

Dombrowski, Nicole A. *Women and War in the Twentieth Century: Enlisted with or without Consent*. Hamden, Conn.: Garland Publishing, 1998.

Gender Violence: The Hidden War Crime. Washington, D.C.: Women, Law, and Development International, 1998.

The Human Rights Watch Global Report on Women's Rights. Human Rights Watch Women's Rights Project. New York: Human Rights Watch, 1995.

Lorentzen, Lois Ann, and Jennifer Turpin, eds. *The Women and War Reader*. New York: New York University Press, 1998.

Mananzan, Mary John, ed. *Women Resisting Violence: Spirituality for Life*. Maryknoll, N.Y.: Orbis Books, 1996.

Russell, Diana, and Nicole Van de Ven, eds. *Crimes against Women: Proceedings of the International Tribunal (Brussels, 1976)*. Berkeley: Frog in the Well, 1984.

Sajor, Indai Lourdes, ed. *Common Grounds: Violence against Women in War and Armed Conflict Situations*. Quezon City, Philippines: Asian Center for Women's Human Rights, 1998. Papers of the Tokyo Conference on Violence against Women in War, 1997.

Scarry, Elaine. *The Body in Pain: The Making and Unmaking of the World*. New York: Oxford University Press, 1985.

Swiss, Shana, and Joan Giller. "Rape as a Crime of War." *Journal of the American Medical Association* 270, no. 5 (4 August 1993).

UN Human Rights Commission. *Sexual Violence against Refugees: Guidelines on Prevention and Response*. New York: United Nations, 1995.

Women's Studies Quarterly: Beijing and Beyond: Toward the Twenty-first Century of Women 24, nos. 1–2 (spring–summer 1996). New York: Feminist Press, 1996.

Violence against Asian Women

Print

Asia Watch and Physicians for Human Rights. *Rape in Kashmir: A Crime of War.* New York: Human Rights Watch, 1993.

(Second) Asian Solidarity Forum on Militarism and Sexual Slavery. *Report.* Tokyo: National Christian Council, 1994.

Brock, Rita Nakashima, and Susan Brooks Thistlethwaite. *Casting Stones: Prostitution and Liberation in Asia and the United States.* Minneapolis: Fortress Press, 1996.

Calica, Dan P., and Nelia Sancho, eds. *War Crimes on Asian Women: Military Sexual Slavery by Japan during World War II: The case of the Filipino Comfort Women.* Manila: Task Force on Filipina Victims of Military Sexual Slavery by Japan, Asian Women Human Rights Council-Philippine Section, 1993.

Dolgopol, Ustinia, et al. *Comfort Women: The Unfinished Ordeal.* Geneva: International Commission of Jurists, 1993.

Her, Kil-cha. "Coming and Going at Sundown." Unpublished script, 1995.

Hicks, George. *The Comfort Women: Japan's Brutal Regime of Enforced Prostitution in the Second World War.* New York: W. W. Norton, 1995.

Howard, Keith, ed. *True Stories of the Korean Comfort Women.* London: Cassell, 1995. Trans. Young Joo Lee, from documents complied by the Korean Council for Women Drafted for Military Sexual Slavery.

Keller, Nora Okja. *Comfort Woman.* New York: Viking, 1997. A novel.

Lang, Daniel. *Casualties of War.* New York: McGraw-Hill, 1969.

Moon, Katharine. *Sex among Allies: Military Prostitution in U.S.-Korea Relations.* New York: Columbia University Press, 1997.

Olson, James S., and Randy Roberts, eds. *My Lai: A Brief History with Documents.* Boston: Bedford Books, 1998.

Perpinan, Mary Soledad. "Militarism and the Sex Industry in the Philippines." In *Women and Violence*, edited by Miranda Davies. London: Zed Books, 1994.

"Sexual Slavery by Japan's Imperial Army." In *Against Prostitution and Sexual Exploitation Activities in Japan.* Tokyo: Japan Anti-Prostitution Association, 1994.

Shim, Jung-Soon. "Elements of a Shaman Ritual as Counter-Imperialist Discursive Strategy in a Korean Comfort Woman Play." *Fu Jen Studies* (Fu Jen University, Taipei) 30 (1997).

Sturdevant, Saundra Pollack, and Brenda Stoltzfus. *Let the Good Times Roll: Prostitution and the U.S. Military in Asia.* New York: New Press, 1992.

War Victimization and Japan. International Public Hearing concerning Postwar Compensation Report. Osaka: Toho Shuppan, 1993.

Watanabe, Kazuko. "Militarism, Colonialism, and the Trafficking of Women: 'Comfort Women' Forced into Sexual Labor for Japanese Soldiers." *Bulletin of Concerned Asian Scholars* 26, no. 4 (1994): 3–17.

———. "Trafficking in Women's Bodies, Then and Now." *Peace and Change* 20, no. 4 (October 1995): 501–14.

Women in Afghanistan. New York: Amnesty International, 1995.

Yasuhara, Keiko, and Aiko Carter, eds. *Remembering Footsteps in the Sands of Time: Report on the Asian Solidarity Forum on Militarism and Sexual Slavery.* Tokyo: National Christian Council, 1993.

Video

Lee, Diana S., and Grace Yoon-Kyung Lee. *Camp Arirang.* New York: Third World Newsreel, 1996. Prostitution at U.S. bases in South Korea.

Violence against African Women

Print

Center for Women's Global Leadership. *Gender Violence and Women's Human Rights in Africa.* New Brunswick, N.J.: Center for Women's Global Leadership, 1994.

Civilian Devastation: Abuses by All Parties in the War in Southern Sudan. Human Rights Watch/Africa. New York: Human Rights Watch, 1994.

Cock, Jacklyn. *Women and War in South Africa.* Cleveland: Pilgrim Press, 1993.

Human Rights Watch Women's Project. *Widespread Rape of Somali Women Refugees in N.E. Kenya.* New York: Human Rights Watch, 1993.

Shattered Lives: Sexual Violence during the Rwandan Genocide and Its Aftermath. Human Rights Watch/Africa. New York: Human Rights Watch, 1996.

Snow, Keith. "Rape as a Weapon of War." *Peacework* 272 (March 1997). Rwanda.

Turshen, Meredeth. "Women and Conflict in Africa." *ACAS Bulletin* 50–51 (winter–spring 1998).

Uganda: "Breaking God's Commands:" The Destruction of Childhood by the Lord's Resistance Army. New York: Amnesty International, 1997.

Violence against Women in South Africa. Human Rights Watch/Africa. New York: Human Rights Watch, 1995.

Video

Jacobson, Mandy. *The Arusha Tapes.* Arcata, Calif.: Internews Network, 2000.

———. *Genocide on Trial: Bringing Justice Home to Rwandans.* Arcata, Calif.: Internews Network, forthcoming.

Violence against Latin American and Caribbean Women

Agosin, Marjorie, ed. *Surviving beyond Fear: Women, Children, and Human Rights in Latin America.* Fredonia, N.Y.: White Pine Press, 1993.

America's Watch and the Women's Rights Project. *Untold Terror: Violence against Women in Peru's Armed Conflict.* New York: Human Rights Watch, 1992.

Brody, Reed. *Contra Terror in Nicaragua: Report of a Fact-Finding Mission, September 1984–January 1985.* Boston: South End Press, 1985.

Bunster, Ximena. "Women and Torture in Latin America." In *Women and Change in Latin America,* edited by June Nash and Helen Safa. New York: Bergin & Garvey, 1985. Also in Agosin.

Chancy, Myriam. *Framing Silence.* New Brunswick, N.J.: Rutgers University Press, 1998.

Danner, Mark. *The Massacre at El Mozote: A Parable of the Cold War*. New York: Vintage Books, 1994.

Esquivel, Julia. *The Certainty of Spring: Poems by a Guatemalan in Exile*. Translated by Anne Woehrle. Washington, D.C.: EPICA, 1993.

Hooks, Margaret. *Guatemalan Women Speak*. Washington, D.C.: EPICA, 1993.

Hopkinson, Amanda, ed. *Lovers and Comrades: Women's Resistance Poetry from Central America*. London: Women's Press, 1989.

Human Rights Watch Women's Project. *Rape in Haiti: A Weapon of Terror*. New York: Human Rights Watch, 1994.

Inter-American Commission of Human Rights. *Affidavits in Support of Communication Respecting the Violations of Human Rights of Haitian Women*. Washington, D.C.: Organization of American States, 1996.

Randall, Margaret. *Sandino's Daughters: Testimonies of Nicaraguan Women in Struggle*. Vancouver, B.C.: New Star Books, 1981.

Sabato, Ernesto, et al. *Nunca Más: The Report of the Argentine National Commission on the Disappeared*. New York: Farrar, Straus & Giroux, 1986.

Violence against European Women

Print

Aita, Judy. "Rape and Abduction of Kosovo Refugees." UN Population Fund. May 1999. Available at kcc-news@alb-net.com.

Allen, Beverly. *Rape Warfare: The Hidden Genocide in Bosnia-Herzegovina and Croatia*. Minneapolis: University of Minnesota Press, 1996.

Amnesty International. *Bosnia-Herzegovina: Rapes and Sexual Abuse by the Armed Forces*. New York: Amnesty International, 1993.

Bassiouni, M. Cherif, and Marcia McCormick. *Sexual Violence: An Invisible Weapon of War in the Former Yugoslavia*. Chicago: International Human Rights Law Institute, 1996.

Chesler, Phyllis. "What Is Justice for a Rape Victim?" *On the Issues* (winter 1996): 12–16, 56.

Epp, Marlene. "The Memory of Violence: Soviet and East European Mennonite Refugees and Rape in the Second World War." *Journal of Women's History* 9, no. 1 (spring 1997).

Gutman, Roy. *A Witness to Genocide*. London: Element, 1993.

Helsinki Watch. *War Crimes in Bosnia-Herzegovina*. 2 vols. New York: Human Rights Watch, 1993.

Hostetter, Doug. "One Woman against Genocide." *Fellowship* (November–December 1996).

Sells, Michael. *The Bridge Betrayed: Religion and Genocide in Bosnia*. Berkeley: University of California Press, 1996.

Stiglmayer, Alexandra, ed. *Mass Rape: The War against Women in Bosnia-Herzegovina*. Translated by Marion Faber. Lincoln: University of Nebraska Press, 1994.

Video

Calling the Ghosts: A Story about Rape, War, and Women. Directed by Mandy Jacobsen and Karmen Jelincic. New York: Bowery Productions, 1996.

Rape: A Crime of War. Produced by International Dispatch. Ottawa: National Film Board of Canada, 1996.

U.S. Militarism

Burke, Carol. "Dames at Sea: Life in the Naval Academy." *New Republic*, 17 and 24 August 1992.

———. "Marching to Vietnam." *Journal of American Folklore* 102 (October–December 1989).

Enloe, Cynthia. *Bananas, Beaches, and Bases: Making Feminist Sense of International Politics.* Berkeley: University of California Press, 1990.

———. *Does Khaki Become You? The Militarization of Women's Lives.* Boston: South End Press, 1983.

Thistlethwaite, Susan Brooks. "Militarism in North American Perspective." In *Women Resisting Violence: Spirituality for Life*, edited by Mary John Mananzan et al. Maryknoll, N.Y.: Orbis, 1996.

Global Responses: The UN and the NGOs

Print

Askin, Kelly D. *War Crimes against Women: Prosecution in International War Crimes Tribunals.* The Hague: Martinus Nijhoff, 1997.

Bunch, Charlotte, and Niamh Reilly. *Demanding Accountability: The Global Campaign and Vienna Tribunal for Women's Human Rights.* New Brunswick, N.J.: Center for Women's Global Leadership and UNIFEM, 1994.

Dunlop, Joan, et al. "Women Redrawing the Map: The World after the Beijing and Cairo Conferences." *SAIS Review* (winter 1996).

International Human Rights Law Group. *Token Gestures: Women's Human Rights and UN Reporting: The UN Special Rapporteur on Torture.* Washington, D.C.: IHRLG, 1993.

Reilly, Niamh, ed. *Without Reservation: The Beijing Tribunal on Accountability for Women's Human Rights.* New Brunswick, N.J.: Center for Women's Global Leadership, 1996.

UN High Commissioner for Refugees. *Sexual Violence against Refugees: Guidelines on Prevention and Response.* Geneva: UNHCR, 1995.

United Nations, *Platform for Action and the Beijing Declaration: Fourth World Conference on Women.* New York: United Nations, 1996.

Video

Look at the World through Women's Eyes. New York: U.S. Ecumenical Women's Network, 1996. Beijing Women's Conference.

The Vienna Tribunal: Women's Rights Are Human Rights. Augusta Productions. Ottawa: National Film Board of Canada, 1995.

Women as Peacemakers, as Nonviolent Resisters

Print

Agosin, Marjorie, ed. *Surviving beyond Fear: Women, Children, and Human Rights in Latin America.* Fredonia, N.Y.: White Pine Press, 1993.

Alonso, Harriet Lyman. *Peace as a Woman's Issue*. Syracuse: Syracuse University Press, 1993.

Breines, Ingeborg, Dorota Gierycz, and Betty Reardon, eds. *Toward a Women's Agenda for a Culture of Peace*. Paris: UNESCO Publishing, 2000.

Hostetter, Doug. "One Woman against Genocide." *Fellowship* (November–December 1996).

King, Ursula. "Spirituality for Life." In *Women Resisting Violence: Spirituality for Life*, edited by Mary John Mananzan, et al. Maryknoll, N.Y.: Orbis, 1996.

Reardon, Betty A. *Women and Peace*. Albany, N.Y.: SUNY Press, 1993.

Rycenga, Jennifer, and Marguerite Waller, eds. *Frontline Feminisms: Women, War, and Resistance*. New York: Garland Publishing, 2000.

Women and the Politics of Peace: Contributions to a Culture of Women's Resistance. Zagreb, Croatia: Center for Women's Studies, 1997.

Video

IFOR Women Peacemakers Program. The Hague: International Fellowship of Reconciliation, 1998.

Index